Anne Henderson grew up and was educated in Melbourne. She taught in Australian secondary schools for seventeen years before joining her husband Gerard Henderson to help create The Sydney Institute. She is currently Deputy Director of The Sydney Institute and editor of *The Sydney Papers*. Anne Henderson is the author of *From All Corners: Six Migrant Stories* (1993), *Educating Johannah: A Year in Year 12* (1995), *Mary MacKillop's Sisters: A Life Unveiled* (HarperCollins, 1997), *Getting Even: Women MPs on Life, Power and Politics* (HarperCollins, 1999) and *The Killing of Sister McCormack* (HarperCollins, 2002). Among her essays of note are 'Dad's Wake' in *Fathers: In Writing* (1997), the biographical chapter on Prime Minister Joe Lyons for *Australian Prime Ministers* edited by Michelle Grattan (New Holland, 2000) and the entry for Prime Minister Joe Lyons in the *New Dictionary of National Biography* (Oxford University Press). She was a contributing editor with Ross Fitzgerald of *Partners* (HarperCollins, 1999).

Also by Anne Henderson

From All Corners: Six Migrant Stories

Educating Johannah: A Year in Year 12

Mary MacKillop's Sisters: A Life Unveiled

Partners (co-editor with Ross Fitzgerald)

Getting Even: Women MPs on Life, Power and Politics

The Killing of Sister McCormack

AN *A*NGEL IN THE COURT:

The Life of Major Joyce Harmer

HarperCollins*Publishers*

Front-cover image: Major Joyce Harmer outside the courts. Back-cover images (*clockwise from top left*): Joyce with local women in Vanuatu; two children the Harmers cared for until their adopted mother died; baby Joyce with her parents and elder brothers Keith and Cecil; Joyce with a male dancer on the Isle of Pines; Joyce with Kathleen Folbigg during Kathleen's trial; Joyce and Hilton Harmer outside the courts; Hilton and Joyce in the early years of their marriage; Joyce as a girl with her sister Joan.

HarperCollins*Publishers*

First published in Australia in 2005
This edition published in 2006
by HarperCollins*Publishers* Australia Pty Limited
ABN 36 009 913 517
www.harpercollins.com.au

Copyright © Anne Henderson and Major Joyce Harmer 2005

The right of Anne Henderson to be identified as the author of this work has been asserted by her under the *Copyright Amendment (Moral Rights) Act 2000*.

HarperCollins*Publishers*
25 Ryde Road, Pymble, Sydney NSW 2073, Australia
31 View Road, Glenfield, Auckland 10, New Zealand

National Library of Australia Cataloguing-in-Publication data:

Henderson, Anne, 1949– .
   An angel in the court: the life of Major Joyce Harmer.
   2nd ed.
   ISBN 978 0 73228 022 2.
   ISBN 0 7322 8022 2.
   1. Harmer, Joyce. 2. Salvation Army – Australia –
   Biography. 3. Salvationists – Australia – Biography.
   I. Title.
287.96092

Image on front cover and spine and image at bottom of back cover by Ross Coffey, reproduced courtesy of *The Australian Women's Weekly* & ACP Syndications. Image second from bottom on back cover by Jon Reid, courtesy of Fairfax Photos; all other back-cover images supplied by Majors Joyce and Hilton Harmer
Cover and internal design by Darren Holt, HarperCollins Design Studio
Typeset in 11/15 Bembo by Kirby Jones
Printed and bound in Australia by Griffin Press.

79gsm Bulky Paperback used by HarperCollins*Publishers* is a natural, recyclable product made from wood grown in a combination of sustainable plantation and regrowth forests. It also contains up to a 20% portion of recycled fibre. The manufacturing processes conform to the environmental regulations in Tasmania, the place of manufacture.

5 4 3 2   08 09

CONTENTS

I dedicate this book to my wonderful husband and soulmate Hilton, and also to my four children, Peter, Bruce, Lyndall and Athol, and my eleven grandchildren, Tanya, Rachel, Timothy, Rebecca, Callum, Lachlan, Dylan, Jordan, Kevin Junior (KJ), Elijah and Jacob.

The love, encouragement and inspiration given to me by them all have been blessings from the Lord, and through them I have enjoyed a journey of richness and joy that has made my life on earth a 'microcosm' of Heaven.

It is my prayer that I have in some way touched their lives in return, so that they will desire to serve Jesus Christ and their fellow man, and that we will one day enjoy a great reunion in the Kingdom of Heaven.

JOYCE HARMER

chapter 1

TAKING THE SALUTE

On Sunday afternoon, 25 July 2004, Majors Joyce and Hilton Harmer concluded their forty-two years of service as Salvation Army officers with an Army 'salute'. A little winter rain had fallen on an otherwise drought-affected city as well-wishers made their way from railway stations and car parks towards the Salvation Army's Sydney Congress Hall in Elizabeth Street.

There had been a media release a month beforehand announcing the Harmers' retirement as veteran court and prison chaplains. Members of the legal profession, some in their wigs and gowns, had said their goodbyes over morning tea, wondering how the couple would ever be replaced, and well aware of the services the Harmers had performed, not only for their clients but for colleagues around the courts as well. Barrister Greg Stanton gave a moving speech linking their practical and professional role with their very special spiritual contribution at the courts over nine years. In Congress Hall for the Sunday salute, judges, magistrates and barristers joined others in the audience whom they had defended or sentenced. As the ceremony got under way, all were welcomed as friends of the Harmers, whether important in the community, or ordinary, or 'struggling with some of life's concerns'.

For several weeks, national and local media had been talking to Joyce and Hilton as they prepared to bow out. While they chatted with host John Kerr for an hour on Radio 2UE's midnight to dawn show, the phone calls had come in from all over eastern Australia — from people who had known them, been helped by them, or who just wanted to say hello.

At the Harmers' retirement salute, the emotion of the day was obvious immediately on arrival at the Citadel entrance. Laughter and bear hugs from Joyce, waves and handshakes from Hilton. Joyce, a small woman with curly grey hair, dressed in the distinctive navy uniform and white shirt of the Salvation Army, greeted every guest alongside Hilton, her tall navy-uniformed husband, sprigs of orchid and frosted ivy leaf on their lapels. They stood for photos with each arrival, grabbed those who might miss out, waved at others to make sure they came over. Not a person arriving missed a welcome hug, or a hand through their arm, or a close-up photo with Joyce and Hilton.

By 3.30 p.m., the two-level hall had filled with a thousand well-wishers. On stage, the Congress Hall Band played strongly, instilling a lively atmosphere, while a huge screen overhead, beyond an illuminated cross hanging from the ceiling, flashed slide after slide, revealing moments in the Harmers' ministry. *At Atherton with friends*; *Hilton and Fred enjoy Christmas lunch (inside)*; *A happy grandma*; *The Family Store staff*; *Joyce and Hilton leave the country*; *At the Downing Centre 2004*; *The Harmers meet the Governor*; *Joyce and Hilton in Alice Springs*; *Joyce and her Mum*. Later the same screen flashed up the words of hymns and songs of praise: 'People Need the Lord; 'How Great Thou Art'; 'We Are Standing on Holy Ground'; 'To God Be the Glory'.

They stood, they sang, they clapped, they listened. Uniformed Salvationists, in their crisp navy uniforms, white shirts and maroon and blue epaulets with the distinctive 'S' on their lapels, stood alongside hundreds of others who had never before been to an Army service. The crowd reflected the magnitude of the couple's working life, a life without sectarian boundaries; work that had ranged from prayerful Sundays leading Salvation Army gatherings to supporting, spiritually and physically, those awaiting judgment for murder, robbery or drug crimes, or the many who had simply lost their way. This occasion had none of the pomp and ceremony that occurs when dignitaries retire from high office, but was the conclusion of careers born out of a commitment to God made early in life, which became a commitment to those most needy in the community.

Speaker after speaker emphasised the energy, the dedication, the uniqueness of Joyce and Hilton Harmer.

For Hilton's brother Ted, a retired Salvation Army officer, their capacity for personal commitment marked them out: 'Their servant nature has prevailed not because of the Salvation Army. They took literally the encouragement of the scripture. Joyce and Hilton never responded to the needy because they wore the epaulets of a particular organisation, and it will be impossible for them to cocoon themselves in retirement and turn a deaf ear to those who plead for someone to come over and help. Only age and infirmity will stop them.'

Jonathon Skye, a friend of the Harmers, had written a special song for the occasion, acknowledging their gentle faith in humanity: *All they need is a little salvation/A tender hand and a beautiful smile/The kind of eyes that speak with kindness/And walk with me a thousand miles.*

Graeme Henson, Deputy Chief Magistrate at Sydney's Downing Centre, spoke of Joyce's ability to focus on those who needed her most. 'With meticulous regularity,' he said, 'and a mysterious ability to decipher what was behind a closed door of a courtroom, Joyce would sidle in and move up alongside some poor distressed member of a family or some poor distressed member of the community about to have their reputation and freedom on the line and out would come the hanky. Behind the hanky I always observed the hand of help. Similarly, whenever I asked if somebody was worthy to be released on bail into a rehabilitation centre or whether they had somewhere to go (and let's not beat about the bush here — many who appear in my court are dishonest and manipulative and would do anything to avoid a confrontation with reality), Hilton's cap would turn in relation to the reliability of the answer to the question. I came quickly to understand the semiotics of that device and its utility in deciding whether I should or should not grant bail and so on . . .

'Joyce and Hilton eventually came not just to manage the people affected by the courts but also those who worked in them. They left a legacy beyond belief.'

Daughter Lyndall Harmer recognised their fearlessness, quoting from a funny email she had received: *Life is not a journey to the grave with the intention of arriving safely in a pretty and well preserved body, but rather to skid in broadside, thoroughly used up, totally worn out and loudly proclaiming, 'Wow, what a ride!'* For Lyndall, her parents had ridden a lot of different roads, some smooth, many very bumpy. But it had been an amazing ride. 'No need is too great, no person too sick, no hour too late and no situation too intimidating for Mum and Dad to take care of someone, always looking for that opportunity to testify to the saving grace of God during the course of their helping.'

In between the accolades came clues to what Lyndall Harmer had referred to as 'very bumpy' roads. The Harmers' ebullient personalities hadn't always suited institutional strictures at Army Headquarters. Choosing his words carefully, Band Sergeant Ian Martin hinted at institutional bewilderment in the face of their abundant personalities: 'Being unique has made it difficult for the Salvation Army to know just what to do with them. At times the Salvation Army has not quite known where to place them. After serving at major appointments at the Sydney Congress Hall and Parramatta Salvation Army Corps, they were appointed as Social Services Development Officers with emphasis on family welfare in Wollongong, without means. They were without resources, without a phone, without a car. Typically, they just did it. When Joyce and Hilton were appointed to the Downing Centre it was as if the Salvation Army thought, Where else?'

Athol Harmer, their youngest son, grasped their core love of God: 'There is one word to describe Mum and Dad — it's passion. They have been passionate about going, being and doing in the name of Jesus.'

Major Daphne Cox, Joyce's sister, gave thanks on behalf of so many they had touched in life. Their grandchildren thanked them on the screen, straight to camera, for treats, for losing races with them and being out of action for a week as a result (Hilton), for showing them a set of false teeth (Joyce), for the times they had their grandchildren to stay for the outings — especially a recent one to *Mamma Mia* — and for just being fun: 'Grandma's very happy and that just makes me very happy,' said young Tim.

On stage, Joyce's beaming face barely dimmed in two hours while sitting next to Hilton, who, with his organiser's eye for detail, and even as the songs were being sung, was capable of noting that a pedestal hadn't been placed at one side of the stage and having it brought out. The anecdotes came and went: the tough times — like Hilton's encephalitis in his early thirties, which almost killed him, and through which Joyce managed their ministry as well as precarious accommodation arrangements for four children including an infant, along with a recuperating husband never again able to sleep beyond a few hours each day. To some, this increased energy made Hilton better than ever. Energy for even more work for the needy. There were other challenges, like Joyce's leadership in the late 1970s of Salvation Army women — some of whom were not ready for change. And always their faith in people in spite of disappointment — for instance, the woman who had been given furniture by the Salvation Army on two separate occasions only to lose it all and end up once again living with her children in an empty house. For Hilton and Joyce, it wasn't good enough to say she had failed to change her bad habits and therefore deserved no more. Whatever her frailty, she needed help. More furniture was delivered.

Then there was Gary, saved by Hilton one Sunday morning. Hilton sat in a car with him and talked him through his anger and resolve to kill himself.

'Hallelujah!' came a voice from the gallery.

'Thanks, Gary,' returned Band sergeant Ian Martin, who was narrating the story.

And Joyce had walked to court with accused child-killer Kathleen Folbigg, and sat with her every day of her trial for the murder of her four babies and later through the two hours of her sentencing. Joyce's gift is her strength and it's in times like these that she gives it generously. 'Put your arm through mine and just look straight ahead,' she would tell her client. And together they would face the cameras, the stares, the ignominy. Arm in arm they'd push on.

But how, asked Ian, could Joyce and Hilton stand with those who had been convicted of murder and other violent crimes? How do you feel about people who have done such wrong? And then he gave the answer. Joyce and Hilton don't think of what that individual has or hasn't done. Each is just a person who needs them at that moment. 'I'm just there for them,' says Joyce. And while never preaching her own beliefs to anyone, she would hand them her business card with clues to where Joyce finds her strength. Turn her card over and you will read:

> Dear Friend, Jesus said 'I am the Light of the World. If you follow me, you won't be stumbling through the darkness, for Living Light will flood your path. (John 8:12) 'Never be afraid to trust an Unknown Future to a Known God.' 'Cast all your anxiety on God because he cares for you.' (Peter 5:7)

In her retirement speech, which she had carefully prepared and practised to combat her nerves, Joyce acknowledged her struggle to commit her life to ministry. Showing no hint of stage fright on the day, she recalled a battle with 'the will of God'. Only in the words of a Christian song could she explain how she had chosen that way: *I struggled and wrestled to win it/The blessing that setteth me free/But when I had ceased from my struggling/His peace Jesus gave unto me.* Telling her audience of that struggle, Joyce seemed calm. Her hours of inner apprehension at the task of speaking never showed for a minute. 'It was not easy, but God the Holy Spirit continued to tap at my heart until I was ready to surrender,' she continued. Only as she spoke of Hilton as her 'gem' did emotion begin to choke her words. 'This is where the hanky might be needed,' she quipped, and recovered herself. 'Jesus placed him in my life when I most needed him. He is my life.' Saying she loved him with all her heart, she broke from her speech to walk over to Hilton and give him a big hug and kiss. Then she spoke of her wonderful children and grandchildren, 'gifts from God'.

Now it was Hilton's turn. At first holding his hands together as he stood at the podium, and later stretching them out to the audience, he began by acknowledging Jesus Christ his saviour — 'I give Him the glory' — saying that he would make many 'understatements' about his life and there would be a need for those who heard him to multiply his experience many times over. But it wasn't long before he had turned his focus to Joyce and called out forty-two red roses in a huge sheath of greenery, which he presented to his overwhelmed wife. Hilton is renowned for giving Joyce roses, what their children call 'no-reason gifts'. 'Why wait till you're dead for flowers?' he'll say. 'I want you to have them while you're alive.' For Joyce, Hilton is a gift himself — her romantic gem. Even so, on this day of all days, he wasn't finished. There was more. Hilton is someone who loves nothing better than springing a surprise. Hinting at something bigger and more lasting, something that had almost cost more than he and his family could manage, he finally presented his adored wife with a ring designed as a circle of tiny diamonds, not quite one for every three years of their service together. Before a thousand pairs of eyes, Joyce squealed like a girl of sixteen.

The retirement ceremony lasted nearly three hours, choreographed, scripted and directed by the Harmer family and their close friends, and closing with a stirring oration from Salvation Army Commissioner Earle Maxwell. Afterwards, most of the audience moved to the fourth floor for a networking and catch-up over coffee and finger food, which ended with a huge chocolate cake presented to Hilton, who had taken his salute on the day of his sixty-fifth birthday, as onlookers chanted 'Hip, hip, hooray!'

One of the guests, who knew Joyce from the Downing Centre, reflected on the words of one speaker — 'Joyce exudes a spiritual fragrance.' For forty-two years and more, with Hilton beside her, that fragrance had filled the lives of thousands just when they most desperately needed it. Those who knew Joyce in her work recognised the fragrance in the way they felt about her; her warmth and empathy moved in the air around them. 'She never judges,' they would say, 'no matter who.' For her it was not a case of bad people, but bad choices; redemption and recovery were always a chance, something to pray for, to work towards with individuals, however hard the road became.

At the retirement ceremony, Hilton's admiration for his wife was palpable. Her strength, her kindly generosity had never faltered. He had known it when he married her in Gympie, forty-five years earlier. And they had walked a hard road many times and seen something of the lows in life, like those they chose to help. This had enlarged their capacity for empathy, but it had not been easy. Hilton had gone through years of depression after suffering encephalitis. And Joyce had stood beside him, unquestioning, when he had fallen out with Headquarters, regardless of the fact that she disliked confrontation and that the disputes had taken significant postings from them. But he continued to marvel at her, more and more in their older years, as if he were discovering her uniqueness all over again.

For in a way, they had won. Not by following career paths to high command. On the contrary, they had won because no matter how much they were sidelined, or how many times they felt almost beaten by physical handicaps, they had never lost sight of the core values of their Christian mission. Against any odds, even when they might have prayed the words of the Book of Job — *Though He slay me, yet will I praise him* — they had made a ministry wherever they were sent.

chapter 2

GYMPIE

Joyce Harmer had grown up a Lipke. Born 13 May 1940, at the Lister Hospital in Shannon Street, Gympie, her parents Reg and Alice Lipke called her Joyce at a time when newspaper and radio reports were swamped with news of war in Europe, the Germans advancing yet again through Belgium on their way to taking Paris as Europe began another world war. 'Joyce,' Alice might have said to Reg as he brought her a morning cup of tea. 'If it's a girl, that's what we'll call her. "Joyce" for "joy".' Soon after Joyce's birth, Reg Lipke, though descended from German grandparents, registered for Allied military service.

Remembered by her peers as something of a quiet little girl, young Joyce had a merry laugh and a strong mind. Elder brothers Cecil and Keith were very different in nature. Cecil clashed with his father regularly and took many beatings, while Keith was more compliant and escaped his father's anger. As an adult, Cecil would live his life in the shadow of memories — those of a hard father who never seemed to have understood him. As Joyce grew older she also found her father a difficult man to please in spite of her generous nature. And Alice, loyal and devoted to her husband above all, left the discipline to Reg, so that neither Joyce nor Cecil could rely on their mother for support.

As a child, Reg himself had taken the knocks hard. He had grown up in Toowoomba with little or no recollection of his father Harry. Before Reg started school, Harry had deserted the family, leaving his wife Maria to raise their six children alone. Like many single parents of the day, Reg's mother had tried to keep her children together, but eventually she had been forced to send the school-aged Reg to a boys' home. She told Reg to let her know if he was unhappy by adding lots of kisses to the end of his letters. Which he soon did. So Reg returned home, but he never forgot the experience. Over the years he was cared for by various older siblings and relatives, some of whom handed out rough treatment to match the orphanage. As a parent himself he was known for his overly strict and sometimes hard ways, especially to his older children. His strap lay on the table at meal-times and hung behind the kitchen door in between. Only with his younger children did he mellow, as if time and an increasingly comfortable life had healed some of the scars from his childhood.

Alice Lipke had grown up a Smith, born in 1912, the sixth and youngest child of Eliza and Charles. Small at birth and frail as a child, her parents had kept her home after her schooling finished. 'We can afford to keep only one lady,' Charles would say. Her mother, Eliza, described Alice as weighing little more than a pound of butter as a newborn. 'I could have carried her round in a milk jug, she was so tiny,' she'd say.

But Alice's pint-sized start in life was no indication of how she would live it. At twenty-one, Alice Smith, barely five feet in height, married the very tall and handsome Reg Lipke, whom she had met at a dance. The Smiths hadn't approved of Reg, although they couldn't stand in the way of his marrying Alice. He was an out-of-towner, little was known of his background and he hadn't much in the way of income or savings to offer their delicate daughter. Reg was working as a forrester at Imbil. He courted Alice by riding his pushbike the thirty-seven kilometres to Gympie on his days off. There would be years of rift before the Smiths grudgingly came to accept their son-in-law.

As newlyweds, Reg and Alice lived at Cooroy, south of Gympie, and then at Dalby in the Darling Downs. The early years of their marriage were financially tough. One old photo shows them in front of a house that looks little more than a shack. Then Reg gave up forestry work to become a gentlemen's hairdresser. Their first two children, Cecil and Keith, came quickly and soon learned to walk and talk, poke and squeal and fight over toys, as little children do, so that in the space of a few years the fragile Alice was coping with quite a handful. A year after the floods of 1939 had swamped the lower lying parts of Gympie and Alice's sister Elsie had died at the age of thirty-six leaving five children, Cecil and Keith welcomed their new little sister Joyce into the world.

Floods were part of memory for a child who had grown up in Gympie, the former gold town 170 kilometres north of Brisbane. When the floods came, a fearful young Joyce Lipke would watch the rising water flowing strongly just below the bridges they had to cross. The floods were bad in Gympie in March 1939. Alice Lipke couldn't remember anything quite like it. The Mary River cut through a vast flood plain on the town's western edges. Gold from Gympie's river had saved the colony of Queensland from bankruptcy in the 1860s, and put Gympie on the map. But all that was long in the past. As the talk of war with Germany began again in the 1930s, Gympie was relying on timber and agriculture rather than gold to survive.

When the family settled in Gympie soon after Joyce's birth, Alice Lipke was glad to be closer to her old home, though Reg still kept his distance. In Gympie, the Lipkes settled into a more comfortable life. The house was small but close to town and Reg had regular employment within walking distance, and was able to drop the children at school on the way to the shop. This was the era of proud housekeeping, of healthy children and home appliances. Advertisements to attract the female customer in local newspapers and magazines portrayed the housewife as shapely but aproned, commanding her kitchen and family behind the walls of a tidy bungalow. Women were offered helpful hints on anything that might be of trouble in the home — from mending a leaky tap or worn washer to serving a hot ham and spreading chocolate icing so that it held its gloss.

Alice's sister Elsie's death in 1939 had been a tragedy. Elsie's five children had been more than their bereaved father could manage and were immediately sent to institutions. But, after fifteen months, grandparents Charles and Eliza Smith, in spite of their ill-health, could not face returning the two girls, Val and Heather, to the orphanage at the end of the holidays. Val was barely three years old. They decided to rear their granddaughters themselves. The little girls lived first in Pring Lane and later at their rambling verandahed home with the hip roof at 11 Rowe Street. Alice and Elsie's unmarried sister Irene, who had been a Salvation Army officer in Sydney, was called home to help. The three boys, though, were left in the Indooroopilly Boys' Home and later went to their father. For years, Val and Heather barely knew their brothers. Eventually they heard news that they were working out west on farms. The siblings had grown up strangers. The girls' cousins, Cecil, Keith and Joyce, took the place of siblings.

For a time, Alice might have thought her own three young children were the complete set. It would be four years before her second daughter, Joan, was born. Yet the once fragile Alice would eventually have seven children. The last three, Daphne, Yvonne and Clifford, were born so close together after a gap of five years that it was as if the older and younger children made up two separate families.

When they first moved to Gympie, Reg and Alice had lived at 29 O'Connell Street, close to the centre of town and across the road from a timber mill and hardware centre. It was a two-bedroomed iron-roofed weatherboard with a sleep-out and a huge macadamia-nut tree at the back. Alice was a mother and wife in the best traditions of the time. She had a live-in home-help, a Mrs Simpson, who shared a bedroom with Joyce. In season, nuts from the macadamia tree would drop onto the iron roof and make a waking din. Eventually Reg chopped it down.

Reg's stint in the Army wasn't to last very long. Shortly before he was to embark for overseas service he was declared unfit, owing to his asthma. He was honourably discharged and returned to his job as a hairdresser, working at Peter Rutkin's shop near Gympie's Memorial Park gates. On Fridays, Reg worked late and Alice would parcel up a hot meal set out on a dinner plate with another plate over the top to keep it warm. Joyce can remember being asked as a small child to run the meal, wrapped in a tea towel tied in a knot, down to the barber's, not very far from the O'Connell Street house.

In time, Reg set up his own business in central Gympie, astutely choosing a shop along the higher parts of Mary Street, well above the flood levels. His shop had long benches and one barber's chair that tilted back, where customers were shaved with a cut-throat razor through a thick lather and dried with fresh towels, collars protected with special paper. Alice would be given a mountain of barber's towels each day to add to the family wash of nappies and toddlers' clothes. In subtropical Gympie with its forty-five inches of rain annually, and well before clothes dryers, it was quite a task always to have them ready for returning to the barber's shop.

With four children putting a strain on the house in O'Connell Street and Reg's income much improved from those early penurious married years, he bought some land to build a larger house on the outskirts of Gympie — at Pilchers Hill.

'It was all bush when we moved in,' recalls Keith. 'We were the first house there. There was only a dirt road to the house for years.'

It was the house all the Lipke kids would remember as the family home. The boys kept pigeons in the back and it looked out over Gympie, well above the town.

'It was weatherboard with a bay window in the front,' Keith muses, thinking back. 'High-set in the front, the steps came down to a little porch and then down again. It had a fibro roof, and fibro inside walls. One thing I'll always remember about that house was how we could see the fire station, and any time there was a fire in Gympie a wartime siren used to sound. It was one howl of a sound. Parts of the city had different codes. The firemen would hear the siren and know the location of the fire. We had fires in Gympie regularly, those old weatherboard houses would go up so easily.'

Gradually more roads were carved out and other people came to live at Pilchers Hill. The Lipkes' address was 5 Somerset Street. Mrs Simpson no longer lived in. A new home-help, an Aboriginal lady called Mrs Conlon, now came on Mondays to do the huge weekend wash. The children remember her as a loving, gentle lady. Days for Alice were full of housekeeping, washing and polishing floors, waiting over her copper for the clothes to boil till they lost every spot. There were three tubs in the wash house and three rinses with the blue bag for shirts. Velvet soap was cut up frugally for the copper and to put in the shaker for the kitchen sink, and there was a wood stove for cooking. A cure for a child's cold was drops of kerosene on a heaped teaspoon of sugar, swallowed quickly. Alice's house was always immaculate, her children disciplined and ready for Dad at the end of the day.

Before long there were home appliances to ease the workload for Alice in the post-war boom: a Mix Master for baking and making ice-cream, a fridge and a floor polisher, but the best toast was still made over the wood fire with a three-pronged toasting fork. Reg, eventually able to indulge his passion to own a car, converted the space underneath his house, so typically Queensland, to garage his regularly traded-in models. Before they had a car, though, the Lipkes used pushbikes.

Joyce recalls how, on Sundays, they would go to church on bikes. 'My father would double my mother, my eldest brother Cecil would double me and Keith would double Joan. We'd walk up the hills together; most of it was dirt roads then. We used the bikes only when we could easily get along on the downhill sections. At one point in the road, near home, the bulldogs from a neighbouring house would come out and everyone's legs would go up as we sailed past.'

Home life was dominated by Reg, who meted out discipline with the strap, given often and quickly. He'd use his black belt or whatever he could reach that would do at the time he exploded. A child did not have to be doing something obviously bad. In fact, the incidents of what Joyce might have done, or not done, to get a belting from Reg are lost to her memory. This is not unusual with fearful events in a life; the memory of them is often wiped away to prevent the sorrow they bring. Joyce might have given a reply that was interpreted as 'answering back' or might not have agreed immediately to do some chore. Her mother would call her a 'cheeky beesom' and would say, 'Wait till your father gets home.' Joyce often would hide in the outdoor toilet about thirty metres from the back door till Reg had been home a while and the dust had settled a bit, so her father might not remember what Alice had told him the girl had done. But it didn't always work, and often out would come the belt.

'If I did not respond quickly enough to a command to do something around the house,' recalls Joyce, 'I would find myself receiving a sharp stroke from the end of the belt he had, or some electric cord. That would bring immediate results for him because I knew that if I did not respond there would be more to follow.' The beatings left her feeling that a cloud of unhappiness hung over her childhood and that she was not loved by her parents. At times Reg even threatened to send her to a 'reformatory'.

One incident of the abuse she received from Reg has stayed clearly in her memory. At the age of five, her father ordered her to her room in a rage. He told her to take off her clothes, as he was going to give her a belting. 'I recall that I yelled out, "No! No! No!" so he belted me over my clothing. But anger was present, and a little girl's heart full of fear.' Those fears left scars that she would carry for life. The abuse was both intermittent and ongoing. It was verbal, physical and emotional. 'Mine was a childhood,' says Joyce, 'where you felt you were walking over eggshells. I had to be continuously on my guard that I did not fall foul of the master of the house, or punishment would be forthcoming.'

Contrasted with this was the warmth Reg could show at times. He was an indulgent father when holidays came. This made understanding Reg even more difficult for Joyce. 'My fear of beatings was mixed with some very happy occasions, when he would take the family to the beach, for holidays and drives. He would buy us Mr Whippy ice-creams when they first came to town. I can remember the green soft serves and chocolate ice-creams he bought for us on outings. And I often wished the happiness that existed on holidays could have been present each day throughout the year.'

The Lipke children attended Gympie Central Primary School and later the local high school. At five, Joyce's father handed her over to Mrs Anderson, the Prep One teacher, who walked the terrified child along the school verandah as Reg turned and left for his shop. Later there was the white-haired Mr Enright, who called Joyce out to the front of the class. Imagining she was about to be severely disciplined for talking, Joyce burst into tears. But a gentle Mr Enright put his arm around her and said, 'Don't cry, I just wanted you to smile at the class and show them your dimpled cheeks!' He gave her his cup and a cold drink and sent her outside to sit on the tank stand till she felt better. At six, she had great fun in the rain as she sloshed to school, and arrived with sopping shoes — like others. The headmistress, Miss Courtney, lined them up and caned them across the palms of their hands.

Joyce recalls feeling inferior at school. She has a sense of being shy and lacking self-esteem. The playground bewildered her with its wild activity, and she often felt left out of groups she could have sat with, as they talked and swapped gossip.

'I remember running through the playgrounds and being bumped on the nose. Often the boys would go crazy and I was always in the way.'

The Lipke children were given small amounts of pocket money once a week to buy fruit for lunch from their aunts' tiny shop. But Joyce would sometimes go to the corner store instead and buy a shilling's worth of conversation lollies, using them in a desperate attempt to communicate with the other children.

'The lollies had little messages written on them. They were shaped like hearts. I didn't see them as desperation, the messages like "I love you" and "I think you're sweet", but I know I was trying to communicate with people, to be wanted, to be needed. I would hand them out and the other children would be friendly. I now know what I wanted was a friend. It's one thing to be friendly, another to be a friend.'

That search for a friend directed Joyce's early years, in more ways than she would realise, till decades later.

chapter 3

THE CITADEL

More than their weekday schooling, it was the Salvation Army Citadel that left a lasting impact on the Lipke kids' development. In the imposing 1939 brick and concrete-rendered building set square on the slope of Caledonian Hill, they attended Sunday school and Corps Cadets weekly. Their social life and the friends they made came from there.

In the post-war era in Australia, Christian churches of all denominations retained their strength, even in some cases excelling in recruiting newcomers, including many from among the steady influx of new immigrants. Families went to church on Sundays; children who attended secular public schools on weekdays still turned up for Sunday school. Social life for many of the young revolved around their church affiliations, whether through Bible studies or youth groups. Newspapers carried columns advertising the times of services and lists of church functions to be held. But among the various denominations, none were as noticeable as the Catholics and Salvationists — for their contribution to the shortfall in government social welfare through their charitable work among the poor and dispossessed; for their distinctive traditions, such as the uniforms their most religious adherents wore; and for their institutional separateness. They were the Christian outsiders to some extent, marked off by funny habits in a country with an established Anglican Church.

Reg and Alice had been married in a Methodist church. And, for a while, the family would attend various churches without belonging to any. But in Gympie, with a growing family, they joined the Salvation Army. As told by son Keith, the story goes that Reg Lipke, who had been brought up in the Salvation Army but had given it away as an adult, was working outside the O'Connell Street house scything his grass, not long after leaving hospital following an operation to remove his appendix. Captain Packer, the local Salvation Army officer, was driving by the house and saw Reg, who he knew was not long out of hospital. He stopped his car and crossed the road.

'You're not supposed to be doing that, you know,' he said, greeting Reg and taking the scythe. Then he rolled up his sleeves and finished the job.

'That,' Reg would recall, 'was a sermon worth more than all others I've heard from a pulpit, that one act of support Packer performed. That's what I call Christianity with its sleeves rolled up. The only sort that matters.' It was enough to convince Reg. He rejoined the Salvation Army as a soldier. The family naturally went with him. Alice had leaned that way for some time, especially when her sister Irene returned to Gympie after being with the Army in Sydney.

The Salvation Army grew out of a breakaway mission from the Methodist Church in England, led by William Booth. In London in 1865, around the time of the Gympie gold rush in the British colony of Queensland, former Methodist minister William Booth, supported by his wife Catherine, who had herself become a renowned preacher, struck out as the leader of a Church founded in the slums. William Booth's bellicose sermons acted like fire in a London that feared revolution among its growing industrial poor.

The foul and fetid breath of our slums is almost as poisonous as that of the African swamp, he wrote in *Darkest England* of the crisis of faith and human depravity he witnessed. *Every year children are killed off by what is called defects in our sanitary system. They are really starved and poisoned.*

This was aggressive language, and such accusations of abuse against civil authorities drew the ire and outrage of mainstream Protestant Churches. William Booth had rejected Calvinism and its belief in the 'elect'. William was very much — partly with the early persuasion of his wife — a believer in 'Christianity with its sleeves rolled up', the Christianity of the streets, where souls (and bodies) needed rescuing. William and Catherine held strongly that sinfulness wasn't innate in poor people, with their drinking, thieving and prostitution, but that poverty was the key to their waywardness. Radically they held also, principally from Catherine, that those to blame for the trade in prostitutes were the depraved men of cities like London. Take the poor out of their downtrodden powerlessness, through saving them for Christ and improving their material circumstances by providing them with food, shelter and clothing, and their sinful lives would be converted to living for God. The Salvationist stood against those other Protestant Churches who shunned the conversion of the poor, unable to forget their past misdeeds. Over decades, William and Catherine Booth brought thousands of poor into their fold and made them leaders and followers in their Salvation Army — an army of foot soldiers and officers to save souls for God.

Although Alice never wore the Salvation Army uniform, Reg and his older children did. In time, Reg became the Colour Sergeant, proudly holding the banner at the front of the band at the weekly Salvation Army open-air meetings on Sunday evening, marching from Rankins Corner through to the Citadel, up Mary Street. So, around the time she started primary school, little Joyce Lipke began attending all-embracing Sundays at the Salvation Army Citadel. In keeping with the belief that Sunday is for God, a Salvation Army family would spend a good part of Sunday at church. For Joyce, a favourite memory is the Salvation Army program each Sunday in the early evening on Radio 4BC. 'The band would strike up and lead us in a bright upbeat half-hour of music. They'd play *O boundless salvation, deep ocean of love/O fullness of mercy Christ brought from above/The whole world redeeming so rich and so free/O come mighty ocean and roll over me.* Meaning, the spirit of God should encompass our lives. And often that would spark my family into getting up and going to church that night.'

When Joyce Lipke started Salvation Army Sunday school at around the age of five, the traditions of the Salvation Army had been modified by time. A more middle-class movement had evolved. The Army still worked with the fringe dwellers of society as it had always done, but in the suburbs and country towns the local corps (church) operated much more like mainstream churches, but with believers who spent more of their time devoted to church activities. The meetings for the Army on Sundays spread across the day, and many soldiers and friends would turn up for corps a number of times. Small children also attended in the afternoons for their Sunday school lessons. That all-encompassing Salvation Army community made a lasting impression on the young Joyce. More than half a century later, Joyce can recall her Gympie Salvation Army Sunday school teacher, Miss Coe, as clearly as if it were yesterday.

'Miss Coe, an unmarried lady, was thought highly of in the community. She was a sweetheart, an angel and she took us for Primary — under-eight-year-olds — as our leader. She fussed over everyone and made us feel wonderful. We would tip our pennies into her lap after the collection and she would count them out in front of us. To collect the money was a great privilege, and we sang, *Hear the pennies dropping/Listen as they fall/Every one for Jesus/He shall have them all/Dropping, dropping, dropping, dropping/Hear the pennies fall/Every one for Jesus/He shall have them all.* It was a thrill for us to be able to write on the blackboard how much we had collected.

'For the Bible story, we sat in a circle of small chairs. Miss Coe would lead the other teachers. "Two strong boys," she would say. "Let me see. Where are two strong boys who can carry the mat?" Two selected boys would carry the mat on their shoulders and unroll it in the centre of the circle of chairs. We'd sit there, nice and quiet, listening to the Bible stories — Abraham and Isaac, the Good Samaritan, Solomon and David, the birth of Jesus the Saviour, the three wise kings, Adam and Eve — taking it all in. It was beautiful. Once you were eight, the class would sing "Happy Birthday" and Miss Coe would escort you around to the senior Sunday school. With a certain ceremony we would be introduced to the class and the Young People's Sergeant Major and Miss Coe would tell them to be sure to look after us. That was very special to a child.'

With her cousins Val and Heather, Joyce would be dressed for Sunday school by their Auntie Rene's friend, whom they called Auntie Maise. Maisie Rudd, a woman Irene had befriended in Sydney, had joined Irene's family in Gympie when Irene had come home to help raise Elsie's daughters, Val and Heather. Maisie had no family of her own and Irene had found her through the Salvation Army, living in an Army refuge. She adored Val and Heather and the Lipke girls. And they adored her.

'All the grandchildren just loved Auntie Maise,' Joyce recalls fondly. 'In a different way from how we loved Auntie Rene. Auntie Maise was such a giver of herself. Sometimes we would stay at our grandparents' for the weekend. That was a treat. Auntie Maise had us sleep in the enclosed verandah. She had her own bedroom there with other spare beds. She would place tiny packages of sweets under our pillows so we knew the fairies came at night. She was such an angel.'

Auntie Maise and Auntie Rene filled some of the emotional gaps. They earned a modest living by running a tiny shop built in the space of an alleyway in Mary Street. Given permission by the auctioneer owner of the lane, they added a front and back wall between two shops either side and set up what became known as the Variety Alcove. With barely space to sit behind the opening onto the street, they sold lollies and fruit, babywear they had knitted or crocheted, iced drinks in summer, toffee apples and flowers. Anything the women could make or grow at home, they sold. Val recalled that when the floods came it was a chance for good takings. While other shops in the main part of Mary Street were flooded out, the Variety Alcove traded well. 'Auntie Rene used to be run off her feet making meat pies and cakes and scones,' says Val. 'I used to bring them down on the front of a pushbike, if you please.'

At other times they made wreaths for funerals and bouquets for weddings, using help from the shop next door to store some of their supplies. The customers literally stood in the street to make their purchases, the shop was so small. All the Lipke kids and their cousins loved the Variety Alcove. They would be given small amounts of money to buy drinks or fruit for school. Stopping by the shop, they were the delight of Irene and Maisie, whose cylinders of fruit juice and jars of lollies worked their magic on the childish imagination. For Joyce, Auntie Maise and Auntie Rene were the warmth and homely comfort, even indulgence, in an otherwise severely ruled and physically contained childhood. Decades later, Joyce would write to Maisie just before the older lady died, to thank her for the magic she had added to her childhood — the lollies under the pillow, the fairies that came in the night, the wonderful times she had sleeping over at the old people's house.

On Sunday mornings at the Smith house or the Lipke house, Auntie Maise prettied up the girls for Sunday school — washed their hair and set it in rags, pressed their clothes and cleaned their shoes. Then she would walk them to Sunday school in the afternoon and bring them home. Later, as they grew older, the girls went to Directory meetings, followed by church, before going home. After lunch they would go back for Sunday school, open-air and prayer meetings, and more church. Families attending the Citadel went home for lunch and at teatime.

Sundays and her contact with Auntie Maise contributed the love and belonging that Joyce Lipke never felt she attracted in other realms of her life as she grew up. Her parents had their burdens and preoccupations. Reg was an asthmatic and was frequently hospitalised in the winters. Alice had younger children to attend to and looked to Joyce to act as a sort of little mother herself. As in many large families, the older children were expected to grow to maturity very quickly. Both parents seemed unaware of the hunger in Joyce and Cecil for recognition of their pubescent selves. The chores were endless and the little ones increasingly occupied their parents' time. Meanwhile, Reg also had his work and his cars.

The strict discipline in the Lipke household was challenged by the strong-willed Joyce and Cecil in their own ways. Joyce can well recall it even now. 'Cecil had to chop the wood for the fire. At 4 p.m. the fire for the oven was lit, religiously. Keith seemed to get off lightly by having to set the table or wheel the baby in the pram. Joan and I would have to do the dishes. I had to wash the saucepans, scrub them with sandsoap so that I could see my face in them. If we dropped a cup or Joan and I were fooling around as we did the dishes, we'd hear our father march out from the bedroom or wherever he was in the house and he'd get the strap off the back of the door and give it to us. On one occasion we just couldn't stop laughing as soon as we broke a cup. "Hear it comes!" we giggled as we waited for our whack.'

Reg was an impatient man. He was the boss at home and outside it. On public holidays, Reg and Alice would pile the children into their latest car and take off on a whim. The cousins and aunts — Val, Heather, Irene and Maisie — would often be invited to join in at the last minute. The phone call would come in the early hours of the Monday holiday.

They'd leave at six, Reg pulling up at the gate well before breakfast, beeping his horn and anxious to get started for a distant picnic spot like Tin Can Bay. There was no complaining because Reg would have been very angry and would probably have said, 'Well I won't ask you again.'

At the Salvation Army Citadel, Reg was the sort of father who looked out for his kids, made sure they got the recognition he thought they deserved. At home, his word kept the children upright and Alice comforted. He did the budgets, set the rules, even determined the home remedies for colds and other ailments. If Alice needed to catch a taxi from the Somerset Street house to visit her parents, it was Reg who doled out the money she needed — and the little extra for such items as bread or milk. Just enough and no more. Mostly Reg would drop Alice off at the Rowe Street house and return for her later, sitting in the car outside and beeping the horn to hurry her up if she didn't appear at the gate the minute he arrived.

At the Citadel on Sundays, the Lipkes would arrive for the 11 a.m. meeting, and by a minute past noon (the service ending at noon) Reg would be in his car out the front honking his horn for the family to pile in. And they did, very quickly, as if to delay would bring down a wrath they would prefer to avoid. Should Reg hear something said in a meeting that he did not like, a view or argument he disagreed with, he would beckon to his family to follow him out and they did, pronto.

'Mum was always the peacemaker,' says Keith Lipke. 'And blessed are the peacemakers.'

Laughing off Reg's quick-to-anger presence wasn't always easy. As Joyce emerged into her teenage years, the two children in the family living next door to the Lipkes often caused her to reflect on how life might have been in a smaller family where there were few babies to take up parents' time and attention — and love. Looking back now, she says, 'It could well have been that I was a difficult child or something. I didn't see myself that way. It might have been where I came in the family, or because of the seven children. It might have been my father's background that I knew nothing of, or his way of disciplining his first three children, or for other reasons.'

In spite of the holidays at Tewantin and the outings on public holidays in Reg's latest car, there was something missing for Joyce at home as she neared the end of her secondary schooling. By sixteen, she was beginning to realise her father was as strict about boyfriends as he was about broken cups. And any career prospects she might have imagined would be overtaken by her mother's need for home help.

'I didn't feel that I was loved at that time,' says Joyce, holding back any acrimony or outright criticism of her parents.

But at church she knew God loved her.

chapter 4

HILTON

Reg and Alice had their last three children very quickly, so that at fifteen, Joyce, as the eldest daughter, was seen as the obvious home-help for Alice.

'In those days you did that. You left school at fourteen or fifteen. I went home to help Mum, who by then had three small children. And while I loved the babies, there was all the rest I hated. Polishing floors on my hands and knees, over and over, washing the lino and buffing it by hand till it shone. My mother was a tremendous housekeeper. Sometimes now I wish she was here so I could ask her so many things there was no time to talk about then — nor desire.'

Joyce remembers a sense of drifting away from her parents in her adolescent years. Their time was occupied with little ones. Reg was a model husband and father with his last three children, getting up in the night to the babies, helping with the washing up. In spite of the strict family observances as members of the Salvation Army, Reg had mellowed a lot in his manner of disciplining the younger children. Daphne and Yvonne, his youngest daughters, loved him as the father Joyce never knew. In her teens, it seemed to Joyce as if the younger children were her parents' main responsibility and interest. As if to be a teenager were to be already grown and ready for adult responsibilities — except, of course, when mixing with the opposite sex.

Adolescence is hardly ever a smooth ride. But for Salvation Army adolescents, like the Lipke children, it came with added restrictions. They were not allowed to enter a cinema or join in just about any mainstream social gathering. Joan Lipke, four years younger than Joyce, hated the rule and often felt the odd one out at school: 'I remember I would have to say, "I belong to the Salvation Army and we don't believe in folk dancing; my parents won't let me take part." And when the other kids were discussing the Saturday afternoon matinée I didn't know what they were talking about.' Daphne Lipke had her own disquiet at being seen to be marked out in an odd way. Standing on the corner of Mary Street for the open-air meetings, she was conscious of friends walking past. 'I always felt a little bit funny about it. Although they accepted me as I was.' And she remembers one Anzac Day when her father stopped them from going to an Anzac Day service because it was held in the local cinema.

The young, for all that, will always find a way. And Joyce was no exception. Looking back on her early life, Joyce can remember Hilton Harmer on the edge of her focus well before he became her true love. Hilton came to Gympie from Nambour at around the age of seven. His father worked for the railways and the Harmer family had moved home a bit over the years. Hilton, born in Mackay, recalls an early life of tough poverty; one house they lived in even had a dirt floor. There were times when the family depended on charity to survive. That early life gave Hilton an empathy for those in dire straits.

The courtship of Hilton's parents, Cliff and Connie, had begun despite a great deal of ill will towards Connie from

Cliff's family. Connie MacDonald had given birth to a child out of wedlock. The child was immediately adopted out, as was the custom — a loss she never got over — and because of the social mores of the time, her reputation suffered. Cliff's sisters would cross to the other side of the street if they saw Connie coming towards them. But Cliff Harmer fell in love with Connie and nothing his sisters could say or do could stop them from marrying.

For the duration of the war, the Harmers and their five children moved around, first to Toowoomba as the Japanese moved south and the north of Australia became a target, then to Nambour and finally Gympie, where they stayed. Unlike the Lipkes, the Harmers managed on a low weekly wage for most of their married life; they had no business to build up and prosper from as Reg had done. But the Harmer family had a closeness and warmth that Joyce found lacking in the house she came from.

The Harmer parents had remained strong Salvationists in spite of their many moves. In Gympie they joined the local citadel, Connie Harmer going on to become a Senior Elder and Corps Treasurer. Their children became part of Corps Cadets and the like, groups that Joyce and her siblings mixed in. There was also the musical drama group, the Sunday gatherings for youth and the meetings they held on weeknights. Church functions filled the social chasm for Salvation Army youngsters. More often than not, Salvation Army teenagers found their future partners at church. Romance blossomed in prayer meetings. A first date could be at a Bible class.

Hilton attended the One Mile School, but he came over to Joyce's junior high for woodwork classes. Before long, the thirteen-year-old Joyce had a noticeable crush on fourteen-year-old Hilton. He made her laugh and his good-humoured temperament attracted her. He was not afraid to be kind, to talk about things with her. Her shyness melted away around him. He wasn't rough like the boys who raced past her in the playground. He was sensitive and cared about people and wasn't afraid to say so. She liked the older Harmers too, his sisters Lillian, Doreen and Beryl — who had been her first Sunday school teacher — and his brother Ted, who played the euphonium in the Army's Corps band.

'The kids used to write *J.L. xx H.H.* and stuff like that over my exercise books,' says Joyce. 'I felt then it was more me interested than him because I felt so unloved at home. I do know I couldn't bear any other girl looking at Hilton Harmer. He was so genuine, so caring and yet so funny in his own way.' She recalls that Hilton also caught her attention with his tendency to 'act up in front of everyone', like the day of the Sunday school anniversary concert. Joyce was wearing her beautiful sky-blue dacron frock. Hilton, still very much a boy, was fooling about as if to seek attention from his peers, in the way young boys will by showing off how well they can do something physically dangerous. Losing sight of where he was headed, Hilton had ridden his bike into Joyce, leaving a black tyre mark right down the front of her skirt. Hilton became upset. He had just been larking about but had obviously gone too far. There were angry words when she got home with the damaged dress.

By their mid-teens, it wasn't only Joyce who was keen on Hilton. Hilton had started to notice Joyce as a friend, someone to talk to. She wasn't a flirtatious sort of girl and Hilton remembers her as always dressing modestly, in longer skirts and high-necked tops, nothing provocative. Her abiding interest in her Christian faith also captured his interest. If Joyce hadn't been a Christian, Hilton admits he would not have had any time for her. Their friendship grew out of their common interests, and issues they shared in their conversations. So unfamiliar in a world of Hollywood films and instant bodily contact. But of course there was eventually the familiar 'she's a girl and I'm a boy' attraction.

The first moment when Hilton was conscious of a physical attraction was the night of the twenty-first birthday party of his twin brother and sister Ted and Doreen. Joyce was sixteen. There was no dancing at this Salvation Army party, but in a session of games they were playing where they had to change partners, Hilton remembers that as he came to partner Joyce from behind he had instinctively, and with feeling, put both his arms around her waist. He noticed this. Like a change of gear. 'But we were not an item then,' he adds.

Hilton had been eager to get into paid work as soon as he could legally leave school at fifteen. He had taken a job with Cullinanes department store, the largest department store in Gympie, which sold items from small goods, haberdashery, clothing, groceries, crockery and manchester to hardware and alcohol. However, Hilton still saw Joyce regularly, both at the Citadel for Corps activities and while riding about town taking orders for groceries at back doors from housewives. He often found himself on the steps at the Lipkes' home at 5 Somerset Street, where Joyce would be helping her mother with the housework and caring for her younger siblings. They would exchange a few words as he took the orders.

In spite of their close friendship, Hilton was sixteen before he was ever invited into the Lipke house as one of Joyce's pals. And in those early years, Joyce never said anything about the way Reg hit them. 'I never knew in those days that he belted his children,' says Hilton. However, he did sense that Reg could rage at a moment's notice with anyone — at home or church. A sentimental chap, Hilton was moved when Joyce finally told him of her rough treatment at home, confiding in him as a person she could trust, someone who would share her unhappiness and make it easier to bear. Hilton never saw Reg hit Joyce, but he often helped mop up the tears afterwards.

'One night I went to pick her up and she was crying. She was telling me about something Reg had done to her. And he crept up behind us in the dark. I didn't hear him coming, he was like that. He heard what Joyce was saying and jumped out at us with, "If you don't like it here, you can get out." '

One Sunday, the tension between Joyce and Reg came to a head. 'It was the last time my father hit me,' says Joyce. 'I was getting ready to go to the Sunday morning prayer meeting which the Salvation Army called Knee Drill. My father thought I should have been home helping my mother get Sunday morning breakfast for the family. When he discovered I was not going to stay home to help, he pushed me into a corner of a room, shouting at me about what I should be doing, thumping me on the arm between the elbow and shoulder. It hurt me a lot and, as usual, I cried. I cried as I walked down the road towards Hilton, who would always come to meet me away from the family home. I refused to go home that day, so Hilton took me to his sister Doreen and her husband Tom, and I stayed with them until I had worked out where I would go in the future.'

In the days that followed, the breakdown in relations between Reg and Joyce was eventually smoothed over, and

Joyce returned home. But now she was ready to go. Shortly afterwards, she packed her bags and headed for Brisbane, where she stayed, working briefly in a Salvation Army hostel. Reg called her again and again, pressuring her to come home. After a few weeks, Joyce said she would, but only if Hilton came to get her, which he did. Once back in the family home in Gympie, Joyce worked for a short time at the Nestles milk factory before moving into nursing work at the Glandore Private Hospital. Later she nursed at the Gympie Public Hospital. Nurses were required to live in at hospitals, so Joyce was able to move out, and this time Reg couldn't bring her home.

Reg was an intolerant man and suspicious of any boy who took Joyce out, but he had a particular grudge against the Harmers. Ted and Hilton believe this had grown out of an altercation Reg once had with Connie Harmer over a difference of opinion on church matters. Connie was an Elder at the Corps and Reg was not one to take any criticism lightly. Their disagreement and its wake certainly made it tough for Joyce and Hilton to see one another.

Hilton recalls a Salvation Army meeting outside Gympie, at Bath Terrace Outpost, when he and Joyce had left the hall to talk, a few yards from the front door of the church. Joyce was sixteen. It was cold and Hilton had thrown his coat over her shoulders when he saw she was shivering. Reg came out, no doubt having noticed his daughter slip away, and demanded to know whose coat she was wearing. The sound of Hilton's name was enough. Reg pulled the coat off Joyce and ordered her to get into his car, leaving Hilton alarmed at what might happen next. Joyce had not long moved into the Glandore Hospital. Hilton reacted quickly to the way Reg had bullied Joyce. He rode his bike to a public phone where he could ring the hospital via an operator. With no money to make the call, he had to persuade the young woman operator to put him through, which she did after recognising Hilton from their days at school. His sense of urgency was acute. But Joyce was fine and the experience brought them closer.

Their serious romance seems to have begun shortly afterwards. 'There was nothing between us when I gave her my coat that night,' Hilton recalls. 'But the way her father spoke to her was a catalyst that sparked my interest. I felt a deep compassion and pity for her because that kind of abrupt and nasty family interaction was completely foreign to me or my upbringing. That did start my interest in Joyce in a way that excluded all others. She went from being a casual friend to everything, and all of a sudden. One week I did not think of her and the next I could not get her out of my thinking.'

Doing deliveries for Cullinanes department store, Hilton loved to catch sight of Joyce on the verandah of the hospital up the hill. He'd give her a wave to let her know he was thinking of her. Joyce, likewise, loved to see Hilton in the distance. 'I'd occasionally walk out on my own to the verandah and he'd wave to me and my heart would jump.'

Around this time, one of the patients at the Glandore Hospital had been encouraging Joyce in a friendship with her son, Ron, who had spent time at the hospital with an injury to his knee. Joyce had gone along with the idea, meeting him when he came to visit his mother, talking to him while he was a patient, going on drives with him later. She had accepted the gifts, the crocheted doilies and other small things. And Hilton hadn't made a definite move, so why not? It must have all seemed a certainty to Ron's mother. Ron lived out of Gympie and came to town rarely, so the night he made a date with Joyce for eight o'clock was a significant occasion. And then Hilton rang.

'Ron was to meet me at eight, as he had to come in from the country. I'm still ashamed with myself at what I did. I didn't even let him know I wouldn't be there. Hilton had rung and asked me to go with him to the Corps Cadets. It would be our first real date. My heart had leaped when he rang. Of course, Hilton was my first choice. I gave no thought to Ron. That was a dreadful thing to do.'

Hilton never forgot the occasion when they first went out together as a couple — 2 October 1956. Meeting up again, though, wasn't so easy. After the coat incident, Joyce had warned him off, saying that their relationship was causing too much trouble with her family. Reg didn't want her dating Hilton Harmer. Hearing this, Hilton says he was mortified at first. But it takes a lot to stop the young from their pleasures. Soon enough they were saying their goodnights beneath Cullinanes furniture factory, Hilton strategically dragging a block of wood to a spot where they could snuggle. 'She would stand on the wood to bring her up to my height. I was so much taller than her and it saved her from looking up at me all of the time. I could kiss her better when she stood on something,' says the still-doting Hilton at sixty-five.

'The first time Hilton took me home after what might be called a date,' remembers Joyce, 'he asked if he could kiss me goodnight. And I said, "Definitely not!" When I got home I thought, you idiot, that's not what you really meant at all. You meant to say yes. You mad thing. But because he had asked I respected him even more. Guys don't generally ask if they can kiss you goodnight. Anyway, I don't think he asked after that.'

By now Hilton was in love. He admits to being insanely jealous of time Joyce spent with any other fellow, however innocent. 'It was my fault, not hers; absolutely anything would set me off — she'd have mentioned talking to a Michael somebody while she was eating in the canteen and I'd say, "What do you have to talk to him for?" Rubbish, you know. Later you mature, thankfully. I was lucky she stayed with me in those early days.'

This was the mid-1950s. The social revolution of Elvis Presley and the Beatles, hit parades and television shows like *Bandstand* were yet to have an impact on Australia, much less Gympie. Joyce saw her teenage self as what she still describes as 'tubby' or 'pear-shaped'. So much so that while she owned a pair of red swimmers she tried to avoid wearing them. 'If we went away with the church group to the beach, I would accidentally on purpose leave them at home, embarrassed about my shape.' But Joyce could certainly dream girly fantasies: 'Me in a two-tone green customline, hair flowing, the blonde, a woman who was free, powerful and part of the future.'

Against this was the Salvation Army identity of being marked out from most of Gympie, of being different in a socially retrograde way. While the saying 'Thank God for the Salvos' was familiar across the nation, the straight-laced moral codes of the Army were a marked contrast with the relaxed and secular nature of Australia generally. In Gympie, the codes came with those Sunday open-air meetings on Rankins Corner, marching with the band. Salvationists would form a circle to sing the hymns and listen to the preaching of firebrands like leader Jock Geddes. Passers-by would throw coins into the circle out of a sense of charity, while the drunks from the pubs chucked heated coins that burned whoever picked them up. But there was also a church community of fellowship, where Joyce could catch up with the adorable aunts Rene and Maise, alongside the many restrictions. There were so many restrictions that for Joyce, an ordinary bike ride one Sunday while staying with her mother's friend Rita became extraordinary — a moment she still recalls vividly so many decades later.

'I got on the bike and thought I was as free as the breeze. I rode down one hill and up another and round to Johnson's store. Halfway there I realised what I was doing. It was Sunday. I wasn't supposed to be riding a bike for the fun of it or even going to a shop. I can't imagine what my parents would have said if they'd known what I was doing. You didn't even knit on Sunday. That day was exclusively for rest, reading, quietness, church worship and Sunday school. But the ride was wonderful.'

chapter 5

THE WORDS OF A SONG

As her relations with home deteriorated, Joyce knelt at her bed one evening and asked God to send her someone who'd love her as she craved.

'During my early days at the Glandore Hospital I was at one time tempted to give it all away as a Christian, until one night I heard some words on a radio broadcast: "*Pass me not O loving Saviour/Hear my humble cry/And while others Thou art calling/Do not pass me by*". So I rededicated my life to God, but needed love more than ever. And I'd say that God sent Hilton Harmer my way when I most needed him. I had my nursing, but that was secondary.'

Their courtship, as such friendships were known in the 1950s, weathered all attempts by Reg to break them up. Joyce continued to live away from home, nursing at Gympie, where she dressed and wrapped up her little nephew Wayne, Cecil's firstborn, in the maternity ward before they took him home. For ten months before she married, she nursed at Nambour. All the while, the tension around Joyce and Hilton's romance continued in the Lipke home. Nearly half a century later, Hilton remembers moments of it vividly.

'One night after I took Joyce home from a Corps Cadet lesson in Bible study, we were sitting on the steps of a church beside the hospital. And Reg's Austin A90 pulled up. I can still remember the registration number was NCS 063. He hadn't noticed us and went straight into the hospital, no doubt to ask where Joyce was. He came racing out after a bit and took off in the car. We decided to split — Joyce went back into the hospital and I went home. But this wasn't unusual. We would often have to put Reg off the scent. We'd say goodnight, see ya later and all that. Then I'd go up the hill to the south and she'd go down Mary Street to the west, and then I'd ride around and come back into the hospital from the other direction. And we'd meet up again.'

Hilton looks back and realises how young they were. He can recollect being so upset when Reg hit Joyce on one occasion that he confronted Reg outside his car and told him that only a rat would do what he'd done to Joyce. Reg started to get out of the car, to come at him for daring to use such language to an adult, but Hilton jammed his leg in the door so he couldn't get out. Then Hilton let go and ran off to his own car, which was full of kids Hilton was driving home from Sunday school.

'If he was alive now, I'd understand him. I'd have more tolerance with him probably. But I was the youngest in our family and only seventeen when Joyce and I started going together. I didn't really know how to handle such people issues.'

But often, neither did parents know how to oversee their teenagers' love life. Joyce once received a letter from Hilton while on holiday with her family at Tewantin. Like a Juliet hearing from Romeo, she'd found it on the front grass, thrown over the fence by the postman. She'd taken it upstairs and read it. A letter from darling Hilton — no more than a letter, but to her a love letter. And then it disappeared. Alice had taken it and kept it. Joyce had no idea what happened to it. But she herself had secrets. Like the Mix Master bowl she had broken while trying to make ice-cream. The pieces of bowl Joyce then got rid of, wrapping them in newspaper and leaving them in the rubbish bin. Only years later had Joyce found the temerity to own up to what had happened to the bowl, her mother's pride and joy. She heard a preacher give a sermon on honesty and felt the Holy Spirit was directing her to tell her mother what had happened. She had written to Alice confessing all. And Alice had written back admitting her own secret. She had taken Hilton's letter, read it and never put it back.

Joyce and Hilton became engaged while on a Salvation Army day out in Brisbane in 1959, Hilton giving Joyce a solitaire diamond ring with a filigree setting. Every time they go to Brisbane, Hilton, ever the romantic, takes her back to the spot on the Brisbane River where he proposed.

But the decision to marry wasn't as simple as it might now appear. It wasn't that the pair weren't devoted to each other. The tussle went much deeper: it revolved around Hilton's conviction that he wanted to join the Salvation Army ministry.

In 1950s Australia, it was unthinkable that a Salvation Army officer's spouse would not be attached to the ministry as strongly as he was. In such a situation, where Hilton wanted to be a Salvation Army minister, the decision was far more complex than whether or not Joyce wanted to spend the rest of her life with Hilton. She also had to be convinced that she wanted to give her life to the work of the Salvation Army as a commissioned officer. This meant much more than deciding on a career or merely, like any young wife of the era, deciding to follow her husband's career moves. For a commissioned officer's wife, the commitment to Salvation Army life had to be as much hers as his, and she needed to feel the call from God to follow that path.

In most Christian denominations, the choice of ministry is the choice of an individual. The Salvation Army, however, remains unique in both its foundation by a married couple — William and Catherine Booth — and in the involvement of married partners in its ministry work. If Joyce had not been ready to make the commitment to ministry, Hilton would have had to choose whether he wanted to make the journey to Sydney alone. But he had no desire to leave Joyce. If he did leave, Joyce could wait for him, and hope he would choose her rather than the ministry. In their youthful and passionate way, they wanted no gulfs between them. But how to remain true to both their love for each other and a commitment to work for God through the Salvation Army?

In 1955, Hilton's brother Ted had gone off to the Salvation Army training college in Sydney to study for the ministry. Before long, Hilton had felt a real calling to do the same. In their early teens and even before, both Hilton and Joyce had made personal pledges that they would give themselves to God in special ways. In the Salvation Army, a child is not baptised or christened as in other Christian churches. Parents instead 'dedicate' their children to God as babies and take on the responsibility for their instruction in the Christian faith. A young person, having grown up with Salvation Army parents, must make a personal decision whether or not to become a Christian at a time when they are old enough to understand what they will be committing themselves to. This practice somewhat parallels the sacrament of confirmation in the Anglican and Catholic Churches, but it is done without a large formal ceremony and far more as an individual choice.

At a Baptist rally in primary school Joyce had felt a special calling. The rally was held in the Gympie town hall and the children had sung a chorus that has remained with Joyce throughout her life. The words of that chorus set her on a path to a special relationship with God. The children sang: '*I met Jesus at the crossroads, where the two ways meet / Satan too was standing there, and he said come this way / Lots of pleasures I can give to you today / But I said NO, there's Jesus here, just see what he offers me / Down here my sins forgiven, up there a home in Heaven / Praise God that's the way for me.*'

At Sunday school, aged twelve, on Decision Sunday with its scripture readings and songs, Joyce had pledged her life to God as a Christian and Salvationist. 'At the peak of the service, you were asked if you wanted Jesus to come into your life, to belong to Jesus and become a committed Christian. If you did, you were asked to come forward to kneel at a special bench called the Mercy Seat. It was explained that the bench was no different from the top of any table or any other piece of wood; it was not magic but a place to kneel and pray. I remember that this Sunday I went towards the Mercy Seat and my cousin Val came and knelt with me and prayed with me. That was the way it would happen. If a person came forward, another person would follow them and offer to pray with them and to make sure you understood what your commitment was. So it was a privilege for my cousin to do that. She told me, "This could be the difference between you being happy at home and not happy." She counselled me along those lines, which to me was very precious.'

Hilton, quite separately, made a similar decision at around the age of twelve or thirteen. 'There was a sort of power struggle in me. I wanted to go forward and give my heart to God but something was making me sit there and not do it. But eventually I went forward and these were the first steps I took on my Christian walk.'

Hilton started to learn the cornet, began playing the tenor horn and, after Ted left for college, took up the euphonium. Hilton was always known for the large heart he had for people, whatever he was doing. At sixteen, he managed to turn his delivery job at Cullinanes into a sort of service for needy mothers at home, riding his bike and taking orders far beyond the usual delivery routine. Good for Cullinanes, and very good for mothers. He earned a reputation for caring about much more than what goods were wanted, using his feelings to sense little ways he could help make life a bit easier for families. But his father often saw his kindness as a weakness.

'I only had three arguments with my father, who was very different from Reg. And two of them were when we argued about my helping the alcoholics. One fellow in central Gympie was travelling by train. I wanted to take him a thermos of tea and some sandwiches so he had something to eat on the way. Another lived under a tank a couple of kilometres from our home and I would take him coffee and sandwiches. My dad would say, "They're just using you up." Not that he wasn't a compassionate man.'

Joyce and Hilton's attendance at Salvation Army services and all the other church activities was about far more than just going along with the social and cultural norms of their group. So, for Hilton, the decision about college had to be made before their decision about marriage.

'It was a big talking point even before we became engaged. We talked about engagement and I said, "Well, we've got to sort out this college thing first." And I know Joyce struggled with it. Then one day the struggle was over. She came to me with the words of a song. *I struggled and wrestled to win it / The blessing that setteth me free.* She'd found the strength to say yes, she'd go to college. It's so often the way for Joyce. The words of a song can help clear her vision. Here they helped her make that commitment to her ministry.'

They were married on Saturday, 5 March 1960 at the Gympie Salvation Army Citadel. Not even Reg had objected to their marriage in the end. Joyce's bridesmaids were Olwin Harris and Rhelma Humphries, Hilton's brother Ted was best man and Keith Lipke was the groomsman. The celebrant was Major John George.

Joyce wore her dark Salvation Army uniform rather than a flowing white dress and veil. She chose a tiara for her brown hair, tightly drawn back into a bun, with some decorative lace sashes to soften the effect of her uniform, and carried a bouquet of white frangipani and roses with a smattering of purple Cooktown orchids tied with silver ribbons. This may say something about her strength of Army commitment or the fashions of the day for Army women. On the day, looking back, Joyce walked on air, but says if she had her chance over again she would do it all differently. Although she admits the cost of the new Army uniforms they had to buy for college the following year would have made them want to save on the expense of a white wedding.

The wedding breakfast was held at the Citadel's function hall below the church. Hilton describes the catering as 'pathetic' after he tried one sandwich, which he thought tasted old and stale. But youth is its own beauty, and to Hilton Joyce looked gorgeous, walking towards him on Reg's arm as the young people's Sergeant Major and Sunday school organist, Mrs Chapman, played 'Here Comes the Bride'. Nothing could dampen his happiness.

Hilton's parents lent them a small car in which they drove off, with well-wishers calling after them and throwing confetti. They were heading for a honeymoon at Noosa Heads. 'Wish I'd bought a couple of the shacks at Noosa then,' says Hilton with a wry laugh. 'Would have made a fortune by now.' They went on to Inverell for a bit, where a number of the Harmer family lived, and then back to Gympie, where they rented a small house for a year while Hilton continued to work at Cullinanes. It was a happy year, with a loving home of her own at last for Joyce. As part of the Harmer clan, too, Joyce felt truly loved and wanted. It would be a cherished attachment, one that she would never find with her own parents.

A year later, true to the promise they had made to each other before their engagement, on the day of their first wedding anniversary they prepared to farewell family and friends at Gympie railway station, ready to take the long journey south to Sydney, where they would begin two years of study towards becoming Salvation Army officers.

chapter 6

GOING SOUTH

Standing before the huge gates of the Salvation Army training school, Joyce swallowed her fears. 'I thought, ah, I'm here, I'm not dead. But Gympie's a long way away.' The Salvation Army officer who had met the Queensland group at Central railway station in the training centre minibus led the way inside.

Joyce and Hilton, neither of whom had ever been further south than Inverell in northern New South Wales, had made the 1200-kilometre journey to Sydney on slow red rattler trains, first from Gympie to Brisbane, where they joined other Salvation Army would-be cadets to take the winding journey down the coast to Sydney, complete with a crossing of the border at Tweed Heads and a change of railway gauge. The train had left the old Gympie railway station on a Sunday, a short article in *The Gympie Times* reporting their departure. A group from the Gympie Citadel had gathered to farewell Joyce and Hilton, led in singing by Sister Vera Chapman who played a piano accordion. The group prayed together and sang the chorus: '*God will take care of you / Through every day / He will take care of you / God will take care of you*'. Hilton remembers it as a defining moment, a final break with home — the moment they took their first step to 'follow the call of Jesus Christ' in their lives. They were seeking a whole new world. It was a farewell filled with emotion — the music and singing of the comrades, of family being left behind, the shriek of the steam engine firing and straining to move out of the station with the carriages clinking and drawing away, the smell of smoke and tears flowing. For both, it was a small personal Calvary.

The rail journey alone took some twenty hours. Trying to stay awake through the night journey to Sydney, they bit hard into nectarines, not quite ripe. They sat up all the way in Salvation Army uniforms in the warmth of early March. The women wore high-necked navy long-sleeved bodices and skirts no more than fourteen inches from the ground, carefully measured at the college for any infringement of the rule. Their thirty-denier stockings were barely visible, enclosed at the ankles by sturdy lace-up shoes. Like Catholic nuns, they had a complete outfit, made from strong serge that buttoned to the neck like a coat. There were no blouses then, just a white band around the high collar. It would be another year before the first of the modifications for summer were allowed — a grey gabardine short-sleeved belted dress. And there was always the Army bonnet with its elaborate bow, whose prototype was designed by Catherine Booth, known as the 'Hallelujah Bonnet'.

In 1961, the Salvation Army training college at 55 Livingstone Road, Petersham, at the top of Addison Street, reminded Joyce of a giant blue and white iced wedding cake behind an eight-foot stone and iron fence. The tall wrought-iron gates clanged shut behind them as they entered, moving up the wide entrance path to a vast door with no portico. The complex consisted of three matching blue and white square blocks. Verandah-less, the impression the architect has created with the building's gothic revival façade is very formal and austere for an Australian setting. Imposing and intimidating in one, the college towers over small brick bungalows in the streets around it.

Among the trainees, there were three married couples from Brisbane and a fourth with an eighteen-month-old daughter from Sydney. In all, there were twenty-nine cadets for the year. Noela Dawkins, whose husband, Alf, had to stay behind for a week in Brisbane while he finished his pilot licence qualifications, had found Joyce and Hilton a warm couple, so easy to befriend. It was a friendship that lasted and Noela looks back on the support they gave her over the years in tough times as very special.

At college, theirs was the first intake of cadets to do a full two years rather than ten months, and, as Noela saw it much later, the college had not fully thought out the consequences. It was an unwritten rule that married cadets were expected not to get pregnant while in training. Sparsely furnished rooms of twin beds sent out the message. The extra length of time added pressures for young married couples eager to start a family. 'Hilton, love,' Joyce had cried in Gympie as they made plans for college, weeping on his lap, 'why didn't we go to college a year earlier, when it was only one year? Now we have to wait another two years before we can have a baby.'

In their room above the college principal's office, Hilton would drop his shoes on the boards at night. The next day, the principal would tersely remind Hilton that the noise of the shoes had distracted him from working in the office below. Joyce and Hilton were young, newly married and now their domestic life was not much better than living in at school. They were woken at 6 a.m. by a male cadet on roster playing a brass instrument outside their door. By 6.30 a.m. they were lined up in separate male and female single lines on parade in the quadrangle below. Announcements would follow, then there would be a 'morning thought' presented by one of the cadets. Next they would recite one of the doctrines of the Salvation Army and say a prayer for the day. After that, all cadets moved off to their 'work sections'. Each person had a chore to do every morning. Breakfast was at 8 a.m., sitting at designated tables. The seating changed each month when new lists went up. Meals ended with a 'returning of thanks' and thanks to God for His goodness. After breakfast, cadets returned to their rooms for private devotions and to prepare themselves for the day. The day's program went through till 8 p.m. By then, most just wanted to go to bed, as they would be exhausted, but there would often be the need to fit in some study or write letters home.

In the Harmers' second year, the college relocated married cadets to a three-bedroom house around the corner in Miller Street. One couple per bedroom. But the boarding-house style culture continued. 'Could we have one of our beds removed?' asked one of the wives. She was a small woman and the couple managed rather well in a single bed. 'We'd like more room for our desks,' she added. Matron's response was a cold refusal. Such a thing was unheard of.

'In the passageways we'd laugh aloud together. When we had to clean the bedrooms and noticed two beds had been moved together (there'd be marks on the floor), we'd tease each other about it,' says Joyce. 'And all so different now, with small apartments for married trainees and no couple discouraged from having a child while studying.'

Meanwhile, Noela and Alf Dawkins were frequently in trouble for not having returned their small car to the college grounds before the gates shut at 10 p.m. They would often collect Hilton and Joyce from their respective corps on the way home, which delayed them all. Locked out, by the time they made it back to Petersham, they would park the car in the street outside the Miller Street house. Noela recalls how the principal, who took a short cut to the college each day along Miller Street, would notice the car outside the house. 'Where was the Dawkins' Austin A40 last night? It wasn't in the car park,' he would snap to the group as they assembled at 6.30 a.m. for parade.

'But we had to do corps work from Balmain to Rozelle to Five Dock. Quite often it was impossible to be back at college before the gates closed. I suppose the idea was that if we had to park in the grounds, we wouldn't be out on the town,' says Noela.

The brigading work the cadets did involved open-air meetings and door-to-door evangelism. At college they studied an intense program of Salvation Army doctrine, Old and New Testament, Army procedures, current affairs, a world view of Army activities, singing, timbrel and music or band practice, public speaking, sermon preparation training, social service or welfare training, creative arts, sectional and combined meetings, a first-aid certificate and worship leadership. In second year, cadets were given specific duties in running a corps.

And there were small opportunities for 'free time', such as Monday afternoons. The Dawkins often spent theirs with a family where they enjoyed a home-cooked meal. Cadets were required to put in a form to say where they would be going and needed to be back by 9 p.m. to sign in and give their time of arrival. A red line was drawn for the 9 p.m. curfew and those arriving after nine signed under the red line and were interviewed the next day as to why they had been late home. One Monday afternoon, like naughty schoolboys, Hilton and a few other cadets took off for the Sydney Cricket Ground to watch a match. They were told to always wear their navy blue uniforms when out, but at the railway station they changed into civvies and headed for 'The Hill' (overlooking the cricket ground). At some stage during the afternoon they spotted one of their training officers coming towards them in full regalia and cap. Without their uniforms, they easily managed to get lost in the crowd.

'It's a wonder we survived college,' says Hilton. 'We went in one end and came out the other. It was akin to being swept along like a piece of paper in a gutter when there's a downpour. We were just pushed along, because it was mostly out of our league. It must have been only the goodness of God that got us through, because Joyce had been made to feel all her childhood that she wasn't anything. She was put down. Her father left a bitter legacy there.'

And those college strictures were bizarre. Hilton was caught in the first week. 'I said to Joyce that I'd see her in our room later because she was going off to class somewhere. The next thing I had the chief side officer calling me in and telling me he'd been told I had called a cadet by her Christian name. He knew it was my wife but that didn't matter. I was instructed never to call my wife Joyce but always to refer to her as "Cadet Harmer". That's how far we've come in forty-two years.'

The move to Sydney had been overwhelming in itself. Hilton couldn't believe all the houses and the area the city covered. They could get from one side of Gympie to the other in fifteen minutes. The scale of Sydney made Hilton nervous, and he was glad to move on when their commissioning was over. But there were, as he puts it, no dramas. They stayed the course.

Joyce made her mark with her ability to sing. And in spite of her reservations about speaking in front of her peers, Hilton remembers she spoke well when it came to her turn. Joyce was, in fact, a natural at group prayer. Her family had always prayed at meal-times. At breakfast, either her mother or her father would read selections from the New Testament in *The Soldier's Guide* and the family would thank God for their food before they began to eat. In the Salvationist way, their faith was for far more than just Sundays. Most Christians attend one service once a week, but by contrast, theirs was an inner life with the Saviour, ever present and outwardly part of their daily routine. They also often sang together at meal-times and Joyce remembers some of the words of a Salvation Army song: *Whisper a prayer in the morning/Whisper a prayer at noon/Whisper a prayer in the evening/To keep your heart in tune/God answers prayers in the morning/God answers prayers at noon/God answers prayers in the evening/And He'll send the answer soon.*

'As children, we had to kneel at our chairs and take it in turns to pray. That's where we began to learn how to pray, probably not realising exactly how important and serious it is but in a childlike way. We would make up a prayer as it came to our turn. Whatever came to your mind. Whatever you wanted to thank Jesus for. A lovely day, keeping us safe during the night, for the food we'd had, to help us at school that day, to help us to be kind to each other. We prayed from a very young age. It was natural.'

Joyce and Hilton had entered the training college with less than four years of secondary schooling behind them. And Joyce had her nurse's training. But suddenly they were expected to take both practical and academic courses. There were assignments to write and modes of behaviour to master. Christians who take on a ministry role must be well versed in their Bible, their church theology and the ritualistic performances they will be required to lead. They must be preachers and listeners, and they are expected to stand before congregations and lead both prayers and singing. At a training college for ministry, that early emotional response to faith, the personal feeling of calling and closeness to God's presence, is acted upon. The coursework undertaken forms the individual into a skilled leader within a spiritual structure. What emerges is a committed professional, ready to be used by the institutional church. None of which comes naturally to all. And for Joyce, so shy in Gympie, it could be terrifying.

'Ours was the first two-year session the training college introduced. Our session was called the "Soldiers of Christ". The session that followed us was given the name "Servants of Christ". The songs we chose, the themes studied were all set around our name as Soldiers of Christ. Our training principal was Colonel Bramwell Lucas and he began our course telling us we'd be packing a lot more into our training than ever before. I was petrified at having to present myself before the others. I would want to stand and say something but I would be so nervous I would end up almost crying. But they say practice makes perfect and I guess in time one isn't so nervous. And I just knew that God had placed His hand on my life and that this was what I needed to do.'

A lot of the academic course work was not only daunting for Joyce, but also frustrating. Her view of officership was the sleeves-rolled-up kind her father had so admired. The long essays weren't her scene. 'Who wants to do that?' she still says.

'I wanted to be doing rather than talking about it; getting out and helping people.' There were lecturers who came and went and they were schooled in the order of various services, with odd moments of unrehearsed amusement. An older officer came to take them through the dedication ceremony for babies. The page of his directory flipped over and he solemnly read out the words of the funeral service instead, so that the pretend baby was buried rather than welcomed into the church. A lesson in itself, really.

It wasn't all seriousness, says Joyce. The camaraderie of the others kept them in good spirits generally. Even when they had to split into male and female groups to go brigading. This happened on Sundays and Tuesdays. Joyce, with other female cadets, went to the Ashfield Corps and later to Balmain and Rozelle and together they would march in file, singing as one on their way to Petersham railway station, one of them with a piano accordion to accompany the group in song. They wore red sashes clipped onto their uniforms and carried bold messages for those who came towards them — *God Saves*, *God Satisfies* — an original sort of T-shirt message.

'We did a lot of that, walking around the streets singing and then standing outside blocks of slums in Redfern and Waterloo. We took our lunches packed in small brown cases. Matron would pack them the night before — tinned fruit, Carnation milk in tins and cold cuts of meat and salad and some bread.'

They would have made good politicians in swinging electorates as they tramped the streets of poorer suburbs, knocking on doors and chatting to locals in the vicinity of Salvation Army churches. They'd introduce themselves and say they were in the area. They'd mention where the children could attend Sunday school if they didn't already go. They'd offer to bring the children home after Sunday school if needed. Some of the locals would ask what they were studying and what they did as cadets. All of which was conditioning them for a lifetime of working with people, most of whom they would meet with little or no introduction.

chapter 7

THE ARMY

The Salvation Army is made up of adherents, soldiers and officers, who technically all share an equal importance. Adherents are like most people who belong to a church. They attend services at a Salvation Army corps, or church, but do not wear any uniform. Alice Lipke was always only an adherent and Joyce now wishes she had asked her mother why she chose not to wear the uniform. In Alice's time, female adherents would sometimes wear a navy dress in place of a uniform. Those who choose to wear the uniform, as Reg did, are called soldiers. The uniform for a soldier is only worn on Sundays and for Salvation Army services. But taking the uniform means making a special commitment to the Salvation Army faith, of recognising individual sinfulness and asking God for forgiveness.

At this point, Salvation Army belief parts company with traditional Calvinism and its belief in the elect who will be saved. For a Salvationist, no matter what the sin or the social stigma of an individual, there can be salvation if an individual turns to God and renounces a sinful life. The uniformed soldier in the Salvation Army must accept Jesus Christ as a saviour, accept all Salvation Army doctrines and abstain from substances and practices regarded as harmful to the body and mind, such as tobacco, drugs, alcohol and gambling. Until recent decades the list of banned harmfuls included cinemas and dancing. When soldiers wish to step up to commissioned officers or take on the role of minister, they must complete the training course to be commissioned. Then they wear the uniform at all times in public, as if on duty.

The image of a Salvationist as a soldier may seem quaint today, but as a marketing tool the army structure and designations have been brilliantly successful over more than a century. From the outset, William and Catherine Booth were crusaders, parting company with traditional church forms. William was fired with a personal fervour and conviction that they could bring lost and forgotten thousands to the Christian message. Beginning their 'mission' with a tent in a Quaker graveyard, the Booths gradually became known throughout London and beyond for their stirring revival meetings and growing legions of followers from among the downtrodden outcasts of industrial England.

The Booth Mission in East London was devised as a 'para-church' group. Its aim, at a time when institutionalised religion was paramount in English lives, was to offer the destitute and socially shunned, those largely abandoned by the established Protestant Churches, a Christianity they could connect with. Catherine and William Booth wanted a movement that was ever fresh and invigorated, as opposed to the staid establishment line of existing churches of the time. Eventually, they dispensed with the sacramental side of Christian worship, believing they could found a long-lasting chain of heroic evangelists devoted to saving souls and reform of the material and spiritual condition of lost people. The souls thus saved would come to Jesus from an inner relationship with God in each Salvationist, a relationship that did not include outward symbols of grace. In mainstream Christian churches such outward manifestations of grace are the sacraments and the ceremonies that surround them.

The soldiers and officers of the Salvation Army raised by the Booths would be bound together by communal social action, largely in their work among the poor and those who had fallen away from respectable society. Hence the dominant roles played in Salvationists' lives for over a century would be the music, the street meetings and evangelising to the unconverted. But, more recently, many in the Army have questioned what they see as an established and settled nature that has developed in Salvationists. They claim that the Army has become much like other mainstream Christian Churches catering for middle-class adherents on Sundays. Some question whether that all-encompassing and hands-on mission of the street has been lost as the Army's defining characteristic.

From the earliest days of Booth's London Mission, his followers were known for their fearless obtrusiveness on the streets, marching, singing and approaching complete strangers. The actual Army structure came later, under the influence of George Railton, William Booth's first Commissioner and the man who framed many of the movement's first documents. A firebrand preacher, by 1873 Railton was regarded as the Mission's ideologist. As such, he urged the Mission towards militant Christianity to counter those respectable and, to him, ineffective Protestant Churches like the Anglicans and Wesleyans. In his preaching he invoked the imagery of war as the Mission's inspiration. With that fire of zealotry, Railton would lead the Army's first official 'invasion' overseas — to the United States, in 1880.

'Where is the holy war?' Railton cried in his preaching. 'Where is the terrible energy displayed in the attacks upon sin? Where is there a hard, unbending advance to exterminate wrong? Is not Christianity today a sentimental attempt to please all men and to give no offence to any? The Christian Mission is war, war to the knife.'

Railton's influence galvanised an already unorthodox movement. Railton took the war and fighting metaphors and mixed them with a more sophisticated view of the world than Booth could manage. The Booth Mission operated in the slums of East London, where London's nineteenth-century population explosion (growing from 1.6 million in 1831 to 3.2 million in 1871), combined with a lack of government refurbishment of outdated infrastructures and living conditions, had produced appalling social decay. The precarious lives and depleted means to any livelihood for tens of thousands forced to live there resulted in high levels of prostitution, crime and squalor.

For Booth there was never any wavering in his faith and his onslaught against what he saw as the evil poisoning society. His engaging personality and ongoing struggle for good attracted officers. His movement appealed to believers whose faith was emotional rather than intellectual. At the annual conference of 1877, Booth proposed the conference be turned into a Council of War. It was at the same council that Booth began to outline his views on plain dressing, blaming 'flashy' dressing for depravity. He was also beginning to think of a uniform for his followers. In November 1878, Catherine Booth announced that the Army would adopt a uniform — a mode of dress that would be simple while distinguishing the evangelists as well as uniting them with the downtrodden they were hoping to save.

Around this time, the rhetoric of war had become a feature of the Army's articles and messages to followers. Booth would send out 'General Orders', such as that issued when his evangelists were so badly paid that there was a fear some were going without food. Booth's 'General Order Against Starvation' urged his followers not to deprive themselves to the point of risking 'the strength and life of the officers, which are of unspeakable value'. By December 1878, the Mission was known as the Army and Booth was called the General, a rank befitting the movement's leader.

It was Railton who had been the first to present the name 'Army', apparently one morning while he was at the General's house, when Booth, still in his dressing gown and slippers, was dictating the orders of the day. Railton, drafting a statement, came up with the term 'volunteer army' as a way of describing the Mission. Bramwell Booth, William and Catherine's eldest son, objected to the word 'volunteer', saying he was a regular or nothing. William Booth then rose from his seat and went over to Railton, where he crossed out the word 'volunteer', writing over it the word 'salvation'. And the Salvation Army it became, with General Booth as its commander-in-chief.

From its earliest years, the Army moved beyond England to become an international movement. Edward Saunders and John Gore arrived in Australia in 1880 and began the mission in Adelaide's Botanic Park, leading a Salvation Army meeting from the back of a greengrocer's cart. The movement withstood initial attacks on its street meetings until, by the early 1900s, the Salvation Army was generally accepted as a force for good. Today the Army operates in Australia as two territories — the Eastern Territory covering New South Wales, Queensland and the Australian Capital Territory (along with Papua New Guinea), and the Southern Territory covering the rest of Australia. There are officer training colleges in both Melbourne and Sydney.

For the believer, Christianity offers a simple and coherent faith. The vivid Bible stories of the Old Testament are reinterpreted by the words of a Saviour, one who comes as the fulfilment of Old Testament prophecy. The stories of the New Testament, a literary masterpiece in its parable and metaphor, re-create the struggle of humanity in the story of one man who offers what the believer sees as a comprehensive way to live with meaning and effect for the good of all. *Love your neighbour as yourself; Love one another as I have loved you; Turn the other cheek; Keep my commandments; The greatest of all the commandments is love; Greater love has no man than this, that he lay down his life for his friends; Blessed are the meek, for they shall inherit the Kingdom of God.* At the peak of all this lies the act of salvation, which is the passion, death and resurrection of that one man, Jesus — a death that is a travesty of justice and undergone for all humanity, so that humanity would be saved from its sin and abuse of this finite world. That is the sacrifice that defines the Christian Salvationist. The life of the Saviour is the life each Salvationist seeks to emulate. And, as for all variants of Christian belief, the final achievement is an everlasting life with the Saviour in Heaven.

Joyce and Hilton had grown up steadfast in their belief in this fundamental explanation of their faith. Close friend and Army leader Commissioner Earl Maxwell and wife Wilma have no hesitation in explaining the Harmers' clear and uncomplicated view of their personal mission: 'In the Harmers you see a couple who share a calling. She says, "I've got it." And he says, "I've got it." Suddenly there is a foundation they can meet on. Then, as they begin their officership, you have a young woman with a community outlook who considers, "How does God fit into it and my Salvation Army role?" For Joyce in particular, it was God first, then family and then the Salvation Army. This should not be interpreted as an inferior ratio given to the Salvation Army, but it was a way of blending God and her family with her work in the community.'

At the end of two years, a commissioning ceremony awarded cadets their rank of Lieutenant. In the 1960s this involved a Covenant Day, which was held at the training college, and where a covenant, or agreement, between each cadet and God was made. Joyce and Hilton would return to their respective covenants with God, made in their first flush of passion for their calling, many times throughout their lives as officers. The years would test their strength of commitment again and again.

The Covenant Day was followed by a huge gathering for the commissioning held in the Sydney Town Hall. It always attracted a crowd of families connected with the outgoing cadets and from the wider community of Salvationists in Sydney. Decades later the location was changed to the Darling Harbour Convention Centre, where it continues to be held. The seriousness awarded to this passing out of new Salvation Army officers is not simply to announce the Army's commissioning of a growing number of officers. It also acknowledges the sacredness of the 'formation' the new officers have undergone.

Attaining ministry is a rite of passage only a select few can undertake. Officership is bestowed only on those who have qualified for the group that leads the faithful, those who will henceforth be a voice of God wherever needed and sent. The completion of the Salvation Army officer training course is acknowledged with the handing out of commissions. These are the appointments the nominated officers will undertake. In this way the officer accepts himself or herself as servant — to go where sent and do what God asks — as much as he or she accepts the role of a leader.

Covenant Day arrived for the Harmers. They had absorbed their theology, finished their assignments at the small desks in their tiny room, overcome all hesitation over leading at meetings and addressing the groups they stood before. The strength of their determination and calling was enough to make them fearless when needed. And the best news of all was that Joyce was three months pregnant. She and Hilton were aching to get on their way to the real thing — to a ministry and a family of their very own.

At the Sydney Town Hall, in front of three thousand people, they were called out. They crossed to stand in front of the Commissioner. 'Lieutenant and Mrs Harmer. You are appointed to Atherton, North Queensland.'

chapter 8

MARCHING ORDERS

Between January 1963 and the end of 1970, Joyce and Hilton lived in four different towns in northern Queensland — Atherton, Bowen, Rockhampton and Mt Isa — most appointments lasting two years. Appointments could send them anywhere in the Eastern Territory, which included Papua New Guinea, New South Wales, Queensland and the Australian Capital Territory. Every alternate year, or thereabouts, Army Headquarters would advise them where they would reside for the next two years. And off they would go.

They left Sydney in January 1963 with all the energy and readiness of rookies everywhere. From the sprawl of Sydney's northern suburbs, they retraced their earlier journey from Brisbane and Gympie, travelling by steam train to Brisbane and then on to Cairns, in an air-conditioned diesel train known as the 'Sunlander'. Joyce, three months pregnant, was sick for most of the journey.

'I had twenty-four hour morning sickness,' she says, pulling a face at the memory of it. And they sat up all the way, as the cost of sleepers was out of the question. It was one in the morning when they pulled into Gympie station, where the train had an extended stop to allow passengers into the refreshment rooms. They got out and walked along the platform for a bit of exercise, their relatives asleep just a few miles down the road. The night air masked the tropical heat of January days. Told in college always to wear their heavy navy blue uniforms in public, Joyce and Hilton were an odd sight as they neared the tropics.

At Rockhampton they were met by Major and Mrs Roy Dawson, who brought them a fish lunch. They stepped out of the cool of the air-conditioned train in their high-necked and heavy navy coats, to a blast of tropical heat that all but knocked them sideways. 'What are you doing in those uniforms?' asked Mrs Dawson, standing on the platform, cool and crisp in her beautifully ironed whites. 'Go and take them off.' They did, and Joyce recalls not wearing hers again until after Peter was born six months later in July.

In Cairns they were met by Major and Mrs Abrahams, who managed the Army's People's Palace. After a night with the Abrahams they caught the Rail Motor, which took them inland up the Kuranda Range through Mareeba and into the beauty of the Atherton Tableland.

The historic settlement of Atherton is the original town on the tableland and has given the area its name. At various times, as in Gympie, timber, mining, agriculture and travellers have sustained the area. Settled a decade before Federation, a century later its population was less than 7000. At an altitude of 753 metres, its climate is temperate after the humidity of the coast, the sort of climate that produced the thick red cedar rainforests that lured Europeans into logging camps there in the 1880s. With the cedar forests long gone, the district is now rich in crops of maize, peanuts, avocadoes, potatoes and macadamia nuts.

Atherton has had its waves of sojourners over the years. By 1900 there were around 1100 Chinese living in the area.

Some went fossicking for gold but most worked for timber cutters or with farmers growing vegetables for the local population. As with many of the Chinese who came to Australia in the nineteenth century, the Salvation Army made contact, and some converts, among them. William Booth had spoken out against the prevailing prejudice of his day regarding the Chinese, that they were opium smokers, saying, 'I know he [the Chinese man] smokes opium, but I cannot forget that the Englishman taught him, and at this moment fattens by his ruin.' The numbers of Chinese in Atherton dwindled after 1907, especially as the effects of the White Australia Policy took their toll. Atherton had seen the Australian Army come and go too. During the war years of the 1940s, as the Pacific onslaught against the Japanese intensified, General Sir Thomas Blamey set up headquarters in Atherton for a short time. Thousands of troops were stationed across Atherton Shire, including Americans.

For the Salvation Army in Australia 1963 was a big year, with a visit by the seventh General Wilfred Kitching and his wife Kathleen to the cities of Brisbane, Sydney, Melbourne and Adelaide; but not a lot was happening in Atherton as Joyce and Hilton arrived in January to take up their first appointment. 'Big Girls Don't Cry' by the Four Seasons had topped the hit parade and Robert Menzies was in his fourteenth year as Australia's Prime Minister. In Atherton, the Salvation Army had only one soldier and a few adherents, but in the outlying hamlets it had a roll of some thirty soldiers. The one attending soldier in Atherton, a young mother with small children, was too busy to meet the Harmers off the train the day they arrived, so a lady from the Country Women's Association collected them instead. Their new home was a cluster of rooms at the rear of the hall they used for services. It had been a while since the Salvation Army had sent an officer to Atherton and the grass at the back of the property came up to Joyce's shoulders in places. The dwelling was a leftover from Atherton's military days and made of corrugated iron.

Joyce's sister Daphne recalls that the Lipkes visited the couple at their new home when Daphne was thirteen. They were all appalled by the conditions. 'You literally walked from the platform at the end of the Salvation Army hall down a few steps and into their lounge room. It was dark and I can't say if there was a window at all. It was not built for people to live in. The rooms were like cubicles. The toilet was outside somewhere near the laundry. But they loved it.'

The kitchen had an old wooden stove to cook on. It rained and rained and the clothes would get mildew. The bathroom was outside, all corrugated iron with no lining and nail holes here and there. The chip heater was burned out when they arrived so they had to buy a new one. And the loo was down a small flight of six steps, well into the back yard. But the countryside was glorious, and with a can or two of paint they freshened up the inside walls. 'Life is where you are,' says Joyce. 'And life is what you make it; so is your home life.'

Joyce soon discovered that her apprehension at her professional role had begun to disappear. She realised suddenly that her shyness had been due to being tested and watched at college. Now, taking the initiative herself and with Hilton by her side, she was more and more excited and ready to go. 'I had no apprehension on arriving at our first posting. I preached, led meetings, did shop league, hotel ministry, jumble sales, women's meetings, visited the hospital and attended to social cases. I felt liberated and free at last from institutional living. Now we could get out and do all that we had been taught in two years of residential training,' says Joyce. And the more she did, the more confident she became.

Their first meeting was a welcome on a Thursday night, with about thirty people in attendance. There were a number of speeches and it was a rather stiff and formal occasion. Joyce felt that one of the ministers of religion was a little distant in his manner, as if he would rather have been at home. The pianist accompanying the singing announced that she was not a member of the Salvation Army but had only turned up to play the piano. It would prove a stark contrast to their farewell gathering two years later, in a crowded hall in the presence of the Shire Clerk. The 'welcome' concluded with cups of tea and then it was over to Joyce and Hilton to build a presence for the Army in Atherton.

It was a small town, and the word soon went round that the Salvation Army was back in the form of two young officers. Throughout the years to come, as the Harmers settled into new postings, Hilton would begin each appointment by introducing himself to the local institutions that might call on the Army's assistance — the police, the fire brigade and the ambulance service. Shops opened and shut at the same times back then. On a weekday early in the posting, Hilton would set off up the main street at 8.30 a.m. introducing himself to the storekeepers and their assistants; up one side and down the other. He and Joyce would drop in on the hospitals and arrange regular visits. Before long the invitations would come for one or other of the Harmers to be present at functions in town. Joyce would attend various church gatherings for women and was sometimes asked to be the guest speaker.

They door-knocked to let folk know they were in town;

they collected kids on the way to 9 a.m. Sunday school in the Kairi hall, twenty kilometres out, and then drove back to Atherton for an 11 a.m. Corps meeting and more Sunday school classes. They took scripture classes during the week. At the Kairi school, Hilton proved so popular the Presbyterian minister complained that the Presbyterian children were attending the Army's classes. At their first Sunday Corps Holiness Meetings around fourteen people came; in time this doubled. Hilton would lead one Sunday and Joyce preach and they would reverse that for the following week. They would always have an 'altar call' during their Sunday meetings, when any person present could put their lives right with God. In their first meeting they had a 'testimony' time, with people sharing their experiences. And, for accompaniment, Hilton would play his piano accordion with Joyce singing as loudly as possible in case he hit the wrong note. He liked to play without music.

They held street meetings on the mezzanine strip of greenery between the two sides of the main street. Passers-by could easily catch sight of them either from the upper footpath or the one below. Joyce was growing more and more pregnant in her white uniform, so hard to keep clean, with its smock-style bodice adapted for her new shape. In spite of her advancing pregnancy she was undaunted, and in fact enthused by her freedom to lead a new misson. Like any modern-day mother-to-be, she continued her professional duties as long as she could. It was unthinkable that she would not.

'Hilton would play the piano accordion and I would play my tambourine. We'd have a two-person open-air meeting — Hilton and I. We both sang and I might do a solo. Hilton would then read from the scriptures and give a mini message of how it applied in our daily lives. Then we'd sing something else, after which I might speak for a few moments, perhaps something topical with a spiritual application.' Like buskers on a sidewalk, it didn't worry them if no one appeared to be listening. Among the *Orders and Regulations for Soldiers of the Salvation Army* is a section called 'Public Speaking', where the philosophy underpinning fearless performance in the streets is spelt out clearly: *Those who have experienced the salvation of Christ are called to be witnesses for Him . . . the convert should be prepared to witness by his word of testimony.* Uninhibited speaking in public is fundamental to the Salvationist's faith. But who would be listening in the main street of Atherton to two uniformed officers conducting a gig about God?

'Well you didn't know who was sitting in cars hearing you anyway,' says Joyce. 'We wouldn't try to catch a person's eyes — just look generally up the street. If anyone stopped to listen we would sing.'

Their enthusiasm owed much to the Salvationist traditions of outback Australia, passed on at corps and by families, like the log books of Captains Florence Whittaker and Ruth Smith, who ran the Number One unit of the Army's outback service in the late 1940s. They told tales of conducting Sunday school in Cobar with twenty-five children in intense heat and a dust storm and then driving in the blizzard to Wrightville, where twenty-two children turned up; shouting in the gritty storm to teach a Bible story and going on to conduct a service that night in a borrowed Methodist church. Or driving out to the families of railway fettlers living in tents along the line and enrolling five children there in a Bible correspondence course; then miles further on to an Aboriginal reserve where the families lived in appalling conditions; conducting meetings on a river bank while the police arrived to break up a drunken brawl. By comparison, Atherton, for the Harmers, was an oasis to work in.

Joyce was right; there were some who took notice. First came a couple of families who were Murray and Pentecostal Islanders, Christians and intermarried. Jimmy and Joyce Blooranta and their large family left the Assembly of God congregation outside Atherton near Yungaburra and began to turn up for Sunday meetings at the Corps. Their eldest son had met Hilton when he gave the boy a lift home from football. The Bloorantas moved closer to Atherton and joined Joyce and Hilton in the street; with music in their bones, they would strum their guitars at a nod. In duets, Hilton and Joyce together, or Joyce with Jimmy Blooranta or Joe Allia, would sing a favourite: '*Tho' some may sing to pass the weary night along/Tho' some may sing to entertain a worldly throng/I sing because I worship God in song/It's in my heart, it's in my heart.*' Joyce gets goose bumps saying the words, remembering, 'Joe Allia had such a loud, penetrating voice that used to go up the main street. Oh, how he sang about the Jesus he loved and who had changed his life.'

And then there was John. The week Peter was born, Hilton conducted the street service alone. It was a Saturday night and the Islander folk were there with him, singing. From the footpath a drunk staggered across, mesmerised by what he was hearing.

'I'm too bad for God to do anything with my life,' said the swaying man.

'What's your name, mate?'

'John.'

'John, I don't think you're well enough to talk about things like this tonight,' said Hilton, taking out a business card. He wrote the times of the church services on the back of the card and popped it into John's shirt pocket. 'I think it would be best if you went home and had a good sleep.'

John moved off into the night air at that, and Hilton went on with his small street meeting. The next morning John must have remembered enough of his chat with Hilton to reach for the card in his pocket. He turned up at the Corps for Sunday service with his mother in tow. 'A darling', Joyce calls her still. A woman who had prayed for years that her sons would become Christians. At the moment in the service when people are called on to make that decision, John went forward to the Mercy Seat and vowed to give his life to Jesus. He became a Salvationist and eventually an envoy, or untrained Salvation Army officer. 'He did good work,' says Joyce. 'And Atherton knew him. Knew the old John and knew the new John.'

Peter, the Harmers' first son, was born on 13 July 1963. Joyce had no worries about her pregnancy while working. She had waited three years for this because of college and revelled in the chance to be a mother, in spite of the constant nausea while pregnant. 'We always envisaged having four children if that was possible. Hilton said it was up to me how many we had, as I was the one to carry them and look after them while they were small. I wanted four children and God blessed me with my desire. I give thanks to Him for this wonderful privilege.' The day Peter was born, Joyce had been on a fundraising street stall selling hot pumpkin scones and handiwork. She believes that her busy life meant she exercised well throughout all her pregnancies, so that her labour, when it came, was reduced — four hours with Peter and five with her other babies. As she lay in her bed after

Peter was born, she heard the night staff talking about the breakfast they were heading off to eat — steak, eggs and chips. They were ravenous. And so was Joyce. But when breakfast came for the new mother, it was four small sandwiches and a cup of tea. Joyce still recalls her hunger for the steak and chips.

Hospital visiting hours were strict — husbands were only allowed for an hour in the evening. When Hilton couldn't visit because he had to collect at the gate of the local show, he sent John, the converted alcoholic, in his place. John brought Joyce a bunch of violets from his mother's garden.

As a baby, Peter loved having Jimmy Blooranta hold him. Peter was as blond as Jimmy was black. And Jimmy would say, 'Hey, Missus, watch him, he's looking up at my big black face.' The Bloorantas became firm friends. There were many evenings, with Peter on his mother's lap or tucked up in his bassinet, when Joyce's little sitting room at the back of the Army hall would fill with Bloorantas, playing their guitars and singing into the night. On free days they would all go fishing at the Tinaroo Dam to catch 'mouth almighties'; Jimmy and Joyce Blooranta called them 'big gobs'.

Sometimes Hilton and Joyce would collect the Islander children for Sunday school and take them home afterwards. Hilton's dad had helped them buy a small utility with a canopy at the back. The children would climb in there and sing their hearts out as they bumped along. A nice little crowd is how Joyce remembers it. Then there was the occasional police officer or school teacher, transferred to the town and looking for a place to worship.

In Sunday Corps meetings, Jimmy Blooranta became their music master. Joyce recalls, 'Hilton would announce unexpectedly, "Now, in a moment Jimmy and Joyce are going to bring us the message in song." So we would hike up to the back of the hall. Jimmy would get his guitar and say, "Missus, what are we going to sing?" I'd say, "Oh come on, get something out that I can harmonise with." He'd say, "Can you do that one?" And off we'd go. In a few minutes we'd be at the front of the church singing. He was a darling.'

They raised money doing the rounds of pubs, Joyce in Atherton, Hilton in towns beyond. They had done the collections in Sydney pubs while at college, so it was a familiar routine, something expected of corps officers in those days. It was a given that the officers in charge of a corps would supplement the basic allowance sent from Headquarters, and even support themselves, with collections and fundraising around the local area. Collecting from pubs, running street stalls, selling cakes and pumpkin scones, whatever could be organised to add to the collections. When Hilton's mother came to stay, on occasion she would bake batches of pumpkin scones just in time for Joyce and Hilton to sell them. And they iced cakes for hours, some days driving them in their canopied ute to Mareeba to set up stalls. The road's dust would be finely sprinkled like cinnamon over the cakes by the time they arrived. There was little choice but to sell them as they were, adding small and large amounts to Corps coffers over time. Pregnant or nursing an infant, Joyce could still manage doing the pubs. Young Katie Blooranta would stay over to help mind Peter on Friday nights while Joyce collected, wheeling him in the pram along the footpath while Joyce went inside the pubs.

'It was a wonderful opportunity, really. Ladies sitting in the beer garden would chat with me. And I was fairly shy in those days. If I was doing it now I would have talked about different things. But approaching them still didn't worry me all that much and the men were very kind and generous to a lady collecting. The uniform also spoke volumes.'

Morning teas raised small amounts for overseas missions. Churches and their guilds supported each other in Atherton. Invitations would go out, the ladies would bake, the food reflecting a theme appropriate to the speaker and a guest speaker would be on hand for the occasion, some passing through from other countries. Camaraderie and community spirit were in plentiful supply.

But at times the money raised for the Corps was insufficient. All their lives as officers, Joyce and Hilton would struggle to find enough to live on. In those days there was no guarantee of a Salvation Army salary, although accommodation was provided and Headquarters would never leave anyone to starve. Some corps managed on Corps Assistance Funding (CAF) but most were expected to exist and continue their work using funds from donations and collections in the area they served. Even in their training college years, Joyce and Hilton had learned what it meant to survive on the little you had. Home on holidays from Sydney as trainees, they travelled to see a chiropractor in Toowoomba when Hilton was suffering from a bad back. They arrived at Toowoomba railway station with just one shilling in their pockets. Until they got back to Gympie they had nothing to eat. No food for a day was part of the sacrifice they had chosen. Later, as corps officers and with a growing family, the sacrifices continued. Joyce recalls how people would come to their door with eggs, fruit, jam, milk, puddings, vegetables and the like, but even so they had to eat 'downmarket' a lot of the time. Meals were basic but nutritious. Windsor sausage and some salad and bread were often on their menu. In desperate moments, Joyce would thicken a can of vegetable soup to eat on toast. Bacon and eggs or ham were out of the question. Lyndall Harmer remembers how her mother would make milk from powdered substitutes and pour it into cartons so her children wouldn't know they couldn't afford real milk. Going without was taken as part of the commitment and never complained about. For Joyce, her faith simply increased as she and Hilton managed to survive. Somehow, God would provide. And He did seem to.

'On one occasion in Atherton we didn't have enough money for our electricity bill,' recalls Joyce. 'It was our regular account. The Keswick Convention for all churches of North Queensland had just been held in Atherton. It had been a great success. Speakers, music, everyone getting together. And then we had a bill we couldn't pay. We went to the post office some weeks later to collect the mail and there was a letter from a Townsville woman who had been at the convention. She wrote that she had no idea why she was sending us some money but that she felt in her heart that God's spirit was prompting her to send it to help us in our work. In the letter was the exact amount we needed to pay our electricity bill. Praise Jesus!'

That sort of occurrence continued to convince Joyce that God answered her prayers. She maintains that the cheque for the electricity bill was one of her first learning experiences of trusting God implicitly for all their needs. When she wrote to thank the woman who gave so generously, telling her that she was blessed, the woman wrote back saying that Joyce should always follow the promptings of God's spirit because they will always be right. From her life experience as an officer with Hilton, Joyce has come to believe firmly that this is true.

Not all of the tough times were simply about small economies. Their faith would be tested by big crises as well in their years ahead as officers, but faith always somehow got them through. 'Oh, it has been hard and very difficult,' says Joyce. 'There've been moments when I've said, "God, where are you?" I would be very untruthful if I said there had not been times like that. There have been times I've had to call on my faith and trust in God even when I have had moments of wondering where He was. But I just knew He was there even while I was in the dark. It was like a tunnel experience. And if, like a small child, I didn't keep holding on to what I believed in and my faith, then it would be like stepping off a train in a tunnel.' Into this explanation Joyce will weave the story of the passion, revived in Mel Gibson's 2004 film spectacular, the sacrifice of Jesus dying on Calvary nailed to a cross to save mankind. 'When I think of that, there's no sacrifice in what I've done,' says Joyce.

With their marching orders at the beginning of 1965, and just two years in Atherton under their belts, Joyce and Hilton were on their way again. The Blooranta children turned up at the Corps to help them pack, too upset to go to school and crying at the idea of losing the Harmers. It was to be the first of many tearful goodbyes for Joyce and Hilton. The Blooranta children, as adults, still keep in touch.

They were next off to Bowen, named after the first Queensland governor, on the coast south of Townsville 1165 kilometres from Brisbane, then a charming and easy-going hamlet and now the gateway to a northern paradise of bays. The area north of Bowen is also renowned for its fifty-kilometre stretch of fertile soils, intensively cultivated for fruit and vegetable growing. From the late 1880s and into the early twentieth century, the Salvationists had converted many Kanakas (Islanders) in their Queensland mission, so much so that in 1911 the Army's magazine, *The War Cry*, referred to Bowen as the first all-black corps in Queensland, in spite of the fact that the Corps officers were themselves white. But such was the attraction of the Army for many Kanakas in that area.

In Bowen, once again the Harmers were accommodated at the rear of the Corps hall, although Joyce recalls the rooms here were nicer, freshly painted and cheerier. Corps soldiers and ladies of the church were more numerous than in Atherton, but divided between older folk and teenagers. That made the task of striking the right note difficult, but a strong musical tradition among Salvationists in Bowen from the Corps' earliest gatherings made it worthwhile. The Bowen Corps had been once described in *The War Cry* as *a real soul-inspiring corps* where *their combined singing was a treat to hear, so much so that the simplest old songs seemed to have new vim and bite in them*.

In the middle of their time in Bowen, Joyce gave birth to her second child, whom they named Bruce, and she now found herself dividing her ministry between caring for an infant and a two-year-old and the demands of the Corps. 'I got fat on stewed mangoes,' reflects Joyce. 'The ladies of the church used to bring them to me. I ate stewed mangoes and ice-cream. I sang duets with an Islander lady, a spiritual gem, at women's functions, and for years she would send me Bowen mangoes at Christmas.'

Their time at postings in Atherton and Bowen had established the Harmers as successful corps officers, full of enterprise and energy. Joyce seemed to thrive on her life as a mother alongside her officer duties, as if one complemented the other. She and Hilton were still learning and very young, but already showing maturity beyond their years, and ready to take in the wisdom of many ordinary Australians they met along the way.

Hilton never forgot the lesson he learned from an old man on the beach in Bowen. 'In 1965, I was walking on the beach. An old bloke who used to gather shells was combing the sand. A lump of seaweed gunk came in and I made to kick it when he yelled at me, "Don't kick that, Lieutenant." I asked why not. He replied, "Inside that is a rare shell, beautiful, and that's how I get them." Don Brown was his name. I told him he could have fooled me. He said to come and see what it was like after he'd worked on it. I did, about six weeks later. He'd put it in chemicals and produced a fantastic mother-of-pearl shell. The Holy Spirit spoke to me then. In my inner being, I always tried to remember that in other people. Never judge them as they come to you but on what they can become through your ministry.'

For Joyce and Hilton, that philosophy would always govern their approach. Before long they were packing once more for a move to Rockhampton, where their little boys would learn to kick balls and sit up straight in services on Sunday. In only a few years, these two fresh-faced trainees evolved into a picture of domestic and professional success, so that after Rockhampton came a much bigger move, in 1969, to the north Queensland mining oasis of Mt Isa.

chapter 9

HOME AS MISSION

In the tradition of William and Catherine Booth, Salvationist couples trained as equals. Joyce and Hilton had both gone to officer training college and had both emerged with the rank of Lieutenant. But married women officers in the ministry, while technically equal to their husbands in rank, were, until recently, not treated that way. Until the late 1990s, Joyce was referred to as 'Mrs' before any rank she held and then never as 'Joyce'. It would be 'Mrs Captain Hilton Harmer' or 'Mrs Major Hilton Harmer'. Her role as wife came before all. Wives, in spite of having completed all the training, were known as 'the officer wife'. And, as with most married working women, Joyce's work for her corps needed always to be balanced with home duties and her role as mother. Hilton, on the other hand, freely admits to being a fanatic about the ministry and relaxed about leaving most of the first-hand caring of the children to his wife. It was the style of the time. Only years later did Hilton take stock of how it must have been for Joyce.

'Our kids for me always came second to the Salvation Army or to the people who came to us needing help. I never worried about the kids. Joyce looked after them. And I was out there doing the Army work. Someone, of course, had to look after them, and if Joyce hadn't done it we would have had a terrible time. Joyce has been a beautiful mother to our children. For all that, our kids have never doubted the love of both of us for them. But there are times when I still believe they underestimate their mother. I became the prominent figure, out there doing it. They haven't always realised what a prominent figure she is.'

The tasks of each day unfolded according to the needs of the public they had been trained to serve. Rising around 6 a.m., they began their days with devotions, spiritual readings and prayers. Early in their married life they did this together, but as the children came along they found it more easily done separately, with one minding the little ones and the other catching a few moments alone. Hilton would breakfast with Joyce and the children but very soon disappear, gone from his home office by 9 a.m., to answer a call for help, attend a meeting or organise an Army function. Sometimes he would drive miles collecting for their monthly jumble sales or delivering furniture, taking food and other basics to needy families, picking up people who needed transport, door-knocking or making house calls to keep in touch with many the Army knew were having a hard time, whether from illness, poverty or abandonment by loved ones. On several days of the week, Hilton and sometimes Joyce would go to local public schools to take classes in 'religious instruction'. These classes ran from 9 a.m. till noon.

They also had a great belief in visiting members of the congregation in their homes, especially those who were sick or having a tough time for some reason. They prepared sermons for Sunday with books spread around them, breaking only for lunch or dinner. They did welfare work — collecting and distributing goods for the needy — and kept the accounts, which needed to be sent in to Headquarters every month. Hospital visits took up more time; they would go from bed to bed wishing people all the best and handing them a copy of the latest Salvation Army *War Cry* magazine. They collected, taking donations as small as twenty cents from shopkeepers and again leaving a copy of *The War Cry*. And there were always the hotel visits on Thursday and Friday nights — collecting donations, speaking to the regulars.

When they had a thrift shop attached to a corps, this would mean hours of unpacking bric-a-brac and clothing as well as setting up the shop with volunteers. When there were no volunteers, Joyce and Hilton ran the shop. They also cleaned the meeting hall for Home League meetings and Sunday services and meetings; the dust storms would often leave a cleaned hall filthy within a few minutes. In Mt Isa they tried to reach what they referred to as 'the unchurched' by hiring a few tennis courts for open get-togethers after their regular open-air meetings on Sunday nights. And they held Sunday school teachers' meetings in their own home. At these meetings the group prepared the worksheets for the 100 children who attended, drawing outlines relating to the Bible teachings for the coming week, which the children would be asked to colour in. These meetings were friendly gatherings of fellowship, which the Harmers looked forward to. Around the Corps, maintenance work was also their responsibility, whether painting walls or mowing lawns. And there were ongoing dedications of babies, weddings and funerals to conduct.

At the end of a day on the road, Hilton might bring home one of the abandoned flock — a baby, a child, someone needing a feed or room for the night. In Rockhampton he had once brought home forty relatives from a funeral he had conducted.

They lived miles apart, out bush somewhere, and hadn't seen each other in years. They needed a cup of tea and somewhere to catch up. Hilton came home to Joyce with them and they stayed talking in groups all over the house and garden for hours. 'I got the cups from the Ladies' Home League,' recalls Joyce. Hilton couldn't say no. He came home with babies whose mothers were sick, on one occasion the daughter of a local fire brigade officer who had attended a crisis where a boy had fallen into the huge pit of a building site and impaled himself on a steel rod. The boy had turned out to be the fire brigade officer's own son. He had collapsed and the mother had also been taken to hospital. Hilton brought their small daughter home to Joyce, who looked after her till the parents recovered. They looked after families who had lost homes in fires, and even a street girl in her twenties, whom Hilton brought home and who slept on the divan in the living room, while Joyce worried what might happen during the night. In true Salvation Army tradition, Joyce and Hilton believed that as officers they were 'public property', there to give of themselves to people who needed them. 'And never,' says Hilton, 'did Joyce complain. And I knew she would manage. She has a marvellous skill for it. Always so calm. So I just left them with her and went off to my Salvation Army work each day.'

They stayed in touch with their extended family mainly by letters, Joyce writing to Alice regularly and keeping up with her sisters and brothers a lot of the time through her mother. Every year during their annual leave, they went home to Gympie, and later also to Brisbane, where the Lipkes moved when Daphne and Yvonne were teenagers. In Gympie they stayed with Hilton's parents, who were relaxed about having young children around them. A broken ornament or scratched piece of furniture was never a worry to Connie and Cliff. While Alice had brought up a large family herself, her fastidious housekeeping made visits difficult. She was never happy with the way grandchildren quickly disordered her tidy rooms. Joyce also felt uncomfortable if Reg was at home, so they would often just visit for a meal with the Lipkes.

It disappointed Joyce not to see her sisters married, but between her four pregnancies and their lives as officers, they couldn't get home for those family weddings. This was not so uncommon in the days before cheap air fares in Australia. In that era, a lot of interstate relatives would be absent at weddings. There was either not enough time or money for the journey, or both.

As the Harmers' appointments had come and gone, the responsibilities had increased, each corps a little bigger, the soldiers more numerous and therefore the responsibilities of ministry more complex. Technically, the postings involved worship ministry rather than the ministry of social support. But wherever Joyce and Hilton went no need could be ignored. They often housed children from homes in distressed situations, a tradition in the Army, where over decades, thousands have been accommodated overnight in officers' quarters or at the back of Army halls on spare mattresses. Joyce and Hilton, though, went the extra mile, taking in motherless infants and children for weeks at a time. In Mt Isa, Joyce cared for seven children (her three and four others) for a month. And they all got the measles. Joyce and Hilton would simply take children in as if they were part of the family.

This meant of course that while Hilton would be at home at night, during the days Joyce took over the management of these extra charges alone. At Mt Isa she also took charge of a newborn baby when its mother couldn't care for it. Did she have home-help? No. There was only Hilton, when he wasn't out and about the town caring for many others in need. Joyce managed, with a penchant for order and strictness that she had learned early in life. She loved her children and was a natural mother for any needy infant, but she did it all with a firm belief that, along with a good dose of love, children must be given definite guidelines and plenty of no-nonsense routine. And it was a firm hand and routine that the Harmer children learned from a week old. Indulgence wasn't in Joyce's vocabulary. Children fed, children dressed, children playing outside or inside, children bathed, children ready for bed; the day would take its own shape, with the children knowing who was boss. Joyce's busy life as wife and officer allowed for nothing less. And for all Hilton's regret at not giving enough of his time to the child-caring, Joyce remembers it a little differently. Whenever Joyce had to do her Army work, meetings for the Ladies' Home League or Women's Fellowship or other activities, Hilton would take over the babysitting, doing some work in his office at the same time if he could. And at night, Joyce made good use of his presence.

'Hilton helped. He would peel the vegetables while I was preparing sermons. He would help me bath the kids in the tub, putting them into pyjamas, cleaning their teeth, settling them into bed. Then we might relax a bit — except if the phone rang.'

At the Harmers' Mt Isa appointment, their duties expanded in a way that allowed Joyce to carry out her officer duties while staying close to the home base and her responsibilities as a mother. The Corps and its accommodation shared a block with a men's hostel. From the early years of the twentieth century the Salvation Army in Australia had made accommodation for working people and the homeless one of its priorities. By the 1970s, the Army was housing a thousand Australians each night. The typical male who depended on this sort of accommodation was an ageing forty-something, unemployed, without roots and a loner. Such a man would stay nowhere for long, his only friends other homeless men like himself. He would have slept rough for years in the open, until falling on the services of the Army for whatever reason — hunger, the bottle, the police after him for vagrancy. These men collected unemployment benefits but drank most of what they took. The Army would clean them up, dry them out and then they would be off again.

The phone rang around the clock at the Mt Isa quarters. People would arrive at any time looking for shelter. It was Joyce who booked them in or handed out food if they didn't want to stay. It was Joyce who administered the hostel's housekeeping, the linen supplies, the meals, the rosters and so on. But Joyce was still very inexperienced with those overcome by alcohol or drugs. She recalls how her welcoming attitude was challenged in Mt Isa when a drunk came knocking on her door while Hilton was out on the road. With the children asleep in the house, Joyce refused to open the door. She admits to being scared of what might have happened if she had. Most people would agree with what Joyce did, but Joyce still feels ashamed that she didn't open her door and help the drunken man.

'You know, I should have been able to do something with him, or just talk to him. But I didn't have a screen door. I had some wire netting on the louvres just beside the front door and I opened them slightly and talked to him. But when he walked away I felt guilty that I hadn't done anything to help him. I could see him going home and saying that the Salvation Army woman wouldn't open the door.'

It's not unusual for children to grow up with the effects of parents' professional choices. The children of seamen have dads who go to sea for months at a time; the children of diplomats move house almost as frequently as the Harmer children did, and from country to country as well. Peter Harmer recalls he attended seven different schools in ten years. But it is unusual for parents to have to house their children in close proximity to clients with mental and social problems, some quite serious. This was not the Harmers' choice. It came about from the work they did for the Salvation Army and the accommodation they were given. To the Army there was nothing odd, it seemed, about housing a couple with small children on the same block as a refuge for alcoholics and itinerant men. Both Joyce and Hilton were savvy about the circumstances for their small children. As much as they extended their generosity of spirit to the needy, they drew the boundaries carefully. Even to soldiers at the Corps who might offer to take their kids out for a break, they'd say, 'No, we'll be right. But thanks all the same.'

While they lived in Mt Isa with the itinerant men's hostel beside their quarters, Joyce had an arrangement with the manager of the local fire brigade across the road. 'If Hilton happened not to be around, I only needed to ring and they would fly over to my assistance. I only did it once but it was good to know I could. Even when I did ring it wasn't a crisis. There was a drunk man wandering around outside the house. I didn't realise he had been booked in. After I rang, three of the firemen bolted across the street as if I was under attack. Afterwards, I felt so stupid.'

While living so close to the men's hostel, Joyce and Hilton instructed five-year-old Peter, who was now at school, to keep an eye on three-year-old Bruce. 'You make sure that Bruce never goes over to the men's hostel,' Joyce would say. 'You *must* not go there. If you see Bruce talking to any of those men, you come running inside and tell Mummy.' Joyce looked out into the yard one day to see Peter dragging Bruce and yelling, 'Mum, Mum! Bruce was taking Lifesavers from that man and he wanted Bruce to go inside.'

As a tag team, the Harmers were exceptional. But with her third pregnancy, in their first year at Mt Isa, the belief that they were public property and their Army-first approach were beginning to catch up with Joyce — although she didn't realise this until Lyndall's birth that year. Joyce's workload was excessive, but always she coped, as Hilton believed she could. She managed the babies who needed mothering and her own besides, the Sunday school classes, the women's groups, the itinerant men's hostel, the sermons and their hours of preparation. In all of it, Joyce simply found an additional bit of energy to make it happen. Her work seemed to invigorate her as it always had, but her blood pressure was high and she was pregnant. She hadn't realised how much the work was taking from her physically.

Lyndall was the daughter Joyce had wanted for so long, but it was not the birth she had expected. 'We had the hostel and something on in the church every night. I had two boys of my own and was often minding other babies that came to us needing care. It was too much. I had a difficult pregnancy with Lyndall and she was born early. My nerves were shot after that.' Events had carried Joyce with them. The birth, a premature infant, return from hospital to the daily round of Corps pressures with three children under seven — and suddenly nothing was as it should have been.

'Lyndall was a perfect baby, but I was nervy and my thoughts seemed to be out of control,' admits Joyce. 'I imagined what I could do to her if I so desired. She was only weeks old but the thoughts continued. I felt as if I was locked in a bottle and couldn't break through. Even the look of the kitchen appeared different.' Joyce recalls how her happy disposition was gone, how she had no wish to associate with people other than her immediate family. On her regular hospital visits in her ministry, she kept up the smile but often looked down on a patient while feeling wretched inside, and she would think how she ought to be lying in a hospital bed herself. The aftermath of Lyndall's birth was a dark tunnel experience.

'As a husband, I knew nothing about postnatal depression,' says Hilton, thinking back. 'I knew Joyce and her capacity to be happy and cheerful in the face of most circumstances. However, this circumstance was different. And I knew that Joyce and the new baby had to become the number-one priority, but the life of the Corps had to go on.'

Joyce found herself acutely frightened of being alone. After a visit to the doctor she was diagnosed as suffering from postnatal depression. 'My thoughts were not normal, and I had given birth to two other children so I knew that something was wrong,' says Joyce of the time after Lyndall's birth. 'I didn't like being alone because I didn't know what I'd do if left alone. I remember standing near the stove, wrenching my hands and saying, "Hilton, don't leave me alone; don't leave me in this house alone!" I was definitely not in my right frame of mind. Thank God I didn't do anything. I can understand and feel for all those other people who have been there. They are to be pitied, not blamed.'

Joyce went to her local doctor. He advised her to 'go to the coast for a bludge'.

'I sat outside the doctor's rooms, with Hilton, in the car. I said, "Well he's told me to get some medication and go to the coast for a bludge." Imagine that. Townsville, on the coast, was 400 miles away. The only place I could have gone to there was a Salvation Army People's Palace. One room in a People's Palace. And in the state I was in. To be told to stay away from my husband and children, languishing in one room. What sort of a bludge was that? I'd go completely mad.'

Joyce and Hilton talked it over. They would manage by themselves as best they could. Hilton undertook to make sure he cared for the children, particularly at night. 'We had a trained nurse in our Corps who had a small family. I called her and she agreed to take Lyndall. I didn't discuss this with Joyce. I just took Lyndall to Dorothy, the nurse. And then I set up the back room for Joyce so she could stay there away from the ebb and flow of a busy officers' quarters. While I knew nothing of postnatal depression, I knew I had a family crisis on my hands.' From then on, Joyce would go to bed at 9 p.m., taking her medication and sleeping in a single bed in the back room. Hilton brought her meals and whatever she wanted, but mostly she wanted to sleep. And so, for a few weeks, Joyce slept her fears away.

'I had my bludge in the back room,' is how Joyce puts it.

'It was a very difficult time for Joyce,' says Hilton.

Her recovery came gradually, and she was eventually able to take care of Lyndall. Hilton had brought the baby home after a week when he realised Joyce was fretting about not seeing her. He still hadn't told her someone else had been caring for the baby. While Joyce was convalescing, Hilton took over the responsibilities for the older children. Peter was at school across the road and the hostel and church were all part of the same block. This helped to make the logistics a little easier. Then, slowly, life resumed its regular routine.

Each Sunday, Joyce and Hilton conducted the services for their Corps. As well, Joyce was in charge of Sunday school classes and their eight Sunday school teachers. The Harmer children attended the Sunday services their parents conducted from the time they were first born. 'Joyce would bring them almost always, regardless,' says Hilton. 'Teething or off-colour. She would bring them out, dress them up accordingly and lie them down on little beds under the seats. That was the go in those days. And she knew what discipline was and what care was needed.'

'Mum's all bluff really,' her son Bruce maintains. 'At the services on Sundays she'd have something in her bag, maybe a blue Bessemer Ware tablespoon. She would get that out and it was an indication that if we didn't quieten down we would get something more at home. But the wooden spoon at home was more of a joke, really. We'd run around the lounge and Mum would chase us till eventually we'd break it. She'd smack something like a chair. We broke several wooden spoons. We'd end up in laughter and hugging each other and all that. Home life was never violent. Mum could never be that.'

However, Lyndall Harmer looks back on a very strict upbringing when it came to standards of right and wrong. 'A lot of it was to make sure we had the right boundaries set. The guidelines were very definite. I had to be covered well at home because Mum would remind me that I had three brothers and a dad living with me. I recall that Dad waited outside for me in the car at my last formal dance at school. But it is a testament to their parenting that all four of us have made good decisions in life.'

Whatever the mayhem of the wooden spoons at home, Joyce did maintain strict control in corps services. 'From a week old they had to learn how to behave themselves. They went to everything with us and they had to be models. I had observed other mothers with children who misbehaved in church and I determined that mine would be trained to behave, without any beatings.' To this she adds an ironic 'Ha, ha', as if the result at times came a bit below the expectations. 'It was a bit of a pain sometimes, because people expected them to be perfect.'

A severe glance at one of her children during a Sunday service could bring compliance. Lyndall still laughs at how her parents would just add the name of one of their children to whatever they were saying to the congregation to let them know that misbehaviour had been noted. 'Dad would be reading out, "We'll now sing the words to *Onward Christian soldiers, marching as to war* — Bruce! — *with the cross of Jesus*. I wouldn't mind — it was always my brothers that were misbehaving.'

Joyce worked to make sure the children had enough distractions to keep them amused. Sweets like soft musk sticks were a fail-safe bribe offered on occasions. She'd provide toys to play with, colouring books and a makeshift area on the floor for the babies. Many in various congregations would help with the child-minding. Bruce recalls he might have occasionally fallen asleep on someone's lap. Peter remembers them sitting in front in their uniforms as children.

Peter can also remember that his father's discipline at home was more physical than that of Joyce. Hilton had a strap. 'Not round the legs. Just on the backsides. That's why we've got a big soft area there. It never hurt anyone,' says Peter, now a father of four himself.

Lyndall has a vivid memory of their Sundays around this time. 'Every Sunday would start off with Mum going straight to the record player and putting on what she called "holy music". We always knew it was Sunday because of that. She still does it to this day. Either band music from the Salvation Army or something else. That would be around 7 a.m. Then we'd be dressed and fed and ready to head off to corps. Whatever corps it was.'

Their first postings, in North Queensland, were all challenges for Joyce. She was being swept along — Hilton, commitment, college, motherhood and ministry. But it wasn't the thrill and uplifting excitement of a conversion experience such as came to the legendary Jock Geddes, *born an atheist and reared a pagan* (as his biographer William Cairns described him in *Padre Jock*), who challenged God till he was convinced by signs that he should become a Salvationist. Joyce's faith was dappled with tiny moments of back-and-forth where Jock was all raging fire and colourful certainty. Joyce's gentle style was a surrendering of the will to the power of God as she believed it to be. She would be an instrument for supporting and guiding others, but she was no firebrand brandishing her Bible. Her shyness hadn't totally abated, yet she gave off a confidence that belied her feelings of inadequacy.

They were isolated physically from the Army proper in the small communities they lived in. Hilton, though, was in his element. 'Hilton can sit at a wedding breakfast beside a guest he has never met and talk all day and night,' says Joyce. 'But I can't do that. I get stuck for words. And it was worse back then. But when I'm in a helping situation I'm not shy. That's a modern miracle, as I see it, that only God could be in control of. Because it's not my temperament or my personality to be game enough to step forward and approach people. To set out to do it. But with the surrender of my will and my life to God, it just flowed from there on.'

As institutions often do, the Army provided fellowship camps so that officers could keep in touch with each other. Twice a year there would be a gathering at a resort centre, somewhere like Yeppoon or Magnetic Island, where families could stay and confer about their work, complete with childminders so the parent officers would be free to attend the sessions. In between the meeting times, families could enjoy a holiday with their children among friends and colleagues. And there was a congress meeting in Brisbane once a year as well.

Noela and Alf Dawkins, the Harmers' friends from Army college, were posted to Longreach as Joyce and Hilton took over the Mt Isa Corps. 'They were isolated postings out there,' Noela recalls. 'I took at least a couple of trips to Mt Isa to stay with Joyce and Hilton when we were at Longreach. I had a young baby and Alf was away on the flying mission every second week. It was over 600 kilometres northwest on the Skinner Bus Service and nearly all dirt road. I was involved a bit with their ministry there and I was hungry for some contact with other women. At Longreach there was only one woman soldier in our Corps.'

On one occasion, Joyce and Hilton made the trip to Longreach to lead a special weekend program. They brought the whole Corps on an old Pioneer coach that broke down a number of times along the way on the dirt road. By the time they arrived, the passengers were coated in dust and very hungry. Noela and Alf Dawkins performed a modern-day loaves-and-fishes miracle, providing them all with fish and chips and a garden tap to wash off the grime. All unforgettable, says Noela. 'The program they gave us took Longreach by storm. There wasn't any television there in those days. It was a small isolated town. The Mt Isa Corps took their open-air meeting to the middle of the main street and marched with the band right through the centre of town. It was like a pageant for the locals. They talked about it for months afterwards.'

Hilton and Joyce had married young, trained and been made officers before they were twenty-five, and were parents of three small children by the time Joyce was thirty. By Hilton's own admission, his energy was of the addictive variety, something he was not aware of until he attended a discussion over a decade later when the psychologist conducting the session turned to him and told him that he had a workaholic personality. Before that, Hilton had not considered it. He never slackened, and believed that was normal. He was a 'now' person: 'Every job must be done now, don't put anything off,' was his motto.

'I was never an alcoholic, drug addict or gambler,' says Hilton, looking back. 'But I was a Workaholic with a capital "W". And for a woman like Joyce who was built for comfort and not speed, built for normality and not for obsessiveness, built for balance in life but living with a totally unbalanced individual, God only knows what pressures were placed upon her. But Joyce, because of her childhood experiences, never confronted me on this.'

'I'm more likely to make a note that something should be done when it's needed,' says Joyce. 'But Hilton will just take off. On the job right away. And with little tolerance sometimes for others who don't see it as so urgent.' Babies needed looking after, Hilton would bring them home. Families needed furniture, Hilton would be in the truck and away, travelling hundreds of miles sometimes. Back at base, Joyce managed the rest.

So it was that Joyce, absorbing rather than flinging back her objections, became the strong central figure of the Harmer family. It wasn't apparent outside. And, Hilton maintains, not even to her children. After all, she was a mother in the same vein as most mothers, and she worked with her husband as a ministering wife, although often this could be interpreted as 'minister's wife'. Within the Salvationist culture, she stood beside or behind her husband. They moved from corps to corps together with their marching orders, but it could appear on occasion that she was following him. He was the more public figure on the road in the towns; she was the compass point that remained fixed at base more often than not, because of the children. And with her peacemaker's ability to absorb the moments of difference rather than confront them, Joyce gained an enormous capacity for calm in the face of crisis. Her life with Reg had some positive spin-off after all. She could maintain her cool and wait out the moments of upset, often praying silently for strength. At her Home League evenings each week, she organised speakers on topics from health to housekeeping, the idea of the Home League being to give disadvantaged women a fellowship where they could be supported and taught ways to better their lives as homemakers and mothers. They shared recipes, read scripture, laughed together and went home not only a little wiser about how to cope but also in cheerier and stronger spirits. 'I had them in raucous laughter one night about our antics in Gympie avoiding Reg,' says Joyce. 'Laughter, I believe, is very therapeutic.'

'I was always very proud of my wife when I saw her loving someone for Jesus,' says Hilton. 'She is such a tender heart and has such a natural way of caring. It is a special gift from God. It was part of our Salvation Army training that the wife of the officer be totally committed, and of course this expectation fuelled my own desire to be everywhere and everything to everyone. Beside all this, Joyce had her own total commitment to being an officer of the Salvation Army, with balance, which I admired greatly and possibly even exploited. All of the care that the public sees in Joyce is exhibited in the home. She is a selfless individual who gives herself unreservedly to us all and anyone who has been blessed to cross her path.'

This recognition of the special aura Joyce has would come to Hilton only in later maturity. In their early years together he took her skills for granted, too busy with corps work to notice how valuable her particular skills of calm parenting were, how they complemented and made possible their professional lives of serving people in need. Remembering the encounter with the man on the beach in Bowen, Hilton can now compare what he learned there with the way Joyce gradually revealed her unique spiritual and healing touch over many years. Hilton can now recognise that, as they lived out their ministry in places like Mt Isa, Joyce was still the diamond in the rough, the shell on the shore covered by a bunch of seaweed. 'When you think of Joyce's early beginnings and what she went on to do, it's an absolute miracle:"A diamond in the rough is a diamond sure enough; before it is ever burnished it is made of diamond stuff."'

Joyce, after eight years as an officer, was still being burnished, but already her skill with people was becoming apparent — her instinctive touch when she heard of a mother in need, the way she absorbed their pain, took care of their children alongside her own without so much as being asked, the way she could empathise and touch the lives of people she barely knew, her joy in the contributions of others — like those of the destitute lady she helped for a time. Joyce had met her in the street, a woman of very low self-esteem. She invited her to the weekly Home League meetings. The woman repaid the Corps for this friendship by unpicking women's gathered skirts donated for their monthly jumble sales, and sewing them into bright pillowslips and covers for the itinerant men's hostel.

As they left Mt Isa in 1971 on their way to a new posting at Newcastle in New South Wales, Hilton's journey to a full recognition of what his wife meant to him had not really begun. The move south was a big step. Newcastle was not only geographically a long way from Mt Isa, it was also a large regional centre. But it was not their work as ministers that would challenge and test their faith from this point on. What happened to them in Newcastle would change Hilton forever.

chapter 10

SAND DUNES

The Stockton Beach sand dunes stretch north for thirty-two kilometres along the coast from the Newcastle harbour. A National Trust treasure set down for preservation in 1972, the dunes are sacred to the Worimi Nation of Australia's indigenous Maaiangal people. They tower in places like small mountains and are sculptured by winds into razorbacks and deep ravines. The sea glitters in the distance as trekkers stand to catch their breath. Behind the dunes is a mixture of dry woodland and swampy forest. The paperbarks sink their roots into wetlands and the wildlife nestles safely — water fowl, grey kangaroos, swamp wallabies, brushtail possums, brown bandicoots and echidnas. Frogs come out after rain, calling to mates. Mosquitos breed easily.

'Boys, how would you like a day at the dunes with Dad?'

Hilton hadn't stopped for his boys in a long while. They were growing, eight-year-old Peter and six-year-old Bruce, and he had hardly had time to notice the changes in them. The Corps absorbed his hours, the endless calls and co-ordinating. He could never say no to a cry for help. And the boys were lively kids, like the Lipke lads before them. Ready for mischief, or a tussle with Dad.

In March 1972, Joyce and Hilton were the officers at the Army's Newcastle City Corps in King Street. Baby Lyndall was toddling about and the family fairly secure in its lifestyle of Army routines. But the work of settling into a new area every two years or so was taking its toll, especially on a dad devoted to his Army duties. A year after they arrived in Newcastle, and with time to realise there was family fun to be had there, Hilton became conscious that he was not spending enough leisure time with his boys. So the boys were thrilled with the suggestion of a trip to the dunes. And off they went one Saturday afternoon. It was a long walk for little legs from the road where Hilton had parked the car, but there was much to observe and talk about for two small lads with a dad. Birdsong like a whiplash broke the quiet and around the small ponds they poked at the water. Tiny creatures scurried under rocks or broke the surface. They watched for kangaroos or wallabies in the scrub. They stumbled on a couple of dead cows. Their walk took them quite a distance, so the return journey was longer than Hilton had planned. Night was falling by the time they made it back to the car, scratching at arms and legs covered in mosquito bites.

It was three weeks later and the week before Easter when Hilton began to feel sick. He conducted his usual Sunday services at the Newcastle Corps with what he calls 'the mother of all headaches'. That night he was guest speaker at a Baptist youth meeting and the headache didn't let up. It was still there when he woke on Monday.

'It's a curse of an ache,' he told Joyce. 'I simply can't shift it.'

'Well, I would tell you to go to bed and call the doctor,' his wife replied, 'but you wouldn't do that.'

'Try me,' said Hilton.

To Joyce, this was serious. Hilton never took to his bed. She phoned the doctor, a young man on call, who diagnosed flu and predicted all would be right after a few days' rest. But Hilton got worse. The headache became unbearable and he started to vomit.

On the Thursday before Easter, Joyce called for help again. This time an older doctor arrived. His face was grave as he told them he suspected Hilton had encephalitis, probably caught from a mosquito bite at the dunes. Water birds are known hosts for the virus. The two dead cows may have added to the danger.

'It's hospital immediately,' declared the doctor. 'You'll need a lumbar puncture so we can be sure I'm right.'

Hilton and Joyce knew little, if anything, about encephalitis, a virus that causes an inflammation of the brain. Hilton had many of the most common symptoms — nausea, severe headache and some disorientation. Encephalitis can also cause lack of sensation in parts of the body. An attack usually lasts about a week and recovery can take months and even years. Some patients are left with permanent disabilities and even brain damage; in some cases a patient will die.

The doctor had gone to the phone, which sat on a small table beside a stool in the hall, and was arguing with someone at the hospital. It appeared there wasn't a bed for Hilton. 'This man is very ill,' he was saying. 'He must be admitted immediately.' Finally, the doctor found a bed. Hilton couldn't argue; the ambulance was called. He was admitted to the Royal Newcastle Hospital and the lumbar puncture was done as soon as it could be arranged.

Hilton went to the hospital insisting he could only stay for a few days. 'I have to be out of here by Saturday,' he said, lying on his side as a doctor numbed his spine in readiness for the needle. 'I have an important part in our Easter play. I'm Peter.'

'You will not be attending any Easter play,' the doctor replied.

The pathology labs were closed for Easter, which slowed down the test results. At one point doctors thought it might be polio, and Joyce wondered if he had meningitis, but when the tests eventually came through the following week it was clear the original diagnosis of encephalitis had been correct.

The worst of Hilton's health crisis lasted four days. In bed, as he woke one morning over Easter, he could not straighten his legs; his knees appeared to be locked together. The paralysis continued for a couple of days. Then, as quickly as it had come, the 'locked' feeling disappeared. During that time, Joyce was told Hilton might have just forty-eight hours to live. In the waiting room she threw herself at God and prayed. Hilton would come through, she just knew it, as God would be her guide.

'I would call that time traumatic,' says Joyce now. 'I don't think I ever doubted, though. I kept my faith and trust in all that I needed to do. And I was six weeks pregnant as well. While I was sitting outside the ward waiting for the doctor, I found a Gideon's Bible. I read Psalm 41, verses 1–4, and it gave me encouragement. I read: *Blessed is the man who considers the poor . . . he shall live and be blessed upon the land.* I took that to my heart and my own circumstances. I saw it as God's message for me that Hilton would come through. I felt that he would continue to be blessed upon the land, because if ever there was a man that considered the poor and the needs of the people that had nothing, it was Hilton. And those words then were very real to me.' As she always did, Joyce calmed herself, in spite of the fear, the turmoil of her thoughts, the 'what ifs'. Prayer and the words of scripture meant everything to her. They were her rock on which she had leaned and from which she had drawn strength over the years. There was the poetry and wisdom of the words, their meaning and her trust in that, and her belief that God would answer her prayers — somehow.

Hilton had never had a grave illness in his life. Now his congregation was rallying in prayer at a special prayer meeting called together by the Corps bandmaster, John Hutton. They were being asked to 'pray for the Captain'. Generally Hilton admits to having reservations about speaking of 'answered prayer', as many prayers are not answered even though the causes are worthy and the prayers offered no less well intended. But, in his case, such was the sudden change in his physical symptoms that he still believes prayer saved him at that point. The psychological after-effects, though, were something else.

Hilton was in a public hospital and told to stay there. The Easter play had come and gone and Joyce appeared to be holding the fort fairly well on her own. But once the danger period had passed, Hilton began what he now refers to as the 'process' of encephalitis. For him, this long period of enduring the effects of the virus on his emotional and psychological system would be even more traumatic than the physical crisis. And the immediate legacy of Hilton's illness would last at least four years. He'd be left with a body that seemed a curse to live with. The danger of those first days in hospital nearly killed Hilton, but what followed left him at times wishing he *had* died.

Within days of being admitted, Hilton began to register the clamour of the ward. The noise made his head throb all the more, so he was moved to a private room with a notice on the door: 'No Visitors Allowed'. Looking back, as Hilton remembers it, the way he lived over the next four years was as if he had put up a 'No Visitors Allowed' sign across his mind and thoughts, such would be his feelings of separation from the old world he knew. Joyce and a few others got in to see Hilton at the hospital, but he was not an easy patient. This was a workaholic whose motto was 'Never get sick or slacken.' Given doses of pethidine, for a while he floated, later telling friends he could understand from the experience why people get hooked on drugs. He felt hooked after a couple of days. Then the doctor took him off it.

'Hilton had been in hospital for three weeks when he decided he'd had enough,' recalls Joyce. 'He wasn't really well enough to go home but he decided he was going. He spruced himself up and sat on the bed and said, "Well, doc, I'm moving home. I feel great." The doctor should have stopped him but he didn't. That's Hilton, I suppose. He insisted on driving the car, wouldn't let me drive, and he couldn't tell a green light from a red light. I had to keep prompting him. I had to tell him when the lights turned green. He was a very sick man.'

Hilton recollects it all with a touch of self-deprecation. 'I managed to con my way out of hospital in time to assist Joyce with a ladies' morning tea. I can recall that I would set up a table and then go out and vomit in an ice-cream container, then go back and set another table up and so on. In reality I should have been in hospital.'

But four weeks had changed everything. Hilton could try to pretend otherwise for a time, but eventually he had to face it. Irritable and grumpy to live with, he kept up the Corps program, preaching on Sundays as always, but his private world was starting to implode.

'I had only two interests in life — one was my calling as an officer of the Salvation Army and the other was my wife and family. And in one foul sweep they were both, in my mind, gone. Because my self-confidence was nil. I could see my once-beautiful family was being affected by this person — me. A person who was quick-tempered, unkind, impatient and so on. I began to hate myself, because I knew better, but I just couldn't stop myself being such a pig of a man. I preached peace on a Sunday but life was a living hell. I knew the standards of a Christian husband and father and I was filled with guilt.'

Hilton had gone from being a jovial, fun-loving husband and father to someone the family barely recognised. Joyce recalls that before the encephalitis, as a married couple they had barely exchanged a cross word. Now she couldn't be sure at any moment what might set Hilton off in a tirade — a noise, a plan he didn't agree with, someone at the Corps who might unwittingly upset him, or things happening too slowly in a day. And then there were mood swings the other way. Even after he seemed to have made a recovery, years later, Joyce can remember Hilton ringing her at Congress Hall while she was conducting her Home League afternoon and asking her to come home to him because he was in bed, under the covers and unable to get over his appalling feelings of isolation and depression. Joyce excused herself from the meeting, saying she had an emergency to attend to, and took a train home to help Hilton recover. At Congress Hall no one ever realised this had happened. Hilton would get back to normal in a day or so and return to his duties as strong as ever. But in the early months, indeed a year or so after his illness, Hilton was irascible and for a long time not able to properly carry out his duties as Corps officer.

Joyce did not condemn Hilton for the cantankerous displays. She carried a picture of him before his illness in her memory and reassured herself that this new Hilton was not the man she had married. This was instead a very sick man who needed time to convalesce and learn to live with a new personality. She recalls that a verse from Proverbs kept her focused: *A soft answer turns away wrath, but grievous words stir up anger.* Given time, she hoped something of the old Hilton would return. Hilton has always appreciated this quality in his wife, that she could rise over the personal hurt of those early years in the aftermath of his encephalitis. He thanks her still, in small ways and large, for what she did for him as he recovered.

Decades later, friends and colleagues would marvel at how Hilton is so demonstrative about his love for Joyce, giving her flowers on the spur of the moment, driving her to the beautician for her lovely nails to be done, spoiling her with a night in a hotel, writing her special love poems on napkins and giving her a diamond ring upon their retirement. These actions are explained by the aftermath of Hilton's encephalitis.

Hilton's agony and his struggle to overcome his demons were torture for Joyce. This was a family who believed strongly in the Christian message from Jesus that told them to *love one another as I have loved you.* Children were disciplined, but not in anger. Mother and father lived out their love in genuine kindness and cherished one another. They weren't saints and Hilton could be impatient, but they knew when to pull back from moments of ill feeling, to discuss their difficulties and work together to support each other in times of need. For Hilton to suddenly roar at the children, to turn his back on Joyce, to be tetchy, unfeeling about Joyce's burdens and selfish about his own was something completely out of character. Hilton could feel the gulf growing between his family and himself, yet it made no difference. He felt it when he ignored the boys' efforts to get his attention and show him what they had done at school, what they had built in the back yard, to tell him anecdotes about a day with their mates. He felt it when he snapped at Joyce after she mentioned what she was doing at the Corps or if she spoke of something the children might need while his mind was ruminating on his lack of interest in his work. He could barely tolerate the children's antics, the sounds they made, getting under his feet, needing time to play. And somehow it was always Joyce's responsibility to keep them under control. As he often saw it then, Joyce and the kids were the problem, not Hilton. And he would bark at them accordingly. His emotions were often out of control, raging one moment with angry words to Joyce or the boys, cutting them like a whip, and then on other occasions the tears would flow without warning, in the middle of a song or a story — any small thing would set him off.

Hilton was losing the plot as he tried to maintain his life's patterns while carrying the effects of his illness. He was no longer able to sleep for very long. In the daytime the children were noisy; at night insomnia took over and there was not much for him to do. He remembers he would wander down to a café in the main street of Newcastle at three or four in the morning and fill in the hours listening to the jukebox. He would sit with the night's street people — prostitutes, drunks, loners. But he would always sit alone or, as he puts it, 'have a pity party or "poor old me" session'. Joyce, back at the house, would be worried sick wondering what might have happened to him. One morning he came to a café with a sign out for breakfast but was told breakfast would not be served for another hour. He snapped at the owner of the café, giving him what Hilton calls a 'verbal', for having a sign out but not being able to deliver the goods. This was not the old Hilton. At home and beyond, it was as if a grizzly bear had taken over his soul.

'I would never take my own life, but for some years I would kneel beside my bed and ask God to take me to be with Him through the night so that I would not have to face another day. All of the Corps work was being handled by Joyce and I was in bed with the covers over my head.' His emotions were all for himself. Where once he had orbited around the calls for help of others and his family, suddenly he was the centre of his own little universe — and a muddled one it was. His self-absorption and his feelings of uselessness and depression soaked up his days in a mist of misery and self-perpetuating bad humour.

Athol was born in mid-November 1972. It was a difficult birth with complications. Athol was born four weeks premature, with an indefinable cerebral irritation. Tests for meningitis came back negative. The case was puzzling. Eventually, the specialist came to Joyce's bedside, in a ward with eight other mothers, and calmly told her that she could expect her baby to have permanent brain damage. As a mother of three other children, he said, she could observe Athol's behaviour at home for what his weaknesses might be. The abrupt coldness of the advice shocked Joyce. As she left Athol behind at the hospital in a humidicrib, not knowing what his future held, she prayed hard and asked her Heavenly Father to come to her help, the divine being who knew 'the beginning from the end and the end from the beginning'.

Then, in spite of the doctor's prediction, Athol came home after three weeks and slowly began to improve. At six months he was a normal baby. And Joyce, with Hilton still very ill and incapacitated, praised God.

Joyce did her best to protect the children from the reality of their father's illness. The physician had told her what to expect and that it would take a lot of time and perhaps years of medication for Hilton to recover to something of his old self. There would be very little left of his relaxation apparatus. Hilton had always been a mobile, get-things-done-at-once sort of person, but now it would be 'snap to it or be snapped at'. And he would not be able to relax easily, no matter how tired. He would be in a sort of perpetual motion of one kind or another. He would have a low boiling point, said the doctor. That was immediately evident where the children were concerned. And Joyce spent months thinking on her feet when the children needed to be kept out of Hilton's way, even standing between them and him if he was really in a bad mood. 'I knew that often what he said didn't mean what it sounded like, whether at Corps or at home,' says Joyce. 'But I could see that others were not able to understand that. I found activities for the children to keep them out of his way. And I prayed hard that I would keep my cool.'

Neither Peter nor Bruce instinctively recalls the time as troubling in the way their parents can, although Peter acknowledges that they were better off staying out of Dad's way. 'Dad has a natural short fuse but after he got sick the fuse was shorter,' recalls Peter. 'I can remember mustering Bruce and Lyndall into the lounge room to watch television, the black and white TV we rented for the first time in 1970, just to stay away from Dad. And although he had always given us the strap when we deserved it, he smacked us harder after his illness. So I dug a hole in the back yard and Bruce and I buried the strap. He never found it. That was fun.' Their lack of memory of the time suggests that the boys have repressed a lot of the detail that was too hard to take.

Joyce stayed firmly by Hilton's side, as true as ever. She was what Hilton now calls the 'angel in the house', who got them all through it. They were the Corps officers, the ministers of religion for the Army's Newcastle 'parish'. It was a vast area to cover and the activities of any week were an enormous responsibility. While Hilton was convalescing, he carried on the appearance of being at work, but in fact was never able to go the extra mile as his old self had. Joyce carried the bulk of the Corps work, presiding at endless fundraising functions, Home League meetings and Sunday school classes, preaching on Sundays, making school and hospital visits, preparing written reports to Headquarters, balancing the accounts and co-ordinating the many Corps meetings each week, whether for Bible classes, the band or Corps Cadets. And along with this she took care of three children and a sick husband who helped a little as babysitter, and carried another on the way. She made gentle attempts to coax Hilton back to normality. Occasionally, in desperate moments when his temper was beyond reason, she added an extra dose of his medication to a cup of tea or coffee. If she waited, she thought, it would come good. She hoped that time would do the healing. With the busy round of a week's commitments, she got through days and months without breaking. And she prayed as never before, alone and with the children. This was her darkest tunnel experience. Who would blame her for calling out, 'Where are you, God?'

'She never retaliated,' says Hilton. 'And loved me through it all. She was officer, wife, carer for me and mother. How she did it I do not know, except to say that she is one hell of a woman and a saint to put up with what I pushed on her in those days.'

Hilton was close to breakdown. Former Corps bandmaster John Hutton believes the Army should have made it possible for Hilton to convalesce over months with the family at a quiet location. But that wasn't how it went in those days, says Hutton. 'Back then, the Salvation Army expected a pound of flesh plus more from its officers.' Hilton and Joyce had a couple of weeks' break with the children at Nelson Bay and then it was home to the Corps at full throttle.

'You could see it in his eyes,' says John Hutton. 'So tired. By the time they left Newcastle at the end of that year, he was still having bouts of the thing. But he never stopped. He had a hand in anything going. He helped so many, and for years after the Harmers left Newcastle people were still being converted because of the Harmers' work there. I don't know how Joyce kept it all going with Hilton's illness, expecting another child and with three small children.'

But with Athol's birth, the Newcastle Corps would be more than the Harmers could manage. The family needed a posting where both parents could ease up a bit. At this point, Joyce and Hilton were called to the Gold Coast, which in 1973 was yet to take on the urban Californian proportions of three decades later. The warmth, the beachside atmosphere, the slower pace of life might be just what they needed.

chapter 11

WHERE GOD CAN USE ME

As always, Joyce prepared the children for Sunday service on the Gold Coast. Baby Athol in a bassinet, little Lyndall with some toys and a rug on the floor, the two older boys in uniform sitting up straight in the front seats close by. And they did this for five months, despite the fact there was obviously something quite worrying about Hilton, who was having injections daily, given by a nursing sister from the doctor's surgery. Joyce, again, was carrying the posting.

'We did the Sunday services as if nothing was wrong. We'd sing as always. I sing alto and he sings the lead or melody. But often, as we sang a duet, it was nothing for Hilton to stop in the middle of it, unable to go on. He'd get too emotional and just break down. I would go on singing. He would just stand there, hoping to get himself together. He did sometimes; other times he didn't. All of this was to do with the brain and the virus, which had affected Hilton's emotions. After five months, we talked with the Army and said we needed some time out. We arranged to take three months' sick leave.'

In the 1970s, most workers forced to take sick leave would have had a house to live in and, more often than not, been entitled to sick-leave payments to live on. This would certainly have been true for those with tertiary qualifications or a profession, such as Joyce and Hilton. But the Salvation

Army was different. Officers moved from post to post, much like Catholic nuns in religious orders. They were called to move every two years or so, when they packed up everything in a month, and did just that. This was a culture born of the nineteenth century, when the poor in their tens of thousands lacked government services and lived in derelict housing with no sanitation. The call of religious workers like nuns and Salvation Army officers was to give their all in the knowledge that others were so much worse off. Moving on command was part of that complete devotion to service.

For officers of the Salvation Army who had a family, moving on command involved not only the adult officers but children as well. Each move in the Salvation Army is carefully co-ordinated, with one set of officers leaving their quarters for others to move in immediately after they leave. And all with the precision of a regular army. Any slight hitch in the chain can cause real problems. In *If Two Shall Agree*, the biography of US Salvationists General Paul Rader and his wife Commissioner Kay Rader, author Caroll Ferguson Hunt records how a crisis developed when the Raders were given marching orders to a posting in Seoul, Korea. As they made preparations to move from the United States, a call came from Territorial Headquarters asking if they could stay in their quarters for another fortnight, as their quarters in Seoul weren't ready. No, we can't, they replied. Their successor at the posting they were leaving was about to move in — a widow with four children. Suddenly, the Raders and their children had no place to live. The problem was eventually solved when they realised they could stop halfway, en route to Seoul, in Hawaii, where there was a Salvationist family with a porch area that could accommodate them. Problem solved, but precariously.

For the Harmers, with a convalescing Hilton, the problem was not so simple. Accommodation came with a posting, the idea being that the quarters were provided for a working officer. But Hilton needed somewhere to take time out, not to work. A caravan on cheap rental in a country-town caravan park might be possible, but Joyce and Hilton were not prepared to accept that sort of accommodation for their children. The boys were at school and needed more stability. Hilton's physical condition required access to medical supervision. They were not simply going on holiday. Then, after five months on the Gold Coast, Uncle Ted got in touch.

'Uncle Ted's on the phone,' young Peter called from the hallway. Ted and Dawn Harmer were by then Salvation Army officers at Toowoomba, west of Brisbane.

'Hello, Ted,' said Joyce in a bright voice that belied her anxiety about where they were going to live. 'Are you calling from home?'

'Yes, as a matter of fact. Might have something you'll be interested in. Don't imagine HQ have found you somewhere to live by any chance?'

'No,' replied Joyce. 'We've knocked back the caravan idea.'

'How would you like to come up here?'

'What do you mean? You haven't enough room for all of us. There's six of us and it would be out of the question.'

'No, I don't mean to our home, but there's a hostel here that might be just enough to get you over the next few months. Put Hilton on and I'll explain.'

Ted had come up with a flat they could live in, attached to a complex that the Army ran as a men's hostel. Joyce could run the hostel and the family would take the flat as their accommodation in return. It was almost as good as being offered an extended vacation. At 800 metres above sea level, set on the edge of the Great Dividing Range overlooking the Lockyer Valley, the city of Toowoomba is renowned for its parks and gardens and civic hospitality. A provincial centre of schools and churches, it offered Joyce and Hilton ideal surrounds. Telling the children they were to move again after only five months worried Joyce, but there was no alternative. They waited till Sunday in church and, as the little boys sat in the front seats, just before the service began and the announcement that the Harmers were moving was made, Joyce explained that Daddy was not well and that they were going to live nearer to Uncle Ted and Auntie Dawn. There would be a new school to go to, but they would be fine. So the Harmers packed their personal belongings yet again and drove to Toowoomba.

'I remember there was no cot for Athol, who was six months old. So I stacked up a little border with blankets around a single bed so he wouldn't roll out at night. And for the next few months I looked after the hostel, which meant giving the men light refreshments and making sure the linen was washed, beds were made and all that sort of thing. It was a marvellous arrangement. Hilton was on a great deal of medication then and slept a lot. He had lost confidence at most things he did and recovery was long and drawn out.' Not that Joyce wasn't fatigued much of the time with the juggling. On one occasion she reached up to a shelf for a headache pill and mistakenly swallowed one of the tablets prescribed for Hilton. 'It knocked me out. I had to leave the children, everything to him,' says Joyce, 'and go to bed and sleep it off.'

It may have been a sign that he was feeling better, but after three months in Toowoomba with no posting Hilton felt he'd recovered sufficiently for a new appointment. He approached their Army superior and suggested he was well enough to get back to work. The response was a negative. You are not ready for heavy duties yet, came the reply. But a posting with lighter duties on the other side of Toowoomba, in a suburb called Harristown, was available. Hilton and Joyce took it up the following January. 'We had a lovely time at this small church,' says Joyce. 'Hilton still wasn't very well. His sleeping patterns were all over the place. Relaxation was very hard to come by. It wasn't like a rash that just clears up. It took time for him to learn how far he could push himself. He was never the same after his illness. Even now, while he seems never to be tired, in fact he can cover his fatigue very well.'

As Salvation Army officers, Joyce and her female colleagues were an early version of the working professional mother. Family life and ministry life were interwoven. Children grew up on the job, so to speak. Athol Harmer says that as kids they just had to accept that home life and Army life were braided together. He can't separate the Joyce as Mum from the Joyce as Salvation Army officer, even though she was the homemaker who cooked the meals and cleaned the house.

This was a feeling that affected Athol, the Harmers' youngest, most of all their children. He got a glimpse of another sort of family life when he met his future wife. 'Kirsten, my wife, and I have been together for thirteen years now,' said Athol in early 2004. 'When I met her family I was struck by how much her mother makes her family the number one priority. It's just like, get out of my way, my family comes first. It was a wake-up call for me. My parents loved us, I know, but we really had to just ride along on the Army journey. They're professional Salvation Army officers and that seemed to me to be their first calling.'

Athol looks back on the many moves the family made and wonders if it left him not as stable about choices as he might have been. He never got time to put down roots anywhere, although he recognises that the moves developed his people skills. His first days at new schools were dreadful, and his name didn't help. A new kid called Athol! In eight different schools! Handling that forced him to front up to the insecurity of new and strange relationships.

For Joyce and Hilton, that calling they had responded to as young adults was their passion. They were servants of the Lord and their entire perspective on life was centred on that choice. They prayed daily, together and alone, that they would accomplish God's mission in their lives. They prayed with their children, Joyce gathering the older ones before they went off to school each morning for a short prayer to start them on their way.

Since the knocks and bruises of their different postings left small legacies, no command was refused. Whatever the trials of the service they underwent, Joyce never blamed the institution. Many have looked back at the conditions under which religious workers such as missionaries, nuns and parish ministers gave their lives to the church and concluded that the exacting labour and penury were a form of abuse. Joyce has never seen it that way. She believed that her dedication to God and commitment to full-time service meant that she accepted things the way they were.

'I was aware that the Salvation Army was insensitive to the feelings and needs of certain officers, but that was not the Salvation Army as a movement but rather personalities within it that clashed. There were, at times, power struggles between individuals.' What was more, Joyce knew that her older relatives, who had themselves been officers, had faced far more privation and narrowness. Compared with theirs, her life was easy.

Hilton is fond of the line 'Man can never place me where God cannot use me.' They would have found a ministry had they been appointed to a bus stop, he reckons. The idea of sudden career shifts imposed from Headquarters is quite foreign to those who live in times of self-direction and self-empowerment, but the practice was not a negative for those who accepted the challenges as they came. With her maturer years, Joyce was finding herself more and more confident at leading. And the years of Hilton's illness had thrust on her responsibilities she would never have experienced with a healthy husband. She was finding her own voice.

By January 1974 the Harmers were back to a full load, with their next posting as corps officers in Maitland, west of Newcastle. Here, alongside their normal Corps activities, they were responsible for organising the Salvation Army's annual Red Shield Appeal from Nelson Bay through to Singleton and the western fringes of the Hunter Valley. In Maitland, Joyce, with the help of pre-school teacher Joy McLeod, began a Women's Fellowship. Joy was muscial, playing piano and singing, and a ball of energy. She stood out as someone Joyce felt would be ideal for organising the functions. 'Joyce and I have always clicked,' says Joy. 'And she does have a special way of just asking you to do something, and getting people in. She sidled up to me at an open-air meeting one Sunday evening and told me she was going to start a Women's Fellowship group. She asked would I help her as the secretary. It was all of a sudden, but I said yes.' They announced the beginning of the group at the Corps on

Sunday and there was a good response. It hoped to attract younger mothers who needed a bit of time for themselves.

They met once a month in the evenings in an old Australian Army hut shaped like a 'T' which had been assembled on a vacant block that the Salvation Army owned at Rutherford on the outskirts of Maitland. A night out for the girls, they called it. There would be a speaker or some local group to entertain. Often there'd be a cultural theme: one night it was all Scottish — decorations, food, costumes and highland dancers — another night it was Indian, with a talk by the local doctor, who came from India, a performance from a belly dancer and Indian food they managed to cook with a little help from the doctor's wife. And sometimes they had 'dress-up' evenings, although the best dressing up involved Hilton himself; for a prank, he crashed one meeting in a wig and golden slippers, and registered as Mrs Brown. The women who noticed him weren't fooled and some quiet laughter began just as the soloist for the evening was singing the mournful 'Old Man River'. When Joyce realised what was happening, identifying Hilton by his broad heels in the slit backs of the gold slippers as 'Mrs Brown' passed by her seat, she was shocked. If Hilton was in the hall, who was minding one-year-old Athol? A local Rotarian's wife apparently, who'd helped Hilton put on his costume.

The communities the Harmers served responded to their warmth and generosity wherever they went. In Hilton there was always something of the music-hall entertainer, in Joyce a capacity for tenderness that never failed. The Women's Fellowship didn't just bring women together. Over time it reached out to different cultural groups in the locality, as well as offering its pool of talented locals a place to put their skills to good use and be recognised. On special occasions they would have a family evening in the old Citadel in the centre of Maitland. They charged at the door and raised sizable sums for the Corps.

In 1976, the Harmers were appointed to the Army's Divisional Headquarters in Canberra; Hilton as Divisional Youth Secretary and Joyce as the Divisional Guard Organiser. This move gave Joyce a position in her own right for the first time. She was now in charge of the Salvation Army's equivalents of Brownies and Guides, which were known as Sunbeams and Guards.

The Sunbeams and Guards are extensive movements for girls of school age within the Salvation Army. They are very much modelled on Girl Guides and Brownies and seek not only to provide wholesome recreation activities for youth but also to build character and purpose in individuals through meeting each week and in outdoor activities such as camps. A sense of service and commitment to others is also part of the culture the Sunbeams and Guards hope to encourage. Leaders of the movement at the time were meant to be upbeat and knowledgable about the rules and codes the girls would have to learn. As a result, Joyce was required to pass a number of Guard Organiser tests of knowledge. And for Joyce that was more than a challenge; it was almost impossible. In fact, ludicrously, for a time Joyce's future as a Divisional Guard Organiser seemed to rest on whether she could memorise petty codes from a girl's Guard handbook. 'I'll never remember that,' she would say in desperation. Gloria Sanders, her deputy, took to throwing things at her to sharpen her memory of particular rules. Sunbeams' and Guards' rituals were strictly observed. The fastidiousness of it all was very foreign to Joyce, but she finally made it through the tests, although she had to go home for her Guard hat before being enrolled as the Divisional Guard Organiser. Enrolment could only take place when a specific hat was worn.

Once she had made it through the petty tests, Joyce took to the job with enthusiasm. Working with youth came naturally to her. She still remembers the words of the ditty they would sing with the girls: 'Be Cheerful Under All Circumstances', or 'B.C.U.A.C.' The words quaintly instilled the Guards' philosophy: *B.C.U.A.C. What more can we be/When things go all wrong we still have a song/We've promised you know wherever we go/To always B.C.U.A.C.*

Joyce's responsibilities as Divisional Guard Organiser required that she manage the training of Guard leaders as well as administer activities and programs for the Guard and Sunbeam groups scattered from the border of New South Wales and Victoria to areas just south of Sydney, as well as in the Australian Capital Territory. In the west, the Division took in Deniliquin, Wagga Wagga and Griffith. Three times a year she would travel by car alone from one end of the Division to the other, visiting the various troops and brigades. The job was so big that before long Joyce's deputy, Gloria Saunders, took up many of the duties in the Wollongong area. Regular rallies for the Guards and Sunbeams were big affairs, held over some days at centres like Mt Keira near Wollongong, where more than a hundred girls would assemble. At the camps there would be an inspection of the Guards on parade by notable Salvation Army officers, with Joyce accompanying the dignitaries in true military fashion to look over the ranks of young women, who would stand to attention in a huge circle with their leaders. They wore grey dresses with two distinctive emblemed pockets on the bodices, and caps that sat on the front of their heads. On parade, the girls would be presented with their patches or certificates for the tests they had passed. Joyce would prepare all these at home in advance and post them out to the various corps. The camps were highly disciplined occasions and often held in the heat of summer. During one inspection of the Guards and Sunbeams, as Joyce led the dignitaries around the ranks of girls, eight-year-old Lyndall noticed her mother's makeup was wilting in the heat. 'Excuse me, Mummy,' she said as Joyce passed, as if to be helpful, 'but your face cream is melting.'

In Canberra, increasingly Joyce and Hilton moved about the Division separately for their own work. It was a vast area to cover. At one stage, Hilton was away four out of five weekends. In turn, Joyce would have to travel for her own meetings in the Division while Hilton maintained the home base. Often she would be away from the family for three days at a time. Through it all, Joyce was enjoying a new confidence. Reg and Alice came down from Brisbane for a visit, only the third time they had stayed over during the decade and a half since Joyce had left Gympie for college. By contrast, Hilton's parents were frequent visitors. Apart from the visits home to Queensland during annual leave, Joyce had only seen her parents while at their posting in Atherton and while she and Hilton were briefly appointed to the Gold Coast after Hilton's illness. But the years and Joyce's growing mastery of her professional focus meant that much of her childhood pain was no longer so acute. A gulf remained between Joyce and Reg, but Hilton does remember the Canberra visit from the Lipke in-laws as being a warm and relaxed one, in fact the closest they ever got. He can even recall Reg said at some point, as if to mend broken bridges, that he would be happy for Hilton to conduct his funeral service when he died. Hilton, never able to forget past scores entirely, was able to amuse himself with thinking it would be a pleasure to bury Reg, and Reg would have probably laughed at the thought too. Humour had taken the place of bitterness at last.

As Athol started school, his mother's work was taking on new meaning. She was hitting her stride, away from home quite a bit, and being seen as an officer in her own right. This may help to explain why Athol was the one who developed a sense that his mother was absent when he felt he needed her. Mrs Captain Hilton Harmer had come through the worst of Hilton's illness and brought the family through it with her. Hilton was still on his medication and slept only four hours a night, but he was more like his old self than when he had struggled through the immediate aftermath of his illness. And he was never still.

Major Philip Cairns, who worked with the Harmers in the mid-1980s, believes Hilton could have slowed down a little. 'Hilton didn't have any boundaries in himself, and he used to go through stages of working and crashing and becoming unwell, then getting better. But that's just the way he was wired. Joyce was more balanced and always totally supportive of Hilton, but just trying to pull him back a little, to help him with that. It was all out of this intense need and passion to be effective, and to try and do something about the need they saw out there.'

In 2004, the Harmers' son Bruce and his wife Carolyn were in charge of the Army's rehabilitation centre in

Fyshwick, Canberra, and living in the same house Hilton and Joyce had worked from in the late 1980s. Bruce reflected on the boundless energy his father seems to have in his work and wondered if Hilton just can't help being attracted to the nerve-ends of humanity, what he jokingly called an appetite for a 'Harmer drama'.

'I've told Dad he's a trauma junkie. He's a bit of a rescuer. We [he and Carolyn] were once in a situation where we had to move from a difficult appointment out of Rockhampton. Dad and Mum came to help. The removalist truck broke down miles out, where it was pretty remote. I thought we were stranded with no van to collect our belongings, but Dad was on to it straightaway. He rang Thrifty and organised another van and a minibus. We loaded up the van, met the truck after it had been repaired and offloaded our belongings. Then went back for the family. Later we got a note from Dad saying thanks for an exhilarating week. If he'd been sitting around having coffee he'd have hated it. But Mum is different; she doesn't go looking for trouble, just throws her all into helping when someone needs her.'

In the 1980s, the Salvation Army entered a new phase of self-searching, like many of the mainstream Churches. Sydney journalist and author of the Salvationist history *Booth's Drum,* Barbara Bolton, describes it as a new battle — *the battle against being taken for granted*. The Salvation Army had been founded by William Booth as an unorthodox movement of the streets. It was a movement that saw itself as a 'mission', not a Church, and it had grown in strength and numbers till it touched all corners of the world. The mission of its officers was to seek out the destitute, the lonely, the socially afflicted, and bring them to a belief in Christianity by helping them both materially and socially. But as the mission settled into localities and towns, set up its corps buildings and territorial headquarters and mapped out its territory, it was no longer so much an army on the march as an institution like any other, with property to manage and officers to house and congregations that were often far from poor and that collected around their local corps and citadels like any congregation did in the parishes of mainstream Christian Churches — exactly what William Booth had not wanted.

Philip Cairns believes that from the 1950s to the late 1980s the Army lost its distinctiveness and became too much like other Christian Churches. And in his view, that was a mistake. 'We need to target again what William Booth called "the submerged tenth" and give more of our ministry to the disadvantaged in society. That's where we began and we've got to rediscover that. What's happened is that the people who got saved and became involved in the Church tended to lift themselves up, to better themselves and become more interested in life, and before long the Army had become a middle-class organisation. And we have tended, I think, to be very middle class. We've got to rediscover our roots. And this is where Joyce and Hilton have remained with the essence of our ecclesiology, because they had a heart for that submerged tenth.'

Joyce and Hilton have thrived on the Booth ethic of working at the coalface. They have never regarded themselves as natural preachers, and Hilton estimates that it took an hour of preparation for every five minutes either of them spoke in a sermon. Yet with people, and especially those who needed their help, they came into their own. But in an institution that had become mainstream and not very much like the original mission of Booth, the way ahead for capable officers who showed above-average leadership skills was to move up the hierarchy; to move away from the coalface and closer to the higher ranks where the positions of power were determined. And this was something that the Harmers, as they worked in their respective leadership roles at ACT Divisional Headquarters, were not afraid of. Being given responsibilities further up the ladder was a privilege, and they were not without ambition to succeed as well as they might in the Army's ranks.

At the time, however, they could not see that their strongly held feelings for the original Booth ethic, of working for and among the most disadvantaged, could become frustrated by too close an association with position and rank. How would they maintain their closeness to the people they most wanted to help if they became more and more successful as officers and moved further into administration and the halls of the organisation itself? This was a conundrum neither saw coming as they completed their Canberra youth leadership appointments.

Hilton had recovered as far as the outside world saw him. And Joyce was showing notable leadership qualities, with the ability to manage a young and growing family alongside extra responsibilities. They would always go wherever sent, wherever needed for the mission. Headquarters had begun to notice their special qualities. But Joyce was as yet unaware of how big their next move would be.

chapter 12

HIGH ROADS

'Shocked' is how the Harmers remember they felt at the news that they had been appointed as the Corps officers at the Sydney Congress Hall in June 1978. They were told of it while at Bundanoon taking a camp for forty-five children as part of their respective Divisional roles in Canberra. Sydney Congress Hall was a huge assignment for two officers still at the Captain rank. Congress Hall officers before them had held the rank of Major. The decision suggested an enormous confidence in Joyce and Hilton on the part of the Salvation Army. The appointment was made by Colonel Petersen and endorsed by Major Earle Maxwell, later to become Commissioner.

In Canberra, Hilton and Joyce had shown they were natural leaders of the young. Clearly the Salvation Army's territorial command had calculated it needed a new approach at its most prestigious corps. Hilton and Joyce had a young family, and a rounded experience of working with youth and teenagers, and were young parents themselves. It all added up to a good move. What was more, they were pragmatic and adaptable to change, and Congress Hall needed some of that in an era of challenge to traditional ways from so many quarters of society generally. If the 1960s and early 1970s had been revolutionary in Western communities across the globe, the decade that followed was one in which organisations everywhere were forced to implement and absorb what had once seemed radical. This was an era of giving youth a voice, of letting younger members be heard, even of taking their ideas on board. Hilton and Joyce were never intimidated by that. They could feel in charge, their authority by no means questioned, while trying fresh activities.

In 1978, Sydney Congress Hall was considered to be the premier Corps of the Eastern Australian Territory. Congress Hall has a proud tradition of excellence. In the late 1970s some 500 people from sixty-eight different Sydney suburbs regarded Congress Hall as their corps. It was as established a centre as any mainstream Christian Church; in some ways more so. In short, the Sydney Congress Hall was a nicely solidified club of very good and fervent worshippers. Many were well educated, some quite wealthy. Congress Hall also attracted quite a number of business people used to handling large accounts. For Joyce and Hilton, it was a huge step up as Corps officers. No more would they have to rely on jumble sales and country-town community nights for their fundraising. Here, well-off soldiers and adherents gave tithes, a tenth of their earnings, as their regular donation to the running of the Corps. Just occasionally, a top-class band performance would also add to the coffers.

'In our day the Sydney Congress Hall Corps was the focal point for the Salvation Army,' recalls Hilton. 'The kind of corps that belonged to Territorial Headquarters. In fact, it paid rent to Headquarters for the space it occupied in the same building. It set the standard, in a way, for the Territory.' A fundraising scheme for the new officer training college in Sydney was successful only after a trend-setting gift from

Sydney Congress Hall of $50,000. In the 1970s, the Sydney Congress Hall Corps had its own uniform, which clearly identified its members. Soldiers wore their uniforms proudly, immaculately pressed and laundered, and smart to look at. But no uniform at Congress Hall was quite as spectacular as that of the senior players of the Congress Hall bands.

Throughout the history of the Salvation Army, the role of its Army band has been central. Begun as an important feature of street worship, over time the Army Band became almost an institution in its own right. Sydney's Congress Hall was very proud of its bands. In 1978, at a time when the Salvation Army band still marked out a Corps' talent and prestige, Congress Hall had a senior brass band of forty players and a junior band of thirty players. The distinctions 'senior' and 'junior' did not reflect the ages of the players. Adults played in either band. It was more a notion of which band was number one and which the second band, although both were highly talented. Band members wore specially tailored uniforms made by a Brisbane tailor by the name of E. Burrows, who worked up a prosperous business outfitting most of the Eastern Territory's Army officers. Band uniforms developed distinguishing and intricate variations of the navy and maroon to display their corps and band membership. Senior instrumentalists, likewise, could outfit themselves in specially designed uniforms.

After 100 years of taking to the streets every Sunday from its base in Elizabeth Street, a few doors south of Liverpool Street, by 1991 the Sydney Congress Hall Band had achieved recognition as one of the best Salvation Army bands anywhere. That year the band made a tour of England with its bandmaster, Ronald Prussing, who was also principal trombonist in the Sydney Symphony Orchestra. In John Cleary's *Salvo*, Prussing is quoted as saying, '*Music is my pulpit.*' Such musical respectability was a far cry from the days when the Army bands holding street meetings were pelted with refuse.

Regulation governed all aspects of Salvationist life, including its music. From the late nineteenth century, Salvation Army music and its songs were available only to Salvationists. An Army music industry was spawned over almost a century. But ossification set in. By the 1960s, Army music had frozen in time and no longer appealed to the people it was trying to influence. Many felt what was needed was cross-fertilisation with modern forms. This was the case for the Sydney Congress Hall Band. In 1981, as if to try something new, it put on 'Brass Encounters', its first 'modern' performance. It featured music from Henry Mancini and Paul McCartney.

The Harmer children were aged between five and fourteen when their parents moved to the Sydney Congress Hall assignment. ABC Radio's John Cleary, who knew the Harmer boys at Congress Hall, remembers them as 'just typical, energetic adolescent boys who found the strictures of the Salvos pretty tough'. He recalls Bruce, now an Army officer, as being the sort a teacher might despair of, saying, 'What do you do with this kid? If he gets past Year Ten I'll be grateful.' The Harmer boys had a reputation for their lively ways, although Joyce recalls they were often at a disadvantage through being the sons of the Corps officers, and would be ragged or quietly picked on by their peers. On one occasion, a fourteen-year-old Peter Harmer rang a radio talk show while his parents were out. The discussion was about workaholics. Peter gave his name and said his father was a workaholic Salvation Army officer. Someone Hilton knew was listening and told the Harmers. It was a message for Hilton that Peter wasn't happy with the way his father's job took him away from the family so much; his pent-up teenage frustrations had led him to tell thousands of radio listeners instead. The boys often clashed with Hilton and, as Cleary remembers it, 'Joyce always gave me the impression of being the one behind the scenes who was keeping things on the rails.' Cleary regards their chafing-at-the-bit-style energies as related to their 'old aggressive working-class genes', but acknowledges that, like their parents, they've turned out fine, channelling their energy into good.

Joyce was expected to preach most Sundays, as well as lead the Home League each week, and the Women's Fellowship every two weeks. These meetings coincided on the same day each fortnight. 'I would see the children off to school,' says Joyce. 'Then I'd take the train to the city for the Home League meetings at Congress Hall, go back home in time to make dinner for the family and return to the Hall for the evening fellowship. I feel tired just thinking of it now.' Band practice would be on the same night and no bandsman ever missed practice. Hilton would often be expected to put in an appearance there, or he'd have another meeting, so sometimes Joyce was able to drive back with him after dinner.

For Joyce, Sunday started on Saturday night, when she laid out all the clothing for the children and herself to wear during their full day at the Citadel. Uniforms had to be pressed and shirts had to be ironed, then all packed to be changed into once they were at Congress Hall the next morning. She had to prepare food for six people, since they would all leave at 8.30 a.m. on Sunday morning and not return home before 9 to 9.30 p.m. As Lyndall remembers it, Joyce would take a stew or roast in her orange crock pot. It would be plugged in after they arrived at Congress Hall to keep the food warm ready for lunch. As Corps officers, Hilton and Joyce had their own small room, somewhere they could warm food and where the family could eat together in the breaks.

'Better wake the kids,' Hilton would say as he turned off the alarm at 6 a.m. each Sunday. 'Peter, Bruce, wake up, lads.' He'd knock on Lyndall's door as he passed. Athol would be chirping away with Joyce, keen to get up like any other five-year-old. Joyce's Sunday music would waft from the player, setting the atmosphere.

'Have you got your briefcase, love?' Joyce would check as they made for the car. Sermons, along with their meeting plans, would have been prepared and typed up during the week. 'Goodness, look at the time, it's gone 8.15. Peter, grab Athol, will you. Has he got something to play with?'

Leaving home around 8.15 a.m., they would arrive at the Citadel after 9 a.m. There'd be people to acknowledge, so that not a lot of time was left to get ready for the first prayer meeting at 9.30 a.m. Meanwhile, the Harmer children would go off to their Directory Meeting, a kind of catechism class.

The entire Sunday moved with the hands of the clock. Like a parliament in a sitting week, the members of Congress Hall and their leaders attended sub-group meetings and Corps gatherings (services and open-air meetings). 'Meeting' is a word used in the Salvation Army for all manner of gatherings of members of its corps. Some meetings were devotional, with readings of scripture, sermons, and songs or hymns, what in other Christian churches would be called a service. Others were merely managerial, concerning the activities of the Corps, whether in relation to the bands, timbrels, uniforms, fundraising, whatever. Hilton and Joyce took brief meals and conferred with colleagues.

The band would meet at 10.30 a.m. in a special band room and be on the platform by 10.50 a.m. ready for the service at 11 a.m. The senior and junior bands did alternative Sunday services in the morning, but the evening service, or 'Salvation Meeting', at 6 p.m. was exclusively the senior band's affair. By 12.30 p.m., the morning meeting or service would have concluded, so everyone made their way to lunch. Warming ovens, urns and other utensils were available to heat food and make tea or coffee. After lunch came junior band practice, timbrel practice, songster practice and the like.

At 2.30 p.m. there would be a 'pleasant Sunday afternoon' until 3.45 p.m., an entertainment which Joyce and Hilton and others were expected to have arranged as part of the Sunday program. Sometimes it would be a talk, on other occasions a musical performance by a known artist or band. The meeting would open with a prayer and hymn and then people would relax while listening to music or a talk around a spiritual theme, perhaps from a missionary officer returned from an international posting or some other visiting Army or Christian leader. While the performance or talk was on, Joyce would attend a group called the Women's Singers, led by Shirley Staines, which visited nursing homes and similar institutions, doing the rounds of wards and recreation rooms to spread a little musical cheer and the Gospel message. Just after 4 p.m., the senior band would march off and the junior band walk to their respective spots for their open-air meetings

— the senior band to St Andrew's Cathedral in George Street and the junior band to Liverpool Street. Dinner was at 5 p.m. and then came the 6 p.m. meeting (service and final prayers), which ended around 7.30 p.m.

'At the end of the last meeting,' recalls Lyndall, 'after a lot of people had caught Mum and Dad for a chat, it was Dad and Mum's responsibility to lock the whole building, which was enormous. It was the old Congress Hall building, not the modern one there now. Flights and flights of stairs. All sorts of doors, here and there. We kids would sit in the car in the lane next to Congress Hall, waiting for Dad to lock the last door. Some time after 8 p.m. we'd see Dad come out the door and finally we could all crash in the car and drive home.' Hilton was not alone in locking up, though. He was always assisted by Envoy Alan Staines, whose small family also waited quietly in their car for him to leave.

'On Mondays, we recovered from Sunday. But also we prepared for what we might focus on for the next Sunday's theme,' says Joyce. 'We were always trying to be interesting and challenging, but we had the same Book (the Bible) that had been used for more than a century by other Army officers. It isn't easy to have to preach every Sunday and be fresh.' Like ministers of religion generally, they had to bring alive well-worn themes. They used their everyday experiences and stories they had read in magazines and books to broaden their scope. They retold Bible stories with new emphasis and interpretation. The lessons to be learned from the old experience of the prophets and the Biblical teachers were matched by messages from the lives Joyce and Hilton led. The true and simple teachings of time, like Psalm 34:12–14: *Would you like to enjoy life? Do you want long life and happiness? Then hold back from speaking evil and from telling lies. Turn away from evil and do good; strive for peace with all your heart.*

Joyce and Hilton would also try to do Monday visits to some of the congregation who had not been able to get to the Sunday worship for whatever reason, whether they were sick or busy elsewhere. The support staff for the office consisted of Maisie Cannings, a secretary Hilton still regards as the best assistant anyone could have had, and retired officer Jock Geddes, who Hilton says was a giant of a man to know.

John Cleary looks back on the years when Hilton and Joyce ran Congress Hall Sydney and can now see what a powerhouse of young talent it catered for, at a moment in the history of the local Salvation Army when certain forces collided. It was an era when families in Australia were still attending corps in healthy numbers, with youngsters who were benefiting from an expanded educational curriculum elsewhere. While many of the parents had missed out on opportunities, their sons and daughters did not. Their public education system, including the tertiary level, was largely free for as long as one studied, and the wholesome life they knew under the Salvation Army banner meant they were directed and encouraged to develop skills and take up the opportunities their parents had lacked. Says Cleary: 'Congress Hall in those days was a magnet for kids. It was huge. You had boys like the Terracinis and a host of other similar families, youngsters with great potential coming out of ordinary backgrounds and bursting with ability. Take the Terracini family. One's now an opera singer, one's a QC and the other is in Amsterdam as a successful composer. That concentration of talent was exploding everywhere at Congress Hall.'

While Hilton was regarded as the pastor of the congregation in the traditional Christian sense, Joyce was every bit his partner in the administration and leadership of the Corps. There were meetings for every variation of Corps life — Band Executive meetings, uniform meetings, Songsters' Executive meetings and so on. Like all institutions, the Salvation Army operates through networks of individuals with their special designations, large and small, each a splinter of authority. The meeting is the transit lane for communication. Mostly it was Hilton who attended the weekly Central Holiness Meeting on Thursdays, leaving home at 7 a.m. and not getting back before 10 p.m. But there were occasions when Joyce was also required to be there. On Fridays, Joyce would take the car and visit 'shut-in' people who belonged to the Corps. She would drop by, read a little scripture and say a prayer with them.

A pet project developed by Joyce in her time at Congress Hall says much about her spirituality and fervent belief in the power of prayer, and also about her ability to find the vulnerable and give support. There was never any faltering in her confidence that God would answer prayer. As she observed it, the hub of Congress Hall life was the bands, which sucked in talent, polished it and sent out a proud Army message to attract non-believers to the Christian path. But all the while, other needs in the congregation were not being serviced. A book she was reading on 'what happens when women pray' set Joyce thinking. Out of this, she began a women's prayer meeting.

'Our women were encouraged to come together with pen and paper,' Joyce explains. 'I would ask them to jot down lists of requests for help — a sick child, a mother with breast cancer, teenage problems, relationship difficulties and so on. Their requests would be recorded in a book. And these calls for help would then be offered to different members of the group, who would agree to pray each day for everyone in the book. The cases recorded would be followed up, and the outcomes were reported to the prayer group. If the prayers were answered, the date would be recorded. Any success, of course, created a great sense of excitement for the group and enthused them to continue in faith and believing for an answer.'

The idea had much support and continued for some years with much success, although over time it became a monthly meeting rather than a weekly one. Joyce had created a momentary spiritual hub at Congress Hall that gave collective support to those whose lives had hit rock bottom. In an Army citadel that had somewhat secured itself against the street and the perils of the world, Joyce was finding ways to confront human tragedy nonetheless.

'I think in some ways Hilton and Joyce are the clichéd Salvo officers,' says John Cleary. 'Not well educated in a formal sense of university and all that, but naturally bright, that good sort of working-class stock who get an honest chance to do good things and manage to do them.'

The status of being leaders at Congress Hall did not mean the Harmers no longer responded to a call for help from the streets. One standout day remains fixed in Joyce's memory. It was the day she had gone to the Billy Graham Crusade, along with tens of thousands of others. Back at Congress Hall, caught by work that had stopped him from attending the Billy Graham event, Hilton learned help was needed urgently in Kings Cross. A man visiting with his wife from New Zealand had collapsed and died. A day or so before, in a Sydney street, the same husband had said to his wife, 'If anything goes wrong while we are here, we can call the Salvation Army.' With her husband dead in a motel room far from home and family and friends, Mrs Alexander had done just that. Hilton, realising he needed Joyce to help comfort the wife, immediately headed off to the Billy Graham Crusade to find her in the throng. And he did. 'See how God works?' says Joyce. They went to Mrs Alexander, and Joyce stayed while they waited for her son to arrive from New Zealand to accompany his mother and dead father's body home. Connections in New Zealand allowed the Salvation Army to continue ministering to the family and arrange the funeral. The Harmers and Mrs Alexander corresponded for years.

At Congress Hall the Harmers were also grateful for the opportunity to catch up with the legendary Jock Geddes, the man who, for the Harmers, expressed the essence of the Army's mission. Jock would come in to lunch with Hilton. 'Skipper,' he'd say when Hilton flicked the phone off the cradle to allow a sandwich in peace, 'what if there is a drowning soul crying out for help and you have the phone off the hook?' So Hilton would connect the phone again. Hilton was at Jock's bedside the night he died and conducted his funeral service. 'Hardened alcoholic men wept in the street the day he was buried,' says Hilton. 'They had lost a true friend.' Jock embodied the founding spirit of the organisation and he was a significant inspiration for Joyce and Hilton.

Like Jock Geddes, as a couple and individually, Joyce and Hilton believed in the fundamentals of the William Booth mission. Their family background and unworldly grasp of Salvationist principles were their guide. They had embraced the Salvationist Christian ethic at its core and never deviated. But, as the Salvationist mission took on a more respectable character, and as Joyce and Hilton moved closer to hierarchical ranks, it was inevitable that they would challenge a number in their congregation, where the essential business was the worship and formalities of Congress Hall. Discussion and debate were overwhelmingly centred on activities relating to the Corps itself rather than any wider community issues.

Managing the day-by-day affairs of Congress Hall required Hilton to be mindful of the seriousness with which his soldiers and congregation took matters relating to the traditions of the Corps. But while older members might want the strength of tradition preserved, new ideas and the pressure of budding talents were also demanding recognition. For Hilton, on a scale of social importance, the matters that caused most dispute within the ranks at Congress Hall were not of any great magnitude. Compared with the monumental task of helping to combat poverty or find housing for the homeless, in-house disputes over band practice or uniforms appeared fairly petty. But in an institution that has nooks and crannies of power, however insignificant these might seem on the outside, there will be tension over administrative matters when personalities clash. And Hilton was still not one for tolerating the tediousness of bureaucracy, the cunning required at times to sit out a challenge to his authority. He was a personality that got things done, even when others expected compromise. And so, in spite of all their energy and youthful enthusiasm for the William Booth ethic, it wasn't long before Joyce and Hilton were sitting on what John Cleary describes as a small volcano waiting to erupt.

chapter 13

LOW ROADS

Errol Woodbury, retired Salvation Army officer and friend of the Harmers, describes them as 'community oriented', people who have always had a vision about the Army's work in the inner-city environment with its dysfunctional poor. At Congress Hall, Joyce and Hilton wanted to be able to respond to the work of the streets, but some in the Corps were unable to accept the fact they divided their time between social work and Congress Hall itself. For these soldiers, a commanding officer was expected to keep to his routine corps obligations and leave the community work to others. Errol Woodbury believes that often Hilton didn't know where to draw the line between community work and work for the Corps, in an organisation that is fundamentally autocratic.

Max Nixon remembers how Hilton stood out at Congress Hall while its commanding officer. He had transformed the spirit of the Corps, had invigorated its younger members in ways previous Corps officers had not been able to. No doubt the pragmatic freshness of his and Joyce's approach was part of the equation. In the 1970s, John Cleary was part of a Melbourne jazz rock band named Solid Rock, which was breaking every Salvation Army rule in the book. He came to Sydney at Hilton's invitation to perform at

Congress Hall. 'Hilton's always ready to take a risk, and he was genuinely popular with the young people of Congress Hall,' says Cleary.

But this was more than some of the regulars felt comfortable with. Nixon remembers that 'apart from being a lot younger, he was very exact and he would speak exactly what he felt. He didn't mess around; this was what he wanted and this was what he'd say. Other ministers we'd had, more mature perhaps, would keep everybody happy. Then Hilton came along. He had a great passion for young people. And he pushed them, encouraged them, got them involved, and some of the old traditionalists were a bit concerned. He held [the Corps] together in a period of great change everywhere. None of that "thou shalt not" as it had always been. And for that he was able to keep many of the younger ones. After he left, a lot of them just drifted off.'

Hilton and Joyce began breathing new ideas into Congress Hall just as debate across all Christian Churches was unfolding. Traditionalists were growing alarmed at an overturning of what they saw as the bricks and mortar of Church existence and authority. For Catholics it had been Vatican II and a break away from the Church of Latin and nuns in medieval dress. A debate had then raged for two decades around contraception and individual conscience in the Catholic Church — a Church of top-down authority from the word of the Pope. For Salvationists, progress was more gradual, with the changing social mores of modern society dragging them along. Writing for *Rally* magazine in 1970, a young John Cleary had queried: *Is the Salvation Army beginning to see its citadels as fortresses of defence rather than bases of attack? Does our emphasis on military paraphernalia, uniforms and*

brass bands conceal a reluctance to realistically face our spiritual needs
and those of our community?

Mainstream Christianity had grown tired and unappealing
in its traditional repetitions. And while some, like Madge
Bevan, also writing for the Salvation Army's *Rally*, saw *a*
marching Army of enthusiastic, sincere, Salvationist young people
flocking to the house of God on Sunday, others thought the
Army had slipped into the same comfort zone as other
Christian denominations, and that this brought no attraction
for would-be adherents and soldiers, potential converts, the
new blood joining up to follow the teachings of the faithful.
Where was the challenge of William Booth's mission to seek
out the forgotten, the wayward, the needy? Where was the
fighting spirit that energised and gathered in new
congregations? At Congress Hall, spirits like Hilton and Joyce
were exactly what a comfort-zone church needed to shake
itself out of its complacency. Alas, as with all ideas ahead of
their time, there would inevitably be friction, but always over
some in-house approach to a matter of Corps life, the
'paraphernalia' John Cleary was referring to.

'The congregation soldiers at Congress Hall were beautiful
people, middle to upper class, with a smattering of battlers,'
says Hilton on reflection. 'The appointment was, without
doubt, the highlight of our forty-two years as officers, from a
church leadership point of view. But we were square pegs in a
round hole, because there is nothing sophisticated about my
Joyce and me. We were from Queensland and not highly
educated, but we had a burning passion for the lost and
hurting of society. There were many conflicts while we were
at Congress Hall that were a result of a difference of emphasis
between us — the commanding officers — and the members

of the Corps. Mostly from me, but impacting on Joyce. I could name them — "the Commonwealth Games saga", "the junior uniform saga", "the cathedral saga". They were endless. The founder of the Salvation Army said, "Go for souls; go for the worst." But to us, Congress Hall was a giant spiritual club, while Joyce and I wanted to be in line with the Army's original mission of working with those who were dispossessed and on the fringes of society.'

Even at Congress Hall, Hilton was one to turn up at the bedside of a person about to undergo surgery at 5.30 a.m. in a suburb an hour's drive from his home, ready to read a few lines of scripture and be a tower of strength. And this took him away from his Corps duties at central office. Meanwhile, Joyce would be getting their children ready for school before going into the city for her day at the Hall. According to Colleen Mahaffe, wife of a Corps Sergeant Major and Sydney Congress Hall soldier, Joyce was the reason why Hilton could be the all-embracing social worker he was at the time. 'She was a very dedicated mother,' says Mahaffe, 'as well as fulfilling her role as Corps officer's wife, a big role within a city corps. Joyce was a lady of dignity and graciousness, with a wonderful heart.'

The social work that Joyce and Hilton refused to give up annoyed quite a few of the movers and shakers at Congress Hall. To these people, this was not part of the role of their officers. Some of those who had become gentrified by their Congress Hall membership (as part of the top Corps, this was how a few felt) might have reflected that mixing work among the downtrodden with Congress Hall activities somewhat lowered the tone around their Corps officer. Pedants, or those who live by the black letter of the rule, flourished in this organisation, which lived by the rules of a military culture. The rules were their comfort, their guide. In their view, those who did not fit within the status quo were to be brought to account.

The saga that would set Joyce and Hilton on a serious confrontational path with that Congress Hall mentality was 'the Band saga'. To an outsider, what happened said a lot about how narrow and inward-looking the Citadel of Congress Hall had become. From the perspective of a quarter of a century later, the matter seems to have consisted of a lot of flak over some very minor matters. But all revolutionary outbreaks, to some extent, flare over relatively minor matters, events that are merely the obvious tips of far bigger icebergs, be it the price of tea in Boston Harbor or the cost of a mining licence on the Ballarat goldfields.

The first big confrontation with church Elders came with a change in status of the women and girls' Timbrel Brigade. Brass bands in the Army were, and to a large extent remain, a male-only phenomenon. Congress Hall's senior band still marched out every Sunday for its rallies, as it had done for nearly a century. All men and all brass. Women could only contribute to the musical performance by playing the timbrels (tambourines) and were never part of the street ministry of the bands. A young woman leader from Congress Hall went to Hilton as the commanding officer and put it to him that the women did a lot of practice, just as the bands did, and performed at concerts, but they were never able to join in the street ministry. Moreover, the bandsmen opposed the women's presence alongside the bands vigorously. But this woman wanted the Timbrel Brigade to be given a place in the Sundays on the street; the timbrels should be allowed to march with the bands. And Hilton agreed. 'From now on,' he said to her, 'you can.'

Band Sergeant Ian Martin recalls how that single decision started a quiet rumbling that quickly became a storm. 'Some of the men from the band went to the Salvation Army hierarchy and complained. The band was a sacred cow. You couldn't touch it. But Hilton simply said he was the commanding officer and that the women would join the band on Sundays. I remember Joyce and Hilton at my home at the time, when we were having a Bible study evening. A Territorial Headquarters officer rang Hilton about the affair, saying the Harmers would be "moved on" and that was an order. But Hilton just said that he wouldn't be threatened and that if they were moved on, they would go willingly wherever, even to the smallest corps in the Territory, and make it the best corps in the world. And he meant it.'

Hilton and the timbrels won the day, and the timbrels still go out with the bands each Sunday. And ever since a visiting Melbourne Timbrel Brigade was given permission to march in front of the band, rather than behind, this is exactly where the Congress Hall ladies have been each Sunday, heading their male colleagues and their brass instruments.

Then came the issue of the Queensland tour for the junior band. In the 1970s, the rivalry between the junior and senior bands was noticeable. The junior band at the time was as highly regarded as the senior band. 'We'd make fun of them and they'd make fun of us,' says Peter Harmer, who played in the junior (or number two) band. 'It was very competitive, and sometimes individuals wouldn't progress to the number one band because the band leader would want to keep them in his band.' The bandmaster of the junior band,

Vita Terracini, has strong views about Salvationist traditions in music and the organisation itself. Asked about changing the Army band's style to a more modern collection of music, Vita will reply, 'That's utter stupidity', and go on to opine that the current decline in corps membership is precisely because of that sort of thinking.

Music was to a large extent the Sallies' theological form. Other Christian Churches had complex theologies of belief and also the sacramental tradition. For the Salvation Army, such intricacies of belief had become distractions from the main point of Christianity — salvation and a life with Christ the Saviour. There was little literature to support the Christian belief structures of the Salvation Army. Its music, the Bible, its meetings, its people, its dedication to Sunday worship and its social work among the disadvantaged had taken William Booth's mission to international significance. Without the theological and ecclesiastical depths of other Christian Churches, the practices of the Salvation Army became its theological form.

John Cleary sees what was happening, and what still is to some extent, as the problem of the Salvation Army's wearing its theology lightly. 'Through all the theological vicissitudes that split Protestantism in the early part of the twentieth century and caused the modernist debate in the Catholic Church, the Salvation Army just went on about its business. The Sallies don't get involved in theological disputation, they're about being Christ in the world. About action and evangelising, not theological argument or philosophy. But once that culture of evangelising starts to break down, as it did in the 1960s, the 1970s and so on, you lose your theology, or for the Sallies their theological form. There's not much left. And yet, at the same time, unless you modify your form, it won't appeal. Now, Hilton and Joyce were never trapped by that.'

With a division of views on such matters, Hilton, as commanding officer, landed himself in the middle of the tug of war. By the end of the tussle, Joyce and Hilton would find themselves removed to Parramatta, although former junior bandmaster Vita Terracini believes the band saga was only a small contributor to the overall tension between Hilton and various Congress Hall members. In his view the Harmers just didn't fit the culture of Congress Hall. They were pragmatic and open to new ideas. They weren't fixed on the inward nature of Congress Hall and its club-like atmosphere. Vita's son Winston Terracini maintains it was said quite widely that Joyce and Hilton had not suited Congress Hall because they 'were more interested in helping people than crawling to bureaucrats and politicians'. And Hilton had shown he was not averse to bucking the authority of his Divisional Commander if he chose. However, it would be the Divisional Commander who authorised the Harmers' sudden move to Parramatta when the band saga was over — a saga that began with a reasonable proposal.

In 1980, Vita Terracini was keen to show off his troupe in the junior band. What about getting some funds together? he suggested. It could be done. His guys were every bit as good as the senior band. Why not try a tour of Queensland for the September holidays the following year? They'd be a hit and it would be great for the band. 'Good idea,' said Hilton. 'Shouldn't be hard to get the funds together. Terrific idea for a holiday excursion for the younger players, and it would be a chance to show what we can do.'

The fundraising began, something Hilton was good at. However, members of the senior band raised objections. Some had what Hilton now calls 'an axe to grind' with the junior band's bandmaster. The junior band's success may also have been part of the problem. Despite this, by April 1981 there was money in the bank for the fares to take the junior band on their proposed tour of Queensland. Then, without warning, Hilton was visited by an officer from Divisional Headquarters to do an audit of the books.

'Unannounced audits were never heard of,' says Hilton. Something was going on. What was the interest at Headquarters in the Congress Hall books? The audit was done. Joyce listened to what was happening with a growing sense of foreboding. Hilton had a right to be annoyed, of course, as he knew the audit was unconventional and probably a tactic to pressure him. But Joyce also knew Hilton's capacity to take on a fight, to get people's backs up by his snappy responses and his impatience with the curly ways of bureaucracy.

'I was summoned to the office of the Divisional Commander,' recalls Hilton. 'He told me that after an investigation of the books, it seemed there was an amount of money collected for the bands that was not being held in the senior band's bank account. It was the money we had raised for the junior band's proposed tour of Queensland. I was instructed to transfer the money to the senior band's account. I responded by reminding him that as the officer in charge of both bands, I would decide what account the money should be in.'

Hilton wasn't in the mood for negotiations. No matter. It was obviously not the answer that had been expected. Hilton had pulled rank with the wrong commander. Within two weeks of refusing to transfer the money to the senior band's account, Hilton and Joyce were given their marching orders to the Parramatta Corps. They were instructed to be there by June 1981.

'The junior band tour was scheduled for September 1981,' recalls Hilton. 'The fund of money raised for the tour's air fares and expenses had reached $10,000. I immediately called the junior bandmaster and arranged for the money to go into a new account, which we opened.' Only the junior bandmaster, the junior band treasurer and Hilton knew where the money was.

Joyce herself was not interested in a tactical win. Her personality is more measured. For all that, she and Hilton were a team and she was with him in his indignation at the rough handling of the junior band. Once again they were on their way, but this time the move felt like a backward one. This was not like the convalescent years when Hilton needed to take some time out; this time they had a sense that they were being cut down to size.

To some extent, Joyce was the collateral damage in a war of wills. 'We moved out of Congress Hall. Joyce had to do her "farewell briefs" at the Corps, take the children out of their schools, pack up the house ready for removal and continue to run the Congress Hall program,' says Hilton, with a touch of the guilts but no regret.

So they moved to Parramatta, after which another audit was done and the money raised for the junior band tour of Queensland was found to be missing. Hilton then received a letter from the Chief Executive Officer of the Territory saying he should reveal what had happened to the money. If he didn't, Hilton would have to accept the consequences. It was a threat Hilton ignored.

'Well, he didn't know me,' says Hilton. 'I didn't care what might happen to me. I called the junior bandmaster. We met in the city, withdrew the money, closed the account and paid the $10,000 to Ansett Airlines for the fares of the band members. I sent a letter to the Territory's CEO explaining what we had done and the junior band's tour went ahead in September as planned.'

Three of the Harmer children went on the band's tour. But their dad, who had raised the money for the tour, wasn't with them. Peter Harmer was most affected, as he knew why Hilton wasn't there. It was a tough initiation into small-world politics for a boy of sixteen. From Townsville, Vita wrote to Joyce and Hilton: *We have arrived all happy and safely!! Thanks to you . . . it is a great disappointment we are not together on this tour.*

Hurt and a bit bewildered, Joyce and Hilton moved on as commanded, believing in the final analysis that Hilton had acted correctly. Then, like some sort of consolation prize, a few months after starting at Parramatta, Hilton was offered the chaplaincy on a *Fairstar* cruise. Off they went together, for a timely escape from Territorial church politics. On their return journey to Sydney they visited North Queensland, where they managed to catch up with Jimmy and Joyce Blooranta, the couple who had been their first new soldiers in Atherton and who remained true friends.

'Joyce and Hilton never got caught up in the trappings of church,' says their former colleague Philip Cairns, evaluating how the Harmers have got by and worked together. 'Hilton can be a good scrounger and make things appear, like raising something from nothing. They certainly get good works started. I would describe them as catalytic people. When you run church growth movements we talk about three sorts of leadership. If you want to get something started you put a catalytic person in the job. William and Catherine Booth were those sorts of people. They can be chaotic but they get something happening. They often make opponents, and might not be popular. Hilton is that sort of person. Joyce is more the oil on the water.'

Joyce and Hilton spent only eighteen months as commanding officers at Parramatta Corps, where they were promoted to the rank of Major. It was the largest corps in the Territory but considered less prestigious than Congress Hall because of its suburban location. For all that, Hilton and Joyce felt closer to the Parramatta soldiers, who were more involved in work with people outside their own corps. In 1982, for instance, Corps soldier Paul Lucas organised Parramatta Corps' second working bee to Indonesia. Paul and Val Lucas had spent holidays in Bali and had befriended some of the Indonesian women from the Salvation Army who worked with the Army's Bali Children's Home. These women had later visited Sydney, staying with Paul and Val, and had addressed the Parramatta Corps about their work. Interest in doing something for the Indonesian mission developed from that. Their first working bee had been in support of the Salvation Army's Bandung Children's Home, with a member of the Corps travelling to Bandung to help do repairs and other work around the Home. In the second working bee, some twenty members of the Corps, including Joyce, took off for Jakarta to help rebuild the Salvation Army's training school building. The men, under Fred Robertson, fixed up the tumbledown building while the women made curtains, pillowslips and other items needed at the school. In spite of being very sick with a gastric attack which slimmed her quickly, Joyce spent the two weeks in Jakarta behind a sewing machine. The Indonesian elections, with their street demonstrations and turmoil, were happening around the group as they sewed and hammered. 'Sometimes we sheltered at the back of the building, it was so dangerous on the street,' says Joyce.

But the Harmers' removal from Congress Hall had left a scar. Congress Hall was celebrating its centenary in 1982 and Hilton and Joyce, as the commanding officers, had been involved in much of the preparation for the celebrations. Now they were gone and their removal, as Hilton sees it, left him with a lot of emotional 'baggage'. He would ruminate on his unfair treatment and the heavy-handed way he had been outmanoeuvred. Joyce was more inclined to let the past go, and to quickly establish new interests and focus in a different posting. Her concern for her children, the need to see them settled into new schools and attend to their everyday needs, also gave her no time for wallowing in what might have been. And she was not that sort of person anyway. Never had been. She was always inclined to count her blessings, just as she had done after Hilton survived encephalitis, when she would say, 'But he's alive, not dead', and grind on with the job of managing life with a sick husband. Joyce didn't have the personality for territorial conquests. She was more inclined to swallow her pride and try to make the best of the relocation.

Hilton, though, continued to smoulder inwardly and view their new posting as the start of a spiral downwards in the ranks. If this was a contradiction in his philosophy about wanting first and foremost to serve the most needy, he couldn't see it. To support his view then, he can still point to the rise of many who had been one-time commanding officers at Congress Hall to prestigious positions in the Salvation Army, and compares that with the way he and Joyce went no further up the ranks. To Hilton, his involvement in 'the band saga' 'sealed my fate for future leadership opportunities within the Salvation Army'.

As if to confirm their being out of favour with Headquarters, the Parramatta appointment was very temporary. After eighteen months, Joyce and Hilton found themselves further reduced in rank when their next farewell orders came through. In January 1983, just as the nation was preparing to face the election campaign that would make Labor's Bob Hawke Prime Minister, they were appointed to Wollongong. But not as commanding officers. Their mission was to start a Wollongong social welfare unit from scratch. 'As I described it to the Commissioner,' says the ever-feisty Hilton, who admits to having an unfortunate way of expressing a truth, 'it was the greatest put-down in the history of the Territory.' They had gone from the glittering prize of being Corps officers at Congress Hall to a post with nothing in place and much less recognition in the organisation, in less than two years.

They would be there for another four. They had quarters to live in but no office set up, no secretary, no vehicle whatsoever, no helpers. And they were expected to pioneer a social-work mission in a large industrial town, with deep pockets of neglected people whom the government had forgotten. How would they distribute goods or organise collections, in spite of a double garage full of second-hand furniture, if they had no vehicle to get around in, no office to co-ordinate the work from? 'We would have died on the vine but for the commanding officer there — Errol Woodbury,' says Joyce. 'We had no bank account and no post office box. Peter and Bruce moved out because we were no longer in Sydney. They were working by then. And Lyndall returned to work in Sydney fairly soon after we moved.' The Harmers' close family life was suddenly gone. Within a few months, their youngest child, Athol, was alone without his siblings. Joyce missed her older children. And before long they were worried about Athol at his new school. He was not settling in and they felt guilty about the nights away from home as they tried to pull together the new project with so little support from Headquarters.

Errol and Dot Woodbury, commanding officers at the Wollongong Corps, were very glad to have the Harmers begin a social-work mission, as the Corps was flat out administering to growing needs in the area. But Errol admits that the welfare unit began with very few resources. 'Wollongong was getting bigger and bigger. We were after volunteers and training people and I was trying to familiarise myself with the whole south. But there was nothing when Joyce and Hilton started.'

Hilton may have believed they were moving to a post with fewer responsibilities, but in fact the scope of their work was immense. With their appetite for a challenge, they began to set up a very effective program, and not only for welfare. They also established refuges and opportunity shops.

Ted Harmer, with a wry smile, will say that his brother shouldn't complain about how his career with the Army has worked out. 'I think it troubles him a little, but he can't altogether blame the organisation. He just hasn't toed the line. If you don't think like others and don't do what the organisation would like you to do then it creates problems. But in their work Hilton and Joyce sustain the good reputation of the Army. They've got great hearts, Hilton and Joyce.'

Joyce looks back on the sudden shift to Wollongong in a more accepting mood. She recalls the acute needs in the community there and how much they could give. 'There was no Salvation Army welfare unit in Wollongong when we arrived — just corps for the faithful. We were to be the Army's inaugural Social Development Officers, based at Auburn Street. In time, we built up an office, a family store of second-hand goods and a refuge for deserted wives and children with a house parent, as well as a youth refuge with house parents by the sea and a welfare centre.'

Joyce was back to what she did best: caring for the most desperate in society. She would think nothing of taking in babies for the weekend to give mothers a break. Looking through her large collection of photos of places where she and Hilton have served, Joyce will come upon one of the children or mothers she has helped. 'Here's another one of those beautiful babies that I minded in Wollongong,' she'll say. 'I just couldn't help it if they were in need and a cute baby was going to suffer or its mother couldn't cope. They'd bring them to the welfare centre. I wouldn't tell them where I lived. We'd just take them home, if they wanted us to, for a few days. One time we minded twin boys and another little one for a night. Athol was the only one of our children still living with us. So I had a baby, Hilton had a baby and Athol had a baby. We'd call out if any one of us had trouble during the night with the baby we were looking after. We certainly enjoyed the opportunity.' On other occasions over the years, they would have to leave their own children sleeping to go out to a call for help. Joyce can remember they left a little lamp on in case one of the children woke up and found them gone. They would know the lamp meant Mum and Dad would be home soon.

One young single mother stands out in Joyce's memory. Tied down, frustrated, with no money, a messy house and a screaming baby. 'All Sue wanted was time out, and I said, "Let me have your baby for the weekend and that will give you a chance to go out for the night. Don't do anything stupid, just go out and have a break." I told her I'd ring her late to check she was okay and to let her know the baby was fine.' The young woman rang late to check on her baby — she was at a disco and having a great time. When Joyce took the baby back to its mother on the Sunday night, the woman had a spotless house she had cleaned that day and was full of thanks to Joyce for giving her time to get her life back to some normality. In a small way, Joyce might well have prevented a tragedy.

They were not all hard times. People came from nowhere to rally behind and support the Harmers in their work, even one man who operated a pleasure flight business. He would take the children Joyce and Hilton knew, who were very underprivileged kids, and give them a treat ride in his aeroplane on a prearranged Sunday. 'We would picnic below and hand out refreshments while the children, two or three at a time, would go up into the sky, kids who had never been in a plane before. They just loved it. And their delighted parents watched their children having pleasures they could not afford,' says Joyce.

When they left Wollongong, driving up the highway towards the escarpment lookout that hangs over the Bulli Pass, Joyce and Hilton could measure their success in terms of tangible gains in a project that had begun at rock bottom. In just four years they had created an oasis for poor people in Wollongong. Hilton recalls that they pulled the car over after they had driven away and leaned on the vehicle, hugging each other and crying at what they had achieved. Looking down on an industrial centre in the midst of the spectacular scenery of the New South Wales south coast, they could say that in just four years, through their faith in Jesus Christ and the strength given them by the Holy Spirit, they had fully established the mission they were sent to. And, despite having been so upset with the post in the first place, even Hilton could say they had had a wonderful time there.

'It is one of the regrets of my life that I did not handle that set of circumstances well,' Hilton says, reflecting on the feelings he had about being sent to Wollongong. 'I should have trusted my Lord more. With our time at Wollongong, we had grown apart from the "Appointments Board" and its private and collective agendas. And it was in Wollongong that I first observed Joyce begin to be an independent individual, with her own specific job. I saw her come into her own there as the person who supervised the welfare clients. She oversaw their visits to counsellors and gave them the money and goods as needed. Although she still feels bad that she had to leave Athol so much at the time because of her work.'

Yes, Joyce was emerging and finding her own voice. Her children were nearly all grown and independent. Athol was making his way through high school, and while he was still having trouble with the constant shifts in home, in Wollongong he had benefited from a change of school, from Fig Tree High to Edmund Rice College. The head of Edmund Rice knew the Harmers and had told them to forget the fees. Hilton had been forced to make another trip to hospital, this time to have a kidney removed, but the effects of his old illness were more under control. Joyce had also coped with the sadness that surrounded her youngest brother's death, at just thirty-four, lost due to a cancer that had spread after he'd found a malignant melanoma on his head.

Balancing her troubles and those of others, Joyce was growing in wisdom and had a capacity for endurance helped by her constant faith in God. Hilton's view is that church work for the Army leaves the officer wife in the shadow of her husband and that only in the wider field could Joyce blossom. But her years of corps work had also helped Joyce refine her people instincts. This wasn't a Joyce who would have refused to open a door to a drunk looking for shelter because she was alone. She was learning to fathom people not from what you asked them, but from how they responded as you said hello. You didn't always need to know the specifics to realise there was something wrong. She was becoming adept at reading the signs of distress in people — young mothers, the addicted, the lonely. And she knew, with more confidence, when to take control and when to step back. She stepped back when a psychiatric patient with an obsession about the Harmers came knocking on the screen door — firmly telling the man to go back to his car and then calling Hilton, who got the man back to hospital. But she could also act on instinct when a depressed young mother came to her, offering to take the woman's baby for a night or two to give her a break. On other occasions, she quickly sensed when parents wanted support but not by leaving children with her. 'I guess for a long time I had felt reliant on other people's opinion, confirming that what I was saying was okay,' says Joyce of her gradual confidence in her own judgment.

In the Harmers' next appointment, which was to Canberra and the Salvation Army's Mancare rehabilitation centre at Fyshwick, Joyce was involved in the Alcoholics Anonymous program that their clients went to as part of their Army program. For a time the centre catered for both males and females, until Joyce found the required policing of contact between male and female clients not worth the time and energy, so the program was reduced to males only. 'Where there is male and female, there is attraction,' says a very practical Joyce. 'And where there is attraction, no one wants to think about a program to get off drugs. They would take off together and do the drugs off the site, with the result that we would have to clean up the mess later.' She and Hilton decided instead to relocate the women to the William Booth clinic in Sydney.

Part of the program required Joyce to attend therapy classes with the rehab clients. As she sat in on these classes, Joyce listened to clinical explanations for various types of behaviour. It was the first time she had heard analysis of this kind. Her college training had been spiritually and socially oriented, her nursing heavily practical. Now suddenly she was taking in psychological explanations for human behaviour she was familiar with, felt herself and saw every day. She was starting to see herself as if looking on from the outside.

'I discovered there were a lot of parallels in the program with my life and how I felt. How insecure I was. How rock-bottom my self-esteem. What was happening to these clients was so similar to me. There was no addiction in my life, but I had similarities to how they felt. They handled their insecurity by drinking and taking drugs; I had handled mine by leaving home early. I related to them very well. And I just loved them so much because they taught me without them even knowing it.'

The clients at the Mancare program would come to Joyce for guidance. She was an authority figure and happily took up the role of adviser. Joyce became aware of the legacy of her own family life in Gympie, of being stood over and made to feel that the only way to survive was to be seen and not heard. She became aware of how that had left her lacking in confidence in her own views. 'I think drug and alcohol rehabilitation management helped me to speak out, to make a decision, and know that it was worth something, that it was okay for me to think like that.'

In 1987, shortly after taking on the Canberra Mancare program, Hilton was offered a place in an eight-week course at the Army's International College for Officers in London. Joyce heard the news and jumped at the chance for both of them. It was a great opportunity to get away on a once-in-a-lifetime and much-needed holiday. Hilton's fare to London would be covered by the Army and the Harmers could put the other on the credit card and pay it off later.

They set off well ahead of Hilton's course for a tour of their own. 'We had the time of our lives,' says Joyce. 'A six-week tour by coach of England, Scotland and Wales.' It was a holiday they had never believed might happen, but one they deserved and an experience these two small-scale adventurers were ready to soak up. Then came sad news. While they were in Scotland, Hilton heard that his mother Connie had died. Half a world away, he could only mourn her passing and regret that he could not be at her funeral.

At the end of the six weeks, Joyce flew out of London for home, stopping off to spend some time with Earle and Wilma Maxwell in the Philippines. She returned to Canberra to manage Mancare alone — Hilton was away for another seven weeks at the International College. Typical of Joyce's evolving capacity for responsibility, the situation just happened and she was forced to step up to the challenge. For Joyce, her time in rehab work was a huge challenge. But it suited her and allowed her to express her talents and make an impact on lives rescued from the streets. Hilton continued to excel in rehab work, although he had a capacity for emotional giving that sometimes exceeded his physical capacities — something for which Joyce and Hilton would pay dearly during their time in Canberra.

chapter 14

TOUGH LOVE

The dog running for the tennis ball had no time to notice the swarthy and unkempt figure of a man, clearly heavy with too much drink, standing half-stoned and contemplating the cold surface of Lake Burley Griffin. He had a length of rope over a shoulder and one pocket in his coat bulged as if containing a bottle.

'Is something wrong? Do you want to talk?' A lady, waiting for the dog, had caught sight of the dishevelled figure and begun to walk towards him, while the dog bounded up, ready for another throw of the ball. Perhaps he's lost something in the lake, she thought.

'Just leave me alone,' snarled the man.

The woman picked up the ball and threw it in the opposite direction, walking with an increasing pace, following the loping dog. She looked back at the man a couple of times but he hadn't moved.

Paul Tank was readying himself for suicide. He was set on it, carrying in his pocket a bottle of weed-killer which he planned to drink and a length of rope to help him jump from a spot where it was deep. He was drunk, but clear-headed enough to know what he was doing. He'd been in and out of the Salvation Army rehab centre in Fyshwick on many occasions. He gave up each time. Tank was a builder by trade, a self-made chap who, as a young man, had migrated from Germany with his wife. A life long in the past now, his business folded and his wife and sons gone, the cars repossessed and the house he'd built for them given over to his ex-wife, complete with mortgage.

The woman with the dog had spoiled his chances. Back at the Ainslie Village, a shelter for homeless people, he hadn't paid his rent. His things had been locked inside his room. He'd borrowed some money to get back in, but as he took stock of what he owned — the grog and the dope — and wondered how he would ever find his next week's rent, he began to cry. He grabbed his shoes and a parka and started to walk to Fyshwick, nine kilometres away. He would go back to rehab.

Paul eventually finished the program and now works for the Salvation Army. There would be two more attempts at rehab for Paul before he finally found himself on a bus to Sydney and the program that would get him off the grog forever. More than a decade later, he looks back on his long journey out of addiction and acknowledges Joyce and Hilton Harmer as the couple who gave him the will to eventually kick the habit. He can still recall a prayer meeting in 1987 in the Mancare chapel in Canberra with Joyce and Hilton. They stood in a circle in the darkened room, each holding a lighted candle. He recalls Hilton's words 'Because He lives, I can face tomorrow.'

Tank had been referred to the Canberra Mancare program by a Salvation Army soldier. He'd tried Alcoholics Anonymous and got nowhere, so he took up the suggestion and introduced himself to Hilton. He was told there was chapel on that night at the centre and he was welcome to join in, so he did. There he met Joyce, and it was that meeting that confirmed Tank's decision to give it a go. 'Mrs Major Harmer was like a mother to the whole centre. They all called her Mother. She was mother to a hundred. She would walk through the workshop and she didn't miss a trick. She made sure everything was nice and clean, but she was very strict. We prayed before we ate and she made sure there were no cigarettes on the table, that we didn't drink out of a can but got a cup or a glass, and we had to take off our caps at the table. It was all part of the discipline of the program, making us care about those details.'

Hilton was famous for his eye for correction. If there was any slippage in the workshop, or goods that walked with a worker, he'd be after them as quick as a shot. But the Harmers had a reputation for being fair. They set the rules and saw they were obeyed. When fights broke out, they took stock before delivering punishment. 'Listen, mate,' Hilton would say after a scrap, 'don't bother about the other guy. I could discharge you for this.' Mostly he would send them back to work. Joyce, likewise, could be indulgent as well as a stickler for the rules. She would let the men buy a few of the second-hand clothes at bargain prices when they fancied something. And if someone came in with nothing, she would take them over to the store and deck them out in new things.

Joyce and Hilton left the Canberra rehabilitation centre a better place than they found it. They worked closely with program director Pat Gates, who had come through the rehab program himself in 1976. Together they pulled the complex into a smoothly run operation over three years. The centre was in two sections — the rehab units and clients with the rehab program, and the family second-hand goods store.

There were practices to improve in the store. It needed a fresh look and better book-keeping to ensure the profits were maximised for the good of the centre. The Harmers turned the business around, sacking some staff and better organising others and opening more stores at Tuggeranong and Kambah.

With her nursing background, Joyce was on call for rehab clients in the detox ward. She also did inspections of the rooms. There'd be reports from a client here or there that other clients were storing banned items and she would move in. It was off to the manager's office, where a decision would be made about whether they could stay or needed to be discharged. Stealing from the Family Store happened from time to time. One chap had a fixation on Buddha statues. An inspection of his room unearthed a horde of Buddhas pinched from the store, along with other goods like cameras.

'Hilton took them all to his office and lined them up on the floor,' recalls Joyce. 'When the chap came home there was a note on his pillow from me: *Please come to the office, you are needed*. He had seen his empty wardrobe and knew he was sprung. At the office, Hilton had no option but to discharge him. But I understand that he went on to turn his life around and is now managing a drug and rehabilitation centre. I thank God he came to his senses. You lose track of so many. But they often go on to other programs that suit them and that's okay. We just want them to get better.'

The men in rehab at the Fyshwick centre were occupied in jobs around the store as part of their rehabilitation and were paid a small wage for the work. Paul Tank had walked into Mancare as the boss of a small business, but going into rehab means beginning again, at the bottom of the social pile. It means entering an institution, surrendering to its routines and strictures, and doing what you are told. For Paul Tank this meant being given the demeaning task of tagging second-hand goods, and he was insulted.

'We had a bed, a cupboard and a curtain to separate us from the others. Many of those there were off the road and glad to have a bed, a small allowance and some food. But I was a builder and had worked for myself. And there I was tagging second-hand clothes and working in the garden. I said to myself, "This is nothing for Paul Tank." After eleven days I thought I was cured. I rang up my wife and she picked me up. But I started drinking again and that's when Major Harmer wrote to me and I went back for a second time.

'We were like a never-ending story,' Paul continues. 'You met them all in rehab. Some of them would disappear and then once in a while come back with long hair and a beard, coming and going. As they left the rehab they'd all say, "Hasta la vista, baby" or "We're black, we'll be back". You hurt yourself when you become dependent on the drugs or the drink. You drink or take more, you can't go to work, you lose your job, you lose your house or flat or wherever you live, you have no money, you end up at Foster House or Edward Eagar Lodge. I did it all. I once stole my son's birthday money sent from his grandmother in Germany just to buy a drink. I abused my body for thirty years. I slept in parks, I was hospitalised, I was clinically dead, I was on a life-support machine, I went into the detox rooms in a wheelchair. And after it all I went back to the drink.'

There are fourteen Bridge Program centres across the Army's Eastern Territory, all in constant demand. Staying the course is not easy. Those infringing the rules are expected to leave. Hilton and Joyce were required to discharge any who couldn't live out the rules, as this could mean a weakening of the program for others. Pat Gates had done the program aged forty-nine. He knew what it took and how hard it could be.

'Hilton used to say to me, "I've just spoken to that fellow there and spent an hour with him. And he's going to stay." The next thing I'd see the bloke going past with his bag. I'd say to Hilton, "If the bloke wants to leave, you can't lock him in. It's better to let him go, and if he can't make it outside, wait till he comes back and we'll see what we can do." But Hilton hated losing any cases. In Pat's view, Hilton needed to harden to the inevitable, but he found it very difficult. Joyce, Pat found, was more practical and accepted their limitations as counsellors.

The program at Mancare was unrelenting, a ten-month, live-in course, with therapy classes at Fyshwick and Alcoholics Anonymous meetings outside. They would be bused to the AA meetings at the Canberra Hospital, where they met others who shared their problems and made them feel less alone. Like the Bridge Program of the Salvation Army, the AA Program is a 'say no' to drugs course and can only be undertaken with complete abstinence. Its Twelve Steps are reviewed daily over the lifetime of any reformed alcoholic in the AA group. The steps are:

1. We admitted we were powerless over alcohol — that our lives had become unmanageable.
2. Came to believe that a Power greater than ourselves could restore us to sanity.
3. Made a decision to turn our will and our lives over to the care of God as we understood Him.
4. Made a searching and fearless moral inventory of ourselves.

5. Admitted to God, to ourselves and to another human being the exact nature of our wrongs.
6. Were entirely ready to have God remove all these defects of character.
7. Humbly asked Him to remove our shortcomings.
8. Made a list of all persons we had harmed, and became willing to make amends to them all.
9. Made direct amends to such people wherever possible, except when to do so would injure them or others.
10. Continued to take personal inventory and when we were wrong promptly admitted it.
11. Sought through prayer and meditation to improve our conscious contact with God as we understood Him, praying only for knowledge of His will for us and the power to carry that out.
12. Having had a spiritual awakening as the result of these steps, we tried to carry this message to alcoholics and to practise these principles in all our affairs.

Joyce recalls that for many the steps were gruelling, but they were the only way to really kick the habit. When the agonising process of searching and recognition was completed, Joyce would take an old tin drum around to the far side of the Mancare buildings. Here she would encourage them to tear up their written recollections of their old selves, throw these in the bin and set them on fire. If they wanted to pray, she would stay with them to ask God to burn out of their minds forever the ugly things they had confessed to Him, just as the paper was burning in the tin. Joyce would offer the men the words 'I pray that it might be burned out of my consciousness, my subconscious, my mind, so that it will never bring me down again because I believe You've forgiven me. I want to burn it out of my mind, never to return again. I want a healthy life, and I want to live for You, and I want to live for other people.' It was a very moving moment and they never forgot it.

'Once they've been through a program,' says Joyce, 'they really can't drink and drug happily again.' That's why, for Joyce and others like her, the AA program accompanied by the Mancare-style live-in program followed by a lifetime of abstinence is the only way. Alcoholics are never really cured of their craving; they just have to replace one craving with a more important one by a daily commitment to a life choice of abstinence.

Joyce Harmer believes she found her strengths during their work at the Mancare program in Canberra. 'The people we cared for came from all over the place, all over the country. When people are addicted they travel, trying to escape or just find a place. They would hear of the Salvation Army rehab centre and come to see if they fitted in because they were sick and tired of doing the same old thing year in, year out. They were tired of affecting so many people's lives and their own; they had nothing to live for; often they had thought of suicide; they would have hurt mother, father, sister, brother, wife, children, whoever came in their way. They were all ages — older men, men past retirement, young people.'

On one occasion a businessman from one of the more fashionable suburbs of Canberra rang and said he needed to do rehabilitation. But he didn't know how to get to the centre from where he lived. 'But I'm over here,' he said, as if he couldn't drive across Canberra for himself.

'Yes. So?' replied Hilton.

'Well, aren't you going to come over and pick me up?' the man asked.

'No, I'm not.'

'Why not?'

'Well, if you are motivated enough to do a program,' replied Hilton, 'you will crawl on your hands and knees if it's necessary to get here. You'd crawl on your hands and knees to get a drink if you had to.'

'Typically, addicted people depend on other people to do everything for them, and that's how we'd find them,' says Joyce. 'That businessman had a young family who were obviously being affected by his drinking. He came to us and did the program. He walked in late at night when we normally don't take people in. He made the grade and became the manager of one of our stores.'

But they did go out and pick up broken-down cases from time to time, says former colleague Pat Gates. 'It was nothing for Hilton Harmer to jump in the car and drive to Sydney to collect someone who had no money to get to Canberra and who wanted to join the program. He'd take people back to the centre after paying their bail. And sometimes Joyce would say to me, "Come on, Pat. We're going for a drive to pick up some donations."'

On other occasions, Hilton and Pat Gates would visit prisoners on remand in Canberra, where there was no jail. Sometimes they went to Goulburn, to the jail itself. They'd conduct interviews. If they found someone who might have a chance with the rehab program, they would apply to the magistrate for permission to take him to the centre on bail, the arrangement being that if it didn't work out the man would be sent back. 'We'd go to the magistrate and there would be terms of the bail laid down,' says Pat Gates. 'If the person left, we'd notify the police immediately and they would be picked up and taken back to jail. We lost a few, but not what you'd call a great many. People knew where their bread was buttered.'

Donny Hilder was one of the cases Hilton drove some distance to help, out to Cootamundra in southwest New South Wales. 'I was lying in gutters,' says Donny with a wistful smile, stirring up fond memories of the Major who saved him from destruction. 'He came to Harden, heard the word and said, "I've got to help this young man".'

'Don,' Hilton had said, 'I am going to help you, but you'll have to help me, know what I mean? I can't help you without your assistance too.'

Donny had been given a week by the police to get himself sorted out.

'You've only got twenty-four hours left,' said Hilton.

'I'll get by,' was Donny's reply.

'Hardly, in your condition, Don. You'll get accommodation with the police, and probably for twelve months. But that's not freedom.'

'How will tomorrow do, to come with you?'

'Tomorrow's no good, Don. You'll be worse by then. You're coming now.'

Twenty years later, Donny is adamant that but for Hilton's taking him to Canberra's Mancare when he did, he'd be 'six foot under now'.

It was Joyce's task to help mentor the men at Mancare as they completed the steps of their rehab program. In the Mancare program, Step Four was the hard one. Each man doing the program would be required to write down his true recollections of himself. Pages of it. 'We lived in with the guys,' says Joyce. 'We would encourage them to go back as far as they could as they wrote their Step Four. The good, the bad; about when they were aged four, aged ten. And then Step Five is to share that with a person they had confidence in. They would choose. It was between them, that person chosen and God. I would be with those who chose me and some would say, "I'm feeling down today. I feel like ripping all of my Step Four up." I would talk to them in a motherly way and say something like, "Well, would you like to wrap your Step Four and put it in an envelope and let me take it upstairs to keep in a cupboard? And if at any time you want to get your Step Four back to tear up I'll give it back to you. It will save you the temptation that it's just sitting there in your cupboard." And afterwards, many guys were so grateful that they had not ripped up their Step Four. When the time came for it all to be put together, I'd go through it with them and they would just read.'

It's something akin to 'tough love', the idea being to kick the habit with will, discipline and support. As such, it is the complete opposite of the injecting-room philosophy or drugs in moderation. With this program there's just black and white: give up completely, forever, or nothing. In Salvation Army centres, the tough-love approach is overseen by officers like the Harmers, and feelings run hot about whether the all-or-nothing approach is best. To Bruce Harmer, managing the Fyshwick centre in 2004, complete abstinence is the only way. 'A lot of other rehab agencies think the Salvation Army is like a modern form of an Amish community, so out-of-date and moralistic. That's just not true. People we have worked with have tried moderation, they've tried a balanced use of drugs and alcohol and they can't do it. An addict is an addictive personality and that doesn't change. They've got to completely stop, not because we think it's bad for you but because we know you, the addict, can't handle drugs.'

Joyce watched the hurt as the rehabs folded back the years of their addiction to their innocent earlier selves. 'It used to bring a lot of pain because, as you can imagine, if they've ill-treated their wife, their children, their mother or father, they're devastated to confront that. I remember one young man who took a long time to do his Step Four. And I went through it with him in his Step Five and as he was reading what he had written it just broke his heart. But that was all therapeutic. That was all good for him. And we made notes and isolated the patterns and we talked about it all.' And afterwards Joyce would pray with the people she sat with. 'I would encourage them, if they could and wanted forgiveness from God as they understood God to be, to pray and ask for God's forgiveness and to ask for the strength to continue to be a drug-free or an alcohol-free person, to allow them to have a decent life and to make amends to those they had hurt.'

In 1998, Australia ranked nineteenth out of fifty countries worldwide for its per capita consumption of alcohol. The same year, 3271 deaths were caused by the consumption of alcohol Australia-wide, while the number of hospital episodes attributable to alcohol consumption was 43,032. Meanwhile, figures on the use of illicit drugs show an increase in the scale of harm, especially among the young. In 1998, just over 1000 deaths occurred as a result of illicit drug use, of which most were young people aged between fifteen and thirty-four. At the same time, almost one in five Australians over fourteen had used marijuana in the previous twelve months.

'There was a difference, in my experience,' says Joyce, 'between the alcoholics and the dependent drug users. The drug users could be more devious and less trustworthy because of their addictions. That didn't apply to everyone, but it was, as I saw it, generally so. But I loved them all, they're God's people. They all have a mother, or had a mother. And they had all destroyed their lives and the families they had come from. AA gives them a hope. And ours is a spiritual program as well. Ours are three steps: I can't, God can, let Him. Those who win out over their affliction hand over their will to God as they come to understand Him.'

Joyce was the one who rang mothers, sometimes getting a short or abrupt response from a mother who thought Joyce was siding with her drug-user son. She would then have to talk her way through, to break down a parent's weariness at the whole drug culture that had enveloped their family's lives through an addicted child or sibling. 'Honey,' Joyce would tell the mother, 'I just want to share your pain. I just want to tell you he's here and getting treatment. I know what's gone before. I feel for you and what you've gone through. I want you to know that I care. I can't do anything for you where you are but I am with your son here and we'll stand by him on the program.'

A man in rehab had to be told one night that his father was dying in a local hospital and that he might like to go and see him. 'I had to do that very sensitively,' says Joyce. 'It was a situation that might be enough to tip an alcoholic or drug user over the edge. Hilton's role was often to be the tough one and mine to be more gentle. So I went to the man's room and talked to him about it. I asked him if he would like to go to the hospital.'

Joyce accompanied him and they drove in the centre's bus to the hospital, Joyce going ahead to speak to the father about who was coming to see him. 'I had to ask him if he would see his son. He just nodded his head. And I remember writing on a little piece of paper as the son approached the room, *If you feel so, tell him you love him*, because it might have been his last opportunity. I just reached over and put that on the other side of the bed for him and then walked outside to allow him to do that.' The man was crying, Joyce remembers, as he came out of his father's room. Then they went back in together and Joyce said a little prayer as they all held hands across the bed.

Joyce and Hilton spent the best part of five years in rehab work. Joyce would get phone calls very late at night from clients who had just been released. 'Generally, an hour or so after they've gone they know they've done the wrong thing. I've sat up in bed after seeing them off with their belongings, checking they had benefits and a bit of money, and I'd be talking to them on the phone.'

'I know you were right,' a chap would be saying. 'I know I should have taken your advice but I don't know where to sleep.'

And then Joyce would tell him where to go for a night's accommodation at the Salvation Army's homeless men's quarters. After putting the phone down, she would ring the quarters and beg them to find a bed.

Not all their troubled charges, by any means, recovered. Of those who couldn't say no, there were many Joyce and Hilton kept in touch with. Like Andy, who remains in Joyce's memory like an epitaph to the whole of her rehab experience. Andy became a Salvationist but, as Joyce recalls, 'lapsed every now and then'. Years after they knew him in rehab, Joyce and Hilton employed Andy in the Mt Druitt Red Shield Industries. But he would miss work for days at a time and Joyce would go round to his unit to check up on him, to see that he hadn't fallen. He didn't always answer the door and on one occasion admitted to having been on the bottle again. 'I was so ashamed,' he told Joyce.

'He was a Scotsman, a lovely guy,' says Joyce. 'I once had to take him to the doctor. "Andy," I told him, "don't do this to me. I'm going to find you dead one day." I had a wheelchair to take him to the car and a man to help me. I put him to bed, got some biscuits and milk, because milk lines the stomach, and I got him his prescriptions. I went back to him that night and he said he would be okay. He had all his medication and was very grateful. I made him give me the key to his unit by saying if he didn't I wouldn't be able to help him any more. I would leave the door a little ajar and knock, saying, "Andy, it's Joyce here" in case he needed to get himself together before I went in.

'The day after I had tucked him into bed, I went back to see how he was. He didn't respond when I knocked. I found him in the lounge and he had slipped down in the lounge chair. His head had slumped forward, cutting off his breathing. I think he was just very drunk and had slipped down. I had found him dead, as I had always feared.'

chapter 15

LIVING WITH RECOVERY

Helping others come to terms with their personalities, Joyce took stock, unwittingly, of her own. 'The guys in rehab and I used to have a lot of fun. They'd say to me, "Oh, if we got you sloshed at a party, you'd be fun." And it was fun that they could say that. No offence was taken. I'd say, "And I'm sure I would be too, but you'll never have the privilege, sorry, mate." Joyce recalled that her mother's brother Stan had been an alcoholic and her own brother Cecil as well. For Joyce, the personality is in the genes. It's how we use it and what we do with it that matters. One way is to destruction, another to a life of energising hard work.

It was Pat Gates who gave Joyce the clue to healing the old sores from her childhood, and brought her to forgiving her father. Reg had died in 1978, just months after visiting Joyce and Hilton in Canberra. During the visit, Joyce never confronted past differences with her father and they managed to have a pleasant time. Pat Gates had worked with Joyce as the program director at Canberra Mancare. There were no secrets. Joyce credits Pat with teaching her a great deal, both in rehab work and life generally.

'One day, he asked me if I had forgiven my father. I was taken by surprise. I realised I hadn't done that. My father had died and I hadn't said I forgave him. We had enjoyed my parents' visit to us in Canberra, but I still couldn't look at Dad without those old feelings about his anger being revived. Even though we were older and the past was gone, I'd never said I had forgiven him. Then Dad died, and only long after did I realise there were experiences in his life that I hadn't understood as a child. Maybe I would have behaved differently if I had known all that.'

Hilton, Joyce and Pat Gates were in the chapel discussing a service they had just finished. It had been a lovely service and the AA Step for the week was 'making amends'. It was then that Pat Gates asked Joyce about forgiving her father. Forgiving him for the anger, the beltings, the mood swings, and his inability to ever talk to her as a fully grown adult. Especially after she had achieved so much herself as a successful Salvation Army officer who supported other adults through their own healing journeys. Joyce can remember the moment as clearly as yesterday. The rehab men had left, the chapel service was over. They were about to follow everyone to the dining room. But instead, they just stood there. Joyce was saying, 'Pat, now I come to think of it, I don't think I ever did forgive my father.' The realisation pulled her up. She waited behind after Pat and Hilton had gone, to pray and meditate, asking God to forgive her for not forgiving her father. In her own life, despite the many difficult episodes, she had emerged strong and assured of her commitments in ways Reg would never know. His burdens had crippled him, as a father and husband. Hers, on the other hand, had not held her back. Because of her ability to withstand the harshness of downswings in her circumstances, she had mastered endeavours beyond her childhood imaginings. And she had her strengths, her love for Hilton, her belief and trust in God and her prayers.

When Joyce and Hilton began their years of rehabilitation work in Canberra, Athol Harmer was fifteen. He would spend his late teens housed in Salvation Army quarters at the rehab centre in Canberra. As officers, Joyce and Hilton believed they should never isolate themselves from the rehab guys or give the impression they were keepers. 'We felt we had to be all or nothing,' says Joyce. 'We had to be a person who loved them and who not only said they loved them but showed they loved them. We felt it was wrong, as in one appointment we had heard of, that the managers ate in the boardroom with someone to serve them. That, to us, was wrong. We would go and sit at the tables with the guys. Hilton would be at one table, me at another. We also had a senior citizens' complex and they joined us for meals as well. The rehabs would wait on the tables and the old folk loved it.'

Looking back, Athol Harmer wonders if the life he led at Mancare affected him as a teenager. His older brother Bruce and wife Carolyn, as managers of Canberra Mancare a decade or more later, never let their four sons go anywhere near the clients. Athol, on the other hand, often spent time chatting with the rehab guys.

'My fascination for the guitar came from the people I was hanging around with at the time,' says Athol. 'People that were teaching me how to roll cigarettes, all struggling with pretty serious addictions, some ex-crims. In some ways, the brothers and sister I didn't have at home I found in the guys on the program. That's why I still have a strong connection with people I meet who have had dependency problems. Many of them would be dead now from their habit.'

Everyone at the centre knew Athol for his guitar playing. Donny Hilder and Sid Oldfield remember Athol well and talk of him affectionately like a member of their family. At a loose end after a day at school, Athol began to spend more and more of his time with various clients, all of whom had stories to fascinate a fifteen-year-old, stories from the road or time in custody. Athol only had to cross the lawn and he was privy to the colourful pasts and rough humour of guys from the 'real' world. He'd go over at meal-times and play cards, bonding with many of them.

'Mum and Dad, at the time, had no idea what I was doing. I can't remember a meal just with them at that appointment; I ate at a table with the guys. I used to come home and play pool with them and just hang out with them. At Wollongong, Mum suffered the most grief about me because I would come home from school and there'd be no one at home. But at Fyshwick I had the rehab guys. They were my role models.'

It was not easy to know what was best for Athol. He was happier at Canberra Mancare than in Wollongong, and Joyce and Hilton didn't want to be overprotective and smother their son as he approached his late teens. Joyce can recall their going on a chance trip to Perth, leaving Athol at home, at his request, to manage on his own. Then the phone call came. 'Over the phone we were told that a former rehab guy had been found wandering around the complex in Canberra with a gun. He had been dismissed or something and held a grudge. And Athol was staying in our house next door. We had to quickly arrange for Athol to move out to another

Salvation Army officer's house till we came home. The guy with the gun was probably under the influence and was threatening all sorts of things.'

With their all-inclusive attitudes and trust in the tough discipline that governed at Mancare, Hilton and Joyce didn't see anything wrong with Athol's mixing with the clients. To them, the rules were being kept, and what harm could come of being friendly? But when Athol later took to smoking pot himself and became addicted, he often wondered if his ease with addicts as a fifteen- and sixteen-year-old had influenced this. 'It may have had something to do with my own addiction later, and the battle myself to give up cannabis. But even now, if I go to church and have the option of sitting with ordinary well-off people or rehabilitees that are struggling, I choose to sit with the rehabilitees every time.'

Athol's years of addiction would be a great anxiety for Joyce and Hilton, their own baby caught by the affliction they'd spent so many years helping others to get over, a lot of times without success. But, twenty years later, Athol is over it and able to reflect on the learning experience that came with his cure from addiction. He notes the recognisable instincts he has for the sort of people he ate with and spent time with at Canberra Mancare. His familiarity with such people, both from his days as a youngster living at Mancare and from what he learned as an addict himself, become his asset. In 2004 he was appointed as the Team Leader of Hillsong Church's Teen Challenge Rehabilitation Centre in Sydney.

At Canberra Mancare, Joyce and Hilton's work schedule was as crowded as ever, all the more so for Joyce, as she no longer had small children to care for at home. They were running rehab programs as well as a growing network of second-hand goods shops. Hilton was manager of the Mancare Rehabilitation Program, with Joyce as 'matron', and between them they had responsibility for a senior citizens' program and the Red Shield Industries network of Family Stores in the ACT. Later, the Salvation Army would divide the load so that the Mancare officers no longer had responsibility for the Family Stores as well. But, after Wollongong, Joyce continued to feel the load was manageable. And her mastery of the rehab program as a director and mentor gave her a stimulus that distracted her from noticing how many hours they were devoting to work. It also often helped Joyce to go with the flow of life's tragedies within her own family. At only thirty-four years of age, her youngest brother Clifford, whom she had helped her mother to care for as a baby, died of cancer in Brisbane around this time, after an illness lasting just a year.

In 1988, as the Harmers' second year at Canberra Mancare started, it wasn't immediately obvious to Joyce that Hilton was suffering, and under some strain. But after a while the physical drain on Hilton, who was once again driving long distances collecting goods or men in need of help at Mancare, began to show. Small signs began returning and Joyce realised that Hilton was working himself to breaking point all over again. He was tearful at times, and at some moments would cry uncontrollably and say he wanted to die. Bruce visited briefly and helped Joyce get through some of the stress. But for the most part, Joyce was left to her nerves of steel and prayers while she waited and hoped it would pass.

'Once again, I had put the bar up too high for myself,' reflects Hilton. 'I couldn't jump it and then would feel defeated. The old fight-or-flight theory came into play. The problem was that it would break my heart when a client would decide to leave the program and go back to alcohol, drugs or gambling. At the same time, I had two trucks that went out each day for the Industries and brought in six tonnes of donated goods. That was thirty tonnes a week. All of that had to be collected, unloaded, categorised, cleaned, priced and placed in the store. And I wanted my Industry to look neat and tidy at all times.'

It couldn't last. Bruce remembers he came home from work one day and his mother told him his father had gone. Joyce says they had disagreed over something very minor. Hilton recollects it was this conversation that tipped him over the edge, though he has no memory of what they were speaking about. They were both working sixteen-hour days.

'I recall Mum just said, "Dad's gone" as I came in the door,' Bruce says. 'I said, "Where?" And then Mum had a cry and I had a cry and we prayed together.' They had no idea where Hilton might have been. What his state of mind might be. What he might be contemplating. Bruce was confident that there had been no heated argument between Joyce and Hilton, as his mother was never that sort of person. 'After Dad's sickness, Mum learned very quickly not to confront Dad at all. And at home, as a young person, she had not had a say. She carried all that baggage around from her father. But she's different now. She can have her say now when she wants to.'

'I put some things into the car and took off,' says Hilton of the time. 'I was going to drive to Sydney and put the car on a train for Queensland. In the end I drove to Temora and then West Wyalong. I was feeling a dreadful failure. I was sick of being a liability on the people I should have been supporting.'

At home, Joyce prayed and kept on with the daily program, once again, as in Newcastle, taking it all on her own shoulders.

In many ways, however, the days of Hilton's disappearance from Mancare were much worse. She had to go on as if nothing were wrong, making out as if Hilton had just gone somewhere on business and would be back in a few days. But her face told anyone who knew her that she felt like death itself. During the day, Bruce would ring and there would be no news.

After two days, the phone rang one evening and it was Hilton. 'Hilton here,' he said down the line as if he were calling from an ordinary trip interstate.

'Love, where are you? We're all worried sick.'

'I'm okay. Don't worry about me. Is everything okay?'

'Love, come home. We'll look after you. You're not well. The boys are worried about you. *I'm* worried about you.'

'I can't. I'm a liability. You're all better off without me.' And he rang off. He had checked into a hostel for men, feeling that was all he was worth. He was no better off than those he hoped to help. Who was he to try and save them? But after four days, he called Joyce again and this time took up her offer and came home. Unshaven, demoralised, unkempt, Hilton arrived home like a derelict at the gate wanting a room and a place in the program.

'I remember Hilton having a difficult time at one stage,' recalls Pat Gates. 'He was always so dapper, but on this occasion he was unshaven, with about three days' growth. I told him he had to do something about himself. Had to pull himself together.' Pat remembers he suggested Hilton take Joyce and get away to a place at Thredbo in the Snowy Mountains, which they did from time to time after that.

The disappearance made Joyce aware that Hilton needed much more than a rest. It was a familiar pattern: Hilton overdoing it and collapsing as a result. But the going away and leaving them to think the worst was quite out of character for Hilton. This time, Hilton needed more than medication. With the assistance of all she was learning from her work in rehab helping broken souls and minds to heal, Joyce was sure it was time Hilton sought proper psychological counselling. He needed to take stock, and to recognise problems in his personality that were fixable. Joyce had faced her own demons — of being too complacent, of nervousness about her own judgment — and gradually recognised her need to take the initiative at crucial moments in the partnership. She had also carefully worked out how to manage her own development around a sick husband and a mother's commitment to four children. She had learned the hard way how to love a husband who was no longer the man she had married. She had practised biting her lip and waiting for calm, appearing to be the follower but so often gently coaxing him to a more sensible option that was not impulsive. Now it was time for Hilton to learn about the psychological extent of his problems — his feeling that he must always respond to requests for help, and his tendency to take too much responsibility for what happened.

Hilton began a course with a psychologist, who started by asking him to tell her honestly: what was the natural thing for an addicted person in a rehabilitation centre to do? The answer was, leave. And what would be the normal condition of an industry receiving thirty tonnes of goods each week? The answer: untidy. From there, the psychologist tried to work into Hilton's consciousness what 'normal' meant.

'She liberated me from the bondage of my two problems, took the weight of my expectations from my shoulders. But I still had emotional difficulties. Then Joyce and I took time out at Thredbo, at a cottage lent by longtime friend and benefactor

David Robertson, who's always been there for us. I relaxed and tried to get in touch with feelings for things beyond work. But I must have seemed suicidal at times.' Joyce knew Hilton was showing those old signs of wanting to end it all, of giving up on the burden he perceived as life. But she also trusted that he would never actually try to kill himself in spite of being very emotional. She was taking no chances, all the same. Years later she confided to Hilton that she had hidden all the knives in case he thought of self-harm. And she also put the keys to the centre's vehicle down her bra, because when he'd returned from his days away, Hilton had told her that on the way back he had been 'tempted' to drive in front of a truck or over a cliff.

As Hilton came through the next few months, some days were hellish. Joyce admits to once again slipping a little extra of Hilton's prescribed medicine into his cup of tea on such days. Then, for two weeks, Hilton went off to Queensland to stay with his brother Ted. A book he read there, sitting in Brisbane's botanical gardens, was a great help; it was called *Healing Without Drugs*. He started to learn to read the signs of his ongoing depression. And Joyce hung in with him, and told him years later that she was able to do that only because she knew him before his encephalitis. That made Hilton worth it.

The year 1989 had not been an easy one. Joyce's mother's death had come suddenly that year. Alice had been quite well in the decade since Reg's death. She had continued living at the family home in Redcliffe, north of Brisbane, until it was too much for her to manage. Then she had moved to Nambour to live with Keith and his wife Doreen. But in the winter of 1989, Alice had been taken ill and was admitted to the Nambour Hospital. Complications from the flu arose and she did not recover. She died on 20 July and was buried at

Redcliffe. Hilton conducted the funeral, which brought the Lipkes together to mourn a devoted mother. 'My mother was a great cook,' reflected Joyce much later. 'Well-organised with her plans for daily meals, long before refrigerators and electric stoves. She was a meticulous housekeeper, and with seven children to cater for and a sick husband, she did a fabulous job. Retrospectively, I understood how much I owed to her fine example.'

In Canberra, Hilton's recovery was precarious. Prior to Christmas 1989 a letter had arrived with a cheque enclosed from the Colonel in charge of the Social Ministries of New South Wales and Queensland. The cheque was for $300 and the letter said that the money was a *goodwill gesture* from Territorial Headquarters for the purpose of giving the men at Mancare ACT a *good Christmas*. Hilton reacted with fury. The money worked out at $7.70 per man. The words with the cheque were unfortunate, but no doubt well meant. If they were clumsy and capable of misinterpretation, this probably said more about Headquarters' remoteness from the coalface than its lack of generosity. Joyce would have reacted by writing her thanks and immediately converting the cheque into a Christmas lunch to remember. Something, in Joyce's eyes, was always better than nothing. She would always try to put things into perspective. There were, for example, Christmases when they had no cheque. But Hilton was not one to let a superior get away with ignorance, and his nerves were obviously far from healed.

'I saw it as the crumbs off the rich man's table,' says Hilton. 'An insult. In a most ungracious letter, I wrote back telling the Colonel that even if I spent five dollars on each man for a gift, that would leave just $2.70 each for Christmas dinner. And that if they were going to send anything, it might at least amount to something that would in fact give what they said they were giving — a "good Christmas" for the men.' The reply was predictable, with the Colonel using the words *tired of having my nose bloodied by your correspondence* and so on. This was, after all, an army, and subordinates did not sound off at their commanders, in print or otherwise. Hilton had stirred the feelings of head office yet again with his daring to speak out and the frankness of the words he chose to use. He had a valid point, no doubt, regarding the smallness of the Christmas offering made. But it was possibly as much as Headquarters could manage all the same. Decades later, Hilton bears no personal grudge against his commanding officer, whom he maintains was 'a nice man'. The commander could have been forgiven for thinking that was not how Hilton felt as he wrote the letter. Hilton's language had personalised the complaint and made it an attack on an individual.

The gloves were off. Territory high command wasn't going to let an officer think he could get away with insubordination in the ranks. When the annual field changes came out in December 1989, the Harmers were told that the Colonel had no place for them in his department. They were put, as it were, on the open market. But not everyone had deserted them at Headquarters. They were talent, whatever disagreements there might be at times. The Divisional Commander of the Sydney Central Division picked them up, offering them jobs as Divisional Social Services Secretaries and officers in charge of the Salvo Care Line at Crown Street, Surry Hills.

Looking back, the argument over the $300 cheque for the men's Christmas may seem a small matter either way. Not worth a major rift between two hard-working and effective officers and Headquarters. But the reaction from the Colonel also suggests a short fuse was developing with some at HQ in reaction to Hilton's independent attitude to high command, and also that Hilton's pugilistic approach to what he saw as stuffy high-handedness from some in the organisation had singled him out as a complete outsider whom Headquarters was at some loss to deal with. There was obviously no attempt to talk the issue through. It was as if the Colonel had decided that no amount of talking would temper Hilton Harmer.

The move to Salvo Care was not a success, and this time both Joyce and Hilton objected to the situation they found themselves thrown into. 'At Salvo Care in Surry Hills,' explains Hilton, 'we were briefed by the outgoing Divisional Commander on how we should introduce changes, but we were not ready for either what we found or for the different attitude of the incoming Divisional Commander.' There were also some deficiencies in work practices. The new Divisional Commander, however, preferred not to confront the situation, and was no support as Joyce and Hilton took stock of the business. The situation for any proper manager was clearly ludicrous.

After a week, Joyce was crying all the way to work and again all the way home. She quit her position after just four weeks, while Hilton was called into endless meetings with the new Divisional Commander and the former manager. 'The issue of "ethics" was on the agenda,' says Hilton, 'put there by me.' Hilton quit the position after nine weeks and wrote a letter to the Divisional Commander saying they could not manage a facility under the conditions he was allowing, and without his support.

For some months, Joyce and Hilton lived on at their Army-supplied quarters in Lakemba without a role in the Army.

Hilton had trouble coping, although Joyce says that in spite of the unsatisfactory conditions at Salvo Care that had led to their withdrawal, this was really a time of much-needed sick leave for Hilton, as he fell into a mini-breakdown. Once again, he needed to recuperate; Joyce made use of the time to watch over him and keep in touch with family and former clients. Then, in September 1990, they were asked by Territorial Headquarters if they would fill in as managers in Morisset, north of Sydney, at the Miracle Haven Farm, another Army rehab centre. This got Hilton back on his feet, and by 1991 they were back into rehab and Family Stores work as they had been in Canberra, but this time at St Peters in Sydney.

They had been given another challenge. The rehab work at St Peters, an inner western Sydney suburb, was vast, and the site of the depot for the collection of second-hand goods when they arrived at the appointment was what they could only describe as a 'tip' — a cluster of ramshackle buildings in the centre of a paddock-like block with piles of discarded and broken furniture and goods littering the ground on all sides of the buildings. A cyclone fence kept the pilferers out while the piles of junk grew higher. Over the next two years, St Peters and the results Joyce and Hilton achieved there would establish their reputations as high-achieving entrepreneurs for good works. And so much of the rehab work they did there would also set them up for their later work in the courts.

By now, the Harmers were very much the empty-nesters. The move to Morisset hadn't suited Athol, who had begun a chef's apprenticeship in Sydney. It was too far for him to travel to and from Sydney each day, so for a time he stayed in the city with Lyndall. He traces his downhill years hooked on cannabis from here. Years that worried Joyce and Hilton, who could only pray and hope he came round like some of the men on the program. Over the next few years, while they could work with the rehab guys who came to Morisset and St Peters, their own son was out of reach.

'I'd gone right away from the church,' recalls Athol. 'Turned my back on the whole thing. Mum and Dad were distraught. I stopped going to church, and working at [Kings] Cross I was exposed to quite a different level of life. But I kept my job. I played in bands around Sydney, took dope and got married at twenty. It was only when our relationship was hours from destruction, after a few years of marriage and me on cannabis, that my wife gave me an ultimatum. She had a bag over her shoulder and was standing at the door.' Athol bounces his six-month-old son on his lap as he looks back. 'She said, "Change or I'm gone." I gave up on the spot. But I know how hard it is for people to give up the drugs and alcohol.' That was in 1998. After seven years, Joyce and Hilton's prayers had been answered.

Athol and Joyce had always been close. His birth at a time of acute illness for Hilton seemed to set their relationship in stone. His decline into drugs had rocked Joyce especially, though neither parent put pressure on their son. The day after he decided to give up, Athol came to see Joyce at work. 'Mum, things are not going very well,' he said before she could ask too much.

'Son, we know. We've always known. Do you want to talk about your problems? We know about your addiction.'

'You didn't tell me you knew. You didn't tell me.'

'Son,' Joyce said in a gentle voice, 'I have lived with alcoholics and addicts for all these years — why wouldn't I know?'

'I've got to get my life back together. I haven't been to church. I've given all that away. My life is a mess and I've got to put it back together again.'

'That's a starting point, son,' Joyce replied.

And then Athol knelt at a little chair in Joyce and Hilton's office where others in distress had knelt. Joyce knelt with him. And she hugged him and he hugged her back. And, as Joyce recalls it, at that moment Athol handed his life over in prayer again. He asked for forgiveness and for God to take his craving from him and help him to get through the situation he was in. Then he told his mother that he wanted his wife Kirsten to come with him back to God and he wasn't sure what her response might be. 'Son, you leave that. I'll pray for that. Ring me tonight.'

Joyce recalls that it happened just as she had prayed for it to happen. 'When Athol rang me that night, he said, "Mum, you'll never believe . . ." I said, "Stop there, I do believe it. I've been praying for it all afternoon. I know what you're going to say. Tell me just what happened." And so he told me, and from then on they started going to church together and eventually became Salvation Army officers.'

Joyce had found herself through rehab work, first in Canberra and even more so at St Peters, her touch gaining a confidence she had never known. Fate and the difficulties with Headquarters had ironically brought Joyce into a field she relished and felt she could do justice to, and where she saw herself make a difference. There isn't anything in life more rewarding than that. No rank in the hierarchy can match it, she says.

chapter 16

GOD'S STOREKEEPERS

In the early 1990s, the Harmers began training in new-look Family Stores, spending time in the United States, over two trips, researching the recycling of merchandise for charitable profit. During one visit to Los Angeles they became part of the relief operation following an earthquake that rocked the city, Joyce handing out babies' diapers until they ran out. Their Salvation Army links meant they could fall into the job of helping wherever they found themselves or a need.

As managers of Red Shield Industries operations, their motto was 'Staff will do what you inspect, not what you expect'. It says much about their commitment to high standards and productivity. The Harmer top-down model of management came with the territory, one where discipline and order were essential. After all, the idea of recycling second-hand goods not only to help the dispossessed but also to bring in income for the Army was still a work in progress. It would succeed or fail on the strength of its management style. A well-run depot and store could deteriorate with the wrong managers or continue to expand with capable ones.

While at St Peters Mancare, Joyce and Hilton eventually administered stores at Hurstville, Campsie and Maroubra. From nothing more than a dump for used goods, they developed an early industry for reusable merchandise — the profits going to support Salvation Army social work. By 1993, Major Charles Strickland was writing to congratulate them on their results: *Your hard work, business acumen and 'hands on' leadership is to be commended. I've appreciated your enthusiasm, vision to see and accomplish these outstanding gains, plus your sense of urgency to 'get on with the issues at hand'.*

Lieutenant Colonel John Major also acknowledged their efforts and success in a letter to Hilton dated 12 January 1993: *I am a 'big picture' person*, he wrote, *and I find helpful the following summary of the gross income for the July–December period for the last three years: 1990 July–December — $.78 million; 1991 July–December — $.94 million; 1992 July–December — $1.37 million. The further fact that in December 1992 alone over one-fifth of a million dollars gross was raised is cause for great rejoicing and congratulations to all concerned.*

But their success had proved too good in relation to their own desire to stay within the area of helping the needy. Hilton and Joyce had shown the Army how to make money out of second-hand goods in a big way. The congratulations were also recognition that they were now a proven money-spinning team for the Army to make much-needed funds for its vast programs. And the Army needed income. It was becoming clear that rehab work was no longer what the Army saw as Joyces and Hilton's forte in the organisation.

Joyce and Hilton are widely regarded as having been among the best when it came to operating Red Shield Industries operations. In 1991, the Salvation Army brought Majors Charles and April Strickland to Australia from the United States to spend two years helping develop its Salvation Army thrift stores, or Red Shield Industries. They were followed by Majors John and Bonnie Jordan. Later

Major John Jordan wrote to Hilton, calling him the 'father' of the Red Shield Industries in the Eastern Territory, such was the success the Harmers achieved in their time as leaders in the field of Army stores operations.

The Harmers were sticklers for professionalism. A store's appearance was half the battle, in their view. They were salespeople in the best tradition. They believed in uniforms for the staff, goods stacked and on display in a layout befitting a good department store, and no slack habits among the workers, whoever they might be. 'What Joyce couldn't see from the office upstairs that overlooked the warehouse and the shop below wasn't worth seeing,' says Sue Combie, who worked with the Harmers later. 'A person only had to slip a piece of paper into a pocket and Joyce would see it. If she saw something from a staffer, she'd be down on the floor in a moment and would whisper in the person's ear, and if they didn't own up to whatever it was they had, they'd be out the door shortly after. Joyce could look left and notice something happening on the right. You'd think, how did she see that?'

But the approach also brought complaints in the past. Joyce was called to account by Headquarters during her time at St Peters. A group of female staff had objected to the strict ways of their madam Major. 'No high standard is achieved without making a few bad friends along the way,' says Hilton. 'We made more than a few because we were trying to turn what had been known as the "Tempe tip" into a well-presented family store. And that took a lot of hard work, believe me.'

In 1992, while at St Peters, Hilton received a call from a senior Army officer responsible for social work. The officer reported that he had received a letter accusing Joyce, principally, and Hilton, as her partner in the business, of a serious matter. The officer would not reveal who had sent the letter but said the accusations were that Joyce had victimised, intimidated and harassed female staff at the St Peters store. There were no specifics, but he asked that Joyce and Hilton attend a meeting to discuss the matter. Major Charles Strickland would also be there.

Joyce and Hilton arrived at Collaroy for the meeting. In commencing the discussion, the officer spoke of 'the seriousness of the charges' and left the meeting open for debate so they might 'move forward on the issue'.

Hilton admits to leading the charge thereafter. 'Who has made these allegations?' he countered.

'I'm not prepared to divulge their names,' replied the officer who had informed them of the complaints, and who had been a close friend of the Harmers for years.

'Well, in what way has Joyce or I victimised, intimidated and harassed staff?'

'I can't tell you that either, because if I did you would know who they were.'

'Well,' said Hilton, 'that should be the end of the matter. If we can't be told who has complained about us, or in what way we are supposed to have victimised, intimidated or harassed these persons unknown, then there is nowhere to go on the issue and this meeting should be concluded.'

After a further thirty minutes, the meeting ended, Joyce and Hilton taking with them a copy of the original letter of complaint. The matter lapsed after that, but the Harmers believed it should be cleared up or it would remain hanging over their heads. As long as the charges and the identity of the complainants were not known, the letter of complaint was clearly defamatory. They engaged a solicitor, who sent Territorial Headquarters a letter in which he insisted that legal action would be taken if the charges were not substantiated or withdrawn within two weeks. If not substantiated, the letter stipulated that the withdrawal of the charges be a) verbal, b) in writing, and c) published in *The War Cry*. The last point seemed to the Harmers a little over the top, and in fact it never happened.

The immediate effect of the solicitors letter was dramatic. The Territorial Headquarters CEO called Hilton at home, very irate. Such a course of action had never been taken by any Salvation Army officer before, he told Hilton. New things can always happen, replied Hilton. The Harmers were berated for not handling the matter 'in-house'. Hilton responded that they had always wanted to resolve the matter in-house but nothing had been done to clear their names and the matter had lapsed. Some plain speaking followed till it became clear that improved communications were all that was needed to fix the situation. The Commissioner and the Harmers resolved to meet amicably and work it all out 'in-house'. The subsequent meeting concluded with the complaint's being withdrawn. Such was the reconciliation that the officer who raised the complaints later joined Joyce and Hilton for a friendly cup of coffee.

Although the Army officer for social work never revealed the complainants, Hilton and Joyce had known all along who they were. The matter being complained about involved the strict standards of dress and behaviour at the St Peters store — standards that Joyce would never compromise. If a woman came to work in jeans, saying her uniform was wet or not able to be worn for some reason, Joyce would provide another uniform and ask her to change. The rules also insisted on no fraternisation between staff who were male clients on the rehab program and the female staff of the store. Joyce came down hard on female staff who sent messages care of the weekly gratuity-payment envelopes to the rehab men who worked there. And then there was the female staffer who took home a 'donated' ring from the store and was told to return it or the police would be called. Resentment at the strictures had led a small group to complain. But the Harmers' objection was at the way the specific matter of complaint had been handled. No one had come to them first to discuss what was being said. Instead, they had been reported to the Commissioner as if they had broken the law.

'No doubt,' says Hilton, 'many staff thought they were being intimidated, victimised or harassed by Joyce and me. When you have fifty to sixty staff with so much activity going on and are at the same time managing a thirty-five bed rehabilitation centre, it is a wonder we are alive to tell the tale. At St Peters, we had seven trucks bringing in around fifteen to twenty tonnes of donated goods every day. It was full-on.' And there was no room for indulgence.

But the matter left a trail. When Joyce and Hilton were given orders to move, Joyce wept.

The marching orders came in November 1992. Orders for the Harmers to move to Mt Druitt, known as the Minchinbury store, where they would be in charge of the major depot for the Red Shield Industries. They were being plucked out of their area of people skills and social work to take over the business of selling and collecting full-time. To the Harmers, in some respects it seemed that they might just as well have stayed in Gympie and opened a business or worked up the ranks at Cullinanes department store to manager level. But, ever the obedient officers, Joyce and Hilton packed their bags for Mt Druitt.

Joyce knew the move meant they would no longer be in charge of a rehab program, just when her work at St Peters was blossoming. At the same time, they were told that the former manager would be staying on at Mt Druitt after they took over there. The idea smacked of the Salvo Care situation, where after some weeks they had felt they could not operate. So Joyce and Hilton refused to go to Mt Druitt unless the former manager was moved away. But in the meantime, they had to move out of their St Peters quarters, as new officers were coming in, and they had nowhere to live if they did not relocate to Mt Druitt immediately. For a time they literally sheltered in a derelict house with few cooking facilities on the St Peters property. They survived with the help of clients of the rehab centre, who brought them meals on trays which they would hand over the fence. Joyce and Hilton stayed in their makeshift digs for ten days before the Army paid out the manager at Mt Druitt and they agreed to move.

'Minchinbury was huge,' recalls Sue Combie, who worked in the office there when the Harmers ran it. 'It employed some fifty-six people and its purpose was to serve all of the western area of Sydney. And Hilton and Joyce had that place cleaned up in no time.'

Joyce and Hilton had been sent to Minchinbury to get it functioning as a serious profit-making operation. And it certainly wasn't functioning as such when they arrived. Stories abounded of second-hand goods that were pilfered or knocked down to almost nothing for favoured dealers, and the centre needed its business mentality spruced up. After the enterprise the Harmers had managed at St Peters, with what had been little more than a dump for rubbish when they'd started, it stood to reason they were right for the job at Minchinbury. But the clean-up had a rocky start. Their reputation for getting a store ship-shape could come at a cost.

The Harmers were certainly different from most of their colleagues, ready to go it alone if they had to. And while Hilton was by any account the real stirrer, it was Joyce who had felt the growing resistance of the organisation in their move to Mt Druitt. 'Joyce always assumed the managerial role if I was sick or away from the job,' recounts Hilton. 'Apparently as we took up the Mt Druitt placement there were people at THQ who did not like Joyce taking over the management role. While we were waiting for the former manager to be cleared at Mt Druitt, Joyce received a call at home from Divisional Headquarters at Parramatta. She was to have an interview with the Divisional Commander. She invited me to go with her. When we got to his office, the Divisional Commander said that Territorial Headquarters had drafted a workplace agreement for Joyce to sign. He added that if she signed it she would be bound by it.'

It was unheard of for an officer of Joyce's commitment and standing in the Army to be asked to sign such an agreement, which said that on arrival at the Mt Druitt Red Shield Industries Joyce's role would be to take responsibility for 'sorting of donated goods' and that she would have no authority outside this area. Joyce read the document and passed it back to the Commander. 'I'm not going to sign that,' was all she said. Hilton admits to being very proud of her as he watched.

And that was the end of the so-called work-agreement idea. Their partnership went on as before. Their strength and success in Minchinbury, in fact, eventually depended very much on Joyce as manager. On occasions, while she managed the Minchinbury operation, Hilton was able to travel to other areas, where he opened new stores.

But the smooth running of the giant Minchinbury Family Store did not eventuate without a huge shake-up after Hilton and Joyce took over. They had had their reasons for wanting a clean sweep of the previous management: the reputation of the store had declined rapidly in the years prior to the Harmers' arrival. In early 1993, as the Harmers took control, a married twenty-nine year-old mother of three told the *Standard*, the local paper, '*I stopped going there two years ago. I would look neat and tidy and the staff would just look at me and make up a price. Some people would walk in there and see a certain former staff member and would go out the back where all the beautiful furniture was, while the rubbish was left for the customers in the shop.*' The Mt Druitt Family Store was overdue for a clean-up, with repercussions quick to follow.

On Wednesday 24 February 1993, the headlines across the front page of the local paper read *DEPOT DISPUTE*, below which the secondary heading was '*Salvos Sack Staff*'. A photo of a weary Hilton leaning sideways, head in hand, was juxtaposed with a photo of four surly sacked staff from the Minchinbury store. The opening paragraph of the accompanying article read: *More than half the staff at the Salvation Army's huge Mt Druitt clothing and furniture depot have been sacked or resigned in an industrial dispute with the new boss*. The article went on to report that Army head office had said that the sackings *were in relation to certain staff and* second-hand-goods dealers getting access to the Army's products before customers. The gist of the argument that followed countered claims of unfair dismissal (one worker a sorter for twenty years) with the exposure of a well-oiled racket that had been going on for years at the Army's and locals' expense. But it was not a good start in the public relations stakes for the Harmers.

The shake-up that followed over the ensuing weeks was a wild ride for Joyce and Hilton. Their actions at times risked payback from a few of the unsavoury characters who had worked up a cosy business ripping off the depot over the years. But threats of legal action and the like over the sackings came to nothing. Fighting back, the Harmers took out a big ad in the *Standard* that sent a clear message. The depot was *UNDER NEW MANAGEMENT* — a slogan they had splashed across the top of the ad under a friendly photo of them both and a large Army Shield. The blurb read: *The Salvation Army Mt Druitt Red Shield Family Store offers bargains for the whole family . . . Your dollar will buy more at the Family Store than you could ever imagine . . . New Family Store opening soon — watch for the announcement in the* Standard.

Hilton also wrote a letter to the editor of the *Standard*, which was published. In it he explained why he and Joyce had introduced thirty-two rules at the depot and concluded: *My wife and I have been Salvation Army officers for thirty-two years. We have given our lives to assist the dispossessed of society and while ever I am the administrator of the Mt Druitt centre, its business will be conducted in the manner which will embody the high ideals and standards which the public have come to expect from the Salvation Army and which is the reason for their continued support. If such a stand makes me personally unpopular, that is the price I am prepared to pay*. The *Standard* was soon reporting a volley of public support for the new management.

The Industrial Relations Department investigated the Army's move against the workers and cleared it of any wrongful doing. Business began to pick up. A new store was opened in March, just a month after the sackings. The report in the local paper was sunny and positive — management and customers with smiles all round. The new building had 20,000 square metres of floorspace, a third of which was laid out like a department store with its trays and racks of clothing and second-hand goods. The Salvation Army Red Shield Industries at Mt Druitt was soon reporting an eighty per cent increase in demand for clothing and furniture from its depot. 'We pride ourselves on being the ultimate recyclers,' Hilton would say.

In her matron-like way, Joyce was the engine for staff presentation. Her stickler-for-the-rules approach continued to make a basic second-hand goods business, often employing men on rehabilitation, seem like a proudly run family firm.

'We used to feel it was essential that if people were going to get their life together they had to look like they were doing it. So we provided two sets of uniforms. Navy shirt and navy trousers, socks, whatever. They had to look immaculate at work and that helped set a tone of respect around them. We didn't allow long hair for the men but we were happy if it was collar length. It was essential that they shaved each day. If they didn't I'd say, "What happened to your chin this morning? You'd better go back and do it, eh?" And back they'd go and shave. They knew they had to because the rules said they had to.'

'Joyce and Hilton cleaned that place up in no time,' says Sue Combie. 'I think only one truck driver remained in the end from the former manager's time.'

Jacinta, who was in the office when the Harmers arrived, became Hilton's backstop until she left to get married. 'I knew nothing about computers at the time,' he recalls. 'Without Jacinta we could never have done it. She knew the business, and was like gold in the office.' Goods were given out where they were needed as they came in and the rest put in the shop to be sold. They had Australia Day sales, when Hilton and Joyce would work around the clock getting goods ready and cleaning up afterwards. These sales topped the takings, year after year. Major John Jordan, writing with his congratulations in 1995, began his letter: *What a superb, splendid and stupendous accomplishment! Just think: in five hours we had sales of $16,000, that is amazing!* He went on to thank the Harmers for their willingness 'to initiate, to try something new, to get out of the rut of the status quo'.

Joyce, says Sue Combie, was beautiful to work with. Firm, even tough, but always so fair she was a pleasure to please. They would laugh at the job, and at the way Joyce handled difficult situations, gently knocking back a mattress with holes in a most polite voice.

'I'm not saying that she never got upset,' says Sue, 'but she never lost her cool. She's a saint. She didn't care where you came from. She didn't care what religion you might have, or even if you went to church at all. She treated everybody the same. When my brother died of cancer, they were there. The day after he died, Joyce and Hilton came to visit and pray with us.'

Joyce and Hilton had arrived at Mt Druitt somewhat reduced in their status from those heady days when they had been appointed to Congress Hall, then Parramatta, with the largest congregation in the Territory. And they knew it. They had taken their orders and made a mission wherever sent. In ten years they had gone from Army careers on a meteoric rise to finding themselves, as Hilton puts it, 'standing outside what the American consultant called the worst Industry he had ever seen', Mt Druitt Red Shield Industries. 'I would be out before daylight,' Hilton says, 'picking up maggot-ridden fruit and other rubbish so as it would look respectable in the eyes of the public and so they would not think badly of my precious Salvation Army. I did that often and, in tears, I would tell the Lord that I would be faithful to Him and His call upon my life, no matter what I had to do.' Hilton and Joyce can chuckle at the fact that Hilton received a letter of commendation from Blacktown Council for the improvement they made to the footpath outside the Salvation Army store in the time they were there.

Even as Hilton begins to sound angry at the way their careers were tossed around in the hierarchy, he acknowledges this is his male ego. It's not how Joyce sees it. 'I just loved rehab and the people I met there,' she will say, seeming not to have regretted for a moment the moves that sent her backwards from high office into life alongside broken people in need of support. And while Hilton can work up a lather at his perception of the injustice, their days at Minchinbury ended with what was becoming a fairly familiar echo of praise for the work the Harmers did wherever sent. Not only had they created a successful business in second-hand goods, but, as always, they had continued to find time for helping needy families as well.

Hilton is the first to acknowledge that the anger of his ego needs to be kept in check. 'Joyce gets on my case from time to time about my bad attitude to the Salvation Army leadership. And I know she hurt for me every time I was in conflict. And Jesus said, if you want to be great, then be a servant and meet the needs of your fellow man. I have a soulmate who is accepting of the circumstances I have found myself in. Between the Holy Spirit and Joyce, I am kept in order.'

At the end of their time at Mt Druitt, they were written up in the local paper, which said they would be *sorely missed*. The report acknowledged the fact that in just three years the Harmers had taken Red Shield Industries from *a tin shack to a huge welfare distribution network extending from Blacktown to Penrith*, and that this had created jobs for fifty people at three distribution centres. For the high-unemployment years of the early 1990s, this was no mean feat.

chapter 17

THE DOWNING CENTRE

In 1993, Major Vic Bailey, standing with his Divisional Commander Major John Major, had looked out of the Territorial Headquarters' windows in Elizabeth Street, Sydney, and across to the building known as the Downing Centre, which housed the local and district courts. 'If you are looking for a new field mission,' he remarked to his commander, 'you don't have to go further than across the street. Over there are thirty-five courts and not a chaplain among them.'

At the time, Vic Bailey and his wife Eileen were working as prison chaplains. The Army had been involved in the prisons in Australia since the 1890s, when Major James Barker started a gate brigade outside Melbourne's Pentridge Prison, meeting released men who had nowhere to go. The mission spread very quickly throughout Australia. Prison chaplains would accompany men or women in custody, on request, when they were called to appear in court. But that was as far as the service went in relation to the courts. Majors Vic and Eileen Bailey recognised that the prison service gave no support to the families of the accused, or the victims and their families, who also had to face the trauma of the justice system and all its ramifications.

'We researched the scope of a mission in the courts, starting with the Downing Centre, its amenities and its courts,' says Vic

Bailey. 'We also found that seventy-five per cent of all court cases in New South Wales were carried out within a couple of kilometres' radius of Territorial Headquarters.' Then Vic Bailey approached the Downing Centre itself. What did the courts think of the idea of a court chaplaincy? Sheriff Dave Lennon, who was in charge of the security of the courts, thought such a proposal was long overdue. It was Sheriff Lennon who eventually helped push the idea of the chaplaincy with the magistracy itself. 'He was the catalyst for it taking off,' says Vic Bailey. 'I cannot emphasise enough the importance of Dave Lennon to the successful establishment of the court chaplaincy service.' The idea of some sort of chaplaincy was immediately supported by the Chief Judge and Magistrate of the Downing Centre, which was immensely helpful in initiating the service.

Courts are highly regimented places. Behaviour in court is dictated by stringent rules and overseen by the commanding eye of the presiding judge. Introducing a new feature to the courts like a chaplaincy service would require careful consideration of where the chaplain fitted within the different roles and areas of responsibility of court workers and officials. Each judge would have to give approval for any chaplain to be allowed into his or her court. In the event, however, there was no real objection. Majors Vic and Eileen Bailey were allowed to begin the chaplaincy service to the Downing Centre as an extension of their prison chaplaincy work.

Thus, the new position of a Salvation Army court chaplain in the Downing Centre, across the road from Congress Hall, evolved. But the proposal needed funding and an application went to the New South Wales Attorney General's Department. A report on the court mission had just been completed by the Salvation Army, with Territorial Commander John Gowans expressing his desire to see the chaplaincy go ahead, should government funding be obtained. At that point, Vic Bailey suggested Joyce and Hilton Harmer would be the ideal people to take the post over from him and his wife. The Baileys had worked with the Harmers in Wollongong and knew their capacity for developing a new position.

The Harmers had been at their Minchinbury appointment for two years, but for all their success at the Industries, being successful retailers wasn't what Joyce and Hilton had joined the officership of the Salvation Army to do. They wanted more and more to get back to being the helpmates of people. They had requested a change of posting and eventually the Commissioner promised them an appointment where they would be in contact with people needing help. Major Bailey's suggestion that the Harmers be the new court chaplains seemed a pertinent one.

In November 1994, Hilton and Joyce were given farewell orders to become the new chaplains in the Downing Centre mission. But the orders were unique. They were to take up the new appointment while continuing their work at Minchinbury. In other words, Joyce and Hilton were to remain managing a vast business at one end of Sydney, below the foothills of the Blue Mountains, while somehow being present daily in the courts, fifty kilometres away, standing by people in need. It would have taken miraculous powers in both of them to achieve this and it was frankly impossible. Anyone else might have split the job — Hilton in the Industries, Joyce in the courts — with the outcome that neither would have been successful in the ways they were expected to be. This was not how the Harmers worked, and they refused to do the job as outlined.

The impossible proposal, however, was more about the lack of funds for the operation in the courts than faulty administrative decision-making. When the Harmers had received their farewell orders, the funding application with the State government for a court chaplaincy at the Downing Centre was still under consideration. For the chaplaincy to take off, it would need seed funding from the Salvation Army. One way around the lack of funds was to use part of the profit from the Minchinbury store. The Harmers' success at the Red Shield Industries in Minchinbury, and the money they brought in, was now being proposed as the base for funding of the Downing Centre chaplaincy.

The tussle went on for some months. The Harmers had replied that they would do one appointment or the other but not both together. Finally, in June 1995, Joyce and Hilton were summoned to a meeting in the boardroom of Territorial Headquarters with Commissioner John Gowans and others. The Commissioner told those present that he had made a decision not all would be happy with. Joyce and Hilton would be leaving the Mt Druitt Red Shield Industries and beginning their chaplaincy at the Downing Centre on 1 August 1995. He was fulfilling a promise he had made to the Harmers long before. In time, he was vindicated in his decision when government funding from the Attorney General's Department was allocated to the position.

Entering the Downing Centre could be confused with lining up to enter the departure lounges of most airports — except for the uniforms at the metal detectors in the entrance foyer, and the wigs and gowns and various other sorts of fancy dress of some who line up to have their belongings checked. All sorts of characters queue for the security checks, some wheeling small cases that look like roll-on hand luggage. Peak hour for entry is the thirty minutes before 10 a.m. Costumed men and women chat together as they wait, as relaxed as if going on holiday. Others stand singly, and are more subdued. Family groups line up, even children.

For many, the courts are theatres; there are actors with their scripts, costumes signifying parts. Some arrive just to watch, like an audience at an event. A few well-known faces in the crowd carry notebooks and mobiles, ready to phone through the outcome of a case to their editors on the news pages of local dailies. On any ordinary day a cluster of cameras and waiting media will congregate just above the stone steps in Liverpool Street.

The Downing Centre was never intended to be a court complex. Designed by architects McCredie and Anderson and built in 1909, it was for almost six decades one of Sydney's landmark department stores, its heyday the 1920s to 1950s, when rail was popular and brought customers to the store's doorsteps from the underground station just across the intersection of Elizabeth and Liverpool Streets. In disrepair in the 1980s after being closed for business since 1968, it was acquired by the New South Wales Justice Department and refurbished to house the Magistrates Courts. Today it is unique as a courthouse in having department store windows in front, displaying occasional amateur artworks, while ornate white-glazed brickwork on the outside of the building's walls has a yellow and orange terracotta trim advertising boldly and permanently, with giant black lettering, *Hosiery*, *Shoes*, *Corsets* and the like.

The modifications inside the Downing Centre leave few clues to its former usage, although some old black and white photographs hanging just off the spiral staircase connecting the ground and first floors give some inkling of the grand days of shopping and glamour the building once knew. Apart from this, there are wide, airy foyers on each floor, left by the space between the outside walls even after the courts had been built in. Between the courts and the corridors that lead to them, and offices on the building's perimeter for regular functionaries and magistrates, various small enclaves have been created, such as that given to the chaplaincy, by enclosing areas of floor space with panels of glass bricks that let in light. These fill up much of the open space of the foyers at each level.

On the lower ground floor are the courts that can be closed for serious or notorious cases, the ones that provoke extreme tensions in the public. The basement below holds the cells, accommodating the accused in custody, who are brought in from the jails for their day in court. The seventeen cells, closed to any contact from relatives or friends, are lonely places, the silence broken only by an occasional noise from a distressed inmate, the clank of a door being shut or the jingle of handcuffs as Correctional Services officers escort inmates to or from the courts. For the visiting lawyer or consultant who needs to see a prisoner, there are small cubicles about a metre square, and only recently heated. Each is divided in half by a glass shield, with walls in pale green and yellow.

As professionals in the courts, Joyce and Hilton needed somewhere to base themselves during the day, an office of some sort. Majors Vic and Eileen Bailey had managed with a table outside the Legal Aid office, but this was only as a beginning, while they were managing other work. For Joyce and Hilton, as the first full-time officers in the chaplaincy, Vic negotiated a small area to serve as an enclosed space on the fourth floor, allotted to them by the sheriff and just large enough for a small desk a cupboard and a few straight-backed chairs.

The Harmers were welcomed to the appointment with coffee and biscuits by the Army's Divisional Command, but across the road, at the Downing Centre, their workplace was still just a tiny space. Hilton began the mission by coming in one Sunday to paint the office walls, after which they purchased a small fridge, a fax and answering machine, a few chairs and some appropriate framed pictures for the walls. That little oasis would be where Joyce could take a client during the day, store material, or disappear for a moment when needed. Later they would relocate to the floor above, into a slightly larger area enclosed by glass tiles and set in the middle of the foyer, bordering similar enclosed spaces for the Legal Aid Solicitor, Commonwealth Matters and the Duty Solicitors. Around them the courts carried on the business of each day.

Joyce and Hilton quickly had to learn officialdom and its ways around the courts. Their arrival was not without a few ruffled feathers in the administration as they staked their claim to their new office, but all was gently but firmly handled. Apart from the adjustment to having a religious fragment inside the courts, small territorial tussles of a more practical nature heralded Joyce and Hilton's presence. Having evolved from more majestic times, to most people the world of the courts is remote and alien, and supported by formalities even more rigorously perpetuated than those of the Christian Churches.

Any relaxing of the rules surrounding the justice setup is fraught with apprehension because of the need to maintain the authority of the courts. Without the aura of this authority, a court might lose its respect.

Dave Lennon is one who believes that a depletion of formality in a court has its problems. The more relaxed nature of the Family Court, he says, without its wigs and gowns and raised benches, and with its sense of egalitarianism, only makes decisions harder to enforce. 'A person comes before a judge and he makes a decision that's going to affect your life, to take your children away, sell your house. In the Family Court, these people are not criminals and another person on the same eye level can leave the defendant thinking, "What right does he or she have to do that?"'

There was an early sorting-out of where the Harmers could operate, as newcomers in an extremely traditional setup where individuals controlled specific areas of responsibility and practices were pedantically defined. 'Like where they could go in the court, small things,' says Dave Lennon, who became involved in working out their status and authority within the courts. The Harmers, as always, wanted to be clear on what they could and could not do, but also wanted space to operate effectively. 'There was a crankiness over it, but it was a nice sort of crankiness,' says Lennon.

Joyce also recalls that it took a few mistakes to learn what the system took for granted — such as 'closed courts'. Except for rare or notorious cases being tried in the special basement courts, nothing more than a small note pasted onto the court door distinguished one court from another as 'closed'. Being closed meant no one could go into that court during the hearing of the case except those taking part in it. Missing the small note on the door, Joyce sidled into a closed court one day early in her chaplaincy and sat at the back. Suddenly legal heads were turning her way, barristers and court officials whispering and stealing glances at the small uniformed woman at the back of the court. Had she something strange on her head? Joyce wondered. Then a court officer came over and pointed out her mistake. Joyce stood up, apologised and left quietly. It would happen a few times before Joyce realised how to notice the small notes on the doors of the many courts. No one had briefed her on what to look for.

Joyce laughs at her first impressions of being a worker in the courts. The notion of higher and lower courts had her completely lost for a long while, until she realised 'higher' and 'lower' did not mean how far the courts were above or below ground level in the building. 'At times it was double Dutch to me. I even thought I would probably forget to say "Your Worship" or "Your Honour" and instead say "Your Majesty".' Yet after she and Hilton had been there a year or so, Joyce was exchanging banter with some of those awesome magistrates. 'I was warned about you,' Magistrate Maloney was heard to say from the bench in a light-hearted way, looking at Joyce, who very soon had started moving about the complex as if she'd been there all her life, the spotless navy and white uniform offering formality and yet opening doors and many pairs of arms.

There had been a small amount of debate when the announcement came that court chaplains were to be appointed at the Downing Centre. Understandably, there was questioning of a chaplain's role at the courts. Would Christian chaplains be appropriate among the multicultural backgrounds of those appearing in the courts? Naturally, stereotypes of religious or church figures played their part. There were some who questioned whether it was appropriate to have vulnerable people cared for by chaplains who might want to proselytise. Shouldn't there remain a separation of Church and State in the courts, in spite of the fact that judicial officers have to take a Judicial Oath on the Bible when they are sworn in and sit under a Royal crest that says *Dieu et Mon Droit*? These and other questions worried a few.

Jackie Milledge, a senior prosecutor when the Harmers were appointed, recalls there was some opposition to the new position. 'I'm not saying that this was widespread, but there was a vocalised sort of "This is wrong". But it wasn't against the Harmers as individuals, only against the Salvation Army having a presence within the complex.'

Jaye Carney is now a magistrate. When the Harmers came to the Downing Centre she was working with Legal Aid clients, many of whom were not the least interested in God, often quite the reverse, and many of whom had been betrayed by religious institutions as children and adolescents. A qualified social worker as well as a lawyer, she recalls questioning to what extent Joyce and Hilton were qualified counsellors. Her idea of counselling was very much in the mould of the university degree background of most professional social workers. She was concerned that a chaplain might bring a religious morality to judge people who had no religion. And then Jaye met the Harmers and watched them go to work.

'When I met Hilton, whom I worked with more than Joyce, and got to know him and the chaplaincy service, I was quite impressed as to what it offered. I had been worried about whether the chaplaincy service was given only in the context of asking people to give themselves over to God, but when you get to know Hilton and Joyce, well, it's all done because they're loving people. They never imposed and at the end of the day I never saw any aspect of conversion. They simply offered the chaplaincy and wonderful practical help.' Jaye was eventually converted to the idea of chaplaincy in the courts.

So Joyce and Hilton had to fill a space only barely chiselled out for them. And one where, in some corners of the complex, the jury was out as to whether it was indeed what the courts needed. At first, various magistrates and judges saw them as retired District Court judge Peter Phelan did — 'just two Salvation Army people in their uniforms at the back of the court'. No more, no less.

The Harmers had been at the courts just a few months when, in October 1995, Joyce took a call from her sister-in-law Vivienne. Cecil, her eldest brother, had died after a long battle with cardio myopathy. A heart transplant might have saved him, but no new heart had been available, and in the end he had spent his last three months in intensive care watched over by the faithful Vivienne. Joyce and Hilton left immediately for Yatala on the Gold Coast. Ted Harmer, Hilton's brother and Cecil's old mate from Gympie school days, conducted a Salvation Army service in a local crematorium. Cecil had not come back to his childhood religion, but as Joyce grieved she knew the good in him, recalling the hard life he had known as a youngster.

As they grew more confident in their work at the Downing Centre, Joyce and Hilton added the Central Courts to their daily routine. Making the most of their ability to share a load, Hilton began to base himself at the Central

Courts, where people are taken after being charged with crimes and where bail or custody is decided. Joyce stayed at the Downing Centre, with its daily routine of cases coming before magistrates and its sprinkling of families caught up in the justice system. In time, they visited suburban Local and District Courts, and even looked in on the Supreme Court between Macquarie Street and King Street, and the Supreme Court at Darlinghurst.

Joyce had begun her days at the Downing Centre cautiously but intently. She had learned to wait out uncertainties and make mistakes as infrequently as possible. Better to be the apprentice and let things bide their time rather than rush in and mess them up. She listened, she questioned the professionals and learned the rituals fast. Her life experiences had taught her to absorb atmosphere carefully, to wait for your moment and to know your job. She had been absorbing pain and distress for decades; now she had it around the clock. A journalist who watched Joyce at work in the courts for years says that while she eventually became recognised for her involvement in a couple of headline-grabbing cases, it was her dogged ability to stand by the most ordinary of people, day after day, listening to them download, bringing them small comforts or helping them get back to normal later, that is her legacy. 'You can achieve a lot with a hug and a hanky' was soon Joyce's motto. Her hanky collection became legendary, at one stage written up as a feature in a women's magazine.

Hilton remembers how they started in the courts by 'floundering' for a while. 'We just walked in and put our stuff in the office and Joyce started at one end of the crowd for the day and I'd start at the other.' From the outset they met everyone connected with the courts. It was impossible to distinguish who was a solicitor and who was a relative standing in the corridor. 'You've got to be prepared to make a bit of a goose of yourself,' says Hilton. They'd walk up to a waiting figure and say, 'Have you got someone in the cells?' and the answer might come back, 'No, I'm an interpreter.' Or, 'No, I'm a solicitor.' Or, 'No, I'm an undercover police officer.' But every so often the reply would be, 'Yes, I've got someone down there.' Then Joyce or Hilton would hand over their card and ask the person to let them know if there was anything they could do to help. In time, it was not unusual for Joyce or Hilton to get calls from people they had handed cards to years before. At first Hilton had begun by going home every night and writing down the names of every meaningful contact they made during a day. He gave it up after a week because of the avalanche of names he collected in those first days.

Before a few years had passed, Joyce and Hilton had drawn up a job description of their chaplaincy service. There were thirty-eight points on their information sheet, and nearly forty kinds of services they offered and frequently provided. They spoke to family members whose loved ones were in trouble, supported victims of crime, supplied counselling in regard to drugs, alcohol, gambling, marriage, family trouble, grief and finance. They sat in court with people stricken with grief, they acted as mediators, they visited jails, they met relatives at airports, train stations, wherever, and helped them get to court or to a prison for visits. They sat in on juvenile interviews with police, made phone calls for people, gave evidence in support of clients, assisted court staff, attended evictions with sheriff officers, oversaw Family Court access visits, went to homes to inform relatives of court outcomes, co-operated with prison welfare officers in assessing people for full-time drug and alcohol counselling, supplied food, travel fares and accommodation, and moved from court to court detecting and assisting people in need. In addition, they helped people who served on juries, took flowers to graves for people in custody, negotiated with landlords regarding financial arrangements for those unable to pay because of court situations, supplied clothing for those in custody awaiting a trial, and at times also withdrew money for people in custody who needed to make fine payments so they could be released. They helped Legal Aid solicitors and others to better meet the needs of their clients, supplied toys and refreshments to people around the courts, cleaned out rooms and units and stored personal effects safely until prisoners were released, conducted weddings, christenings and funerals, and handed out many hankies when needed. Their work was 24/7; they offered contact at any time to those affected by the courts, or 'court users' as Joyce would call them.

By the time they left, Joyce and Hilton had an intimate knowledge of the courts and had won the confidence of their court colleagues. 'I had a relationship with them that they could pop into the office and we talked about issues,' says Sheriff Gary Byles. 'Issues mainly related to the welfare of my officers, which has been very informative and has allowed me to take certain actions in certain services.'

The Salvation Army's court chaplaincy appointment was not highly regarded in terms of positioning in the Army's hierarchy of jobs, but it grabbed Joyce and Hilton's interest from the outset. In their rehab work they had known many on bail. Others they had saved from a stretch in prison. Regardless of its low status in the Salvation Army organisation, to the Harmers their appointment to the courts was a high-opportunity mission.

For Joyce, with all her children well into their own adult lives, married and long gone from home, it was also her time like never before. She did miss Lyndall, who had moved to the United States, where she had trained as a Salvation Army officer and then married one of her American colleagues. Hilton had done extra work at night as a cleaner to help pay their airfares so they could get to the wedding. Lyndall chose to wear her white Salvation Army uniform as a bride, coming down the aisle on her proud father's arm, after which Hilton performed the wedding ceremony. It was a wrench to know that Lyndall would now settle permanently so far away. But one of Joyce's greatest surprises would be when Hilton secretly organised a phone hook-up with Lyndall for Joyce's surprise sixtieth birthday party, and then in early 2002 arranged a surprise visit from Lyndall to Sydney. The joy of her daughter's homecomings overtook the sadness at losing her to the other side of the world.

Meanwhile, in her Downing Centre work as a chaplain to the courts, Joyce was discovering that, through her gentle loving of people with stories of distress, she could speak to thousands through her work.

chapter 18

AN ANGEL IN THE COURT

Jake was youngish, in his late twenties perhaps, a big tall guy with thickset muscles, known around the courts for his hardened ways and contempt for the justice system. He could fake psychological disorder and hide behind the *Mental Health Act*; he was heartless in his criminality. He had hidden in women's toilet blocks and ripped handbags from the floor of nearby cubicles; he'd made bomb threats against an airport. Some said he was another Martin Bryant just waiting to go off. He was in court for the umpteenth time, and the magistrate was beginning his judgment in the case of Jake, who stood before him. The court was four floors up, in the Downing Centre.

'Well, I'm sorry but I'm going to have to send you to jail,' began the magistrate, looking slowly up from his notes towards the defendant.

'No you're not,' was Jake's unexpected reply. And before anyone in the room could stop him, Jake was out the door and making his way across the foyer to the Legal Aid office, where for some unaccountable reason a window was open. He climbed onto the ledge of the window. 'I'm going to jump. I'm going to jump.' It was a Code One, a top-priority emergency operation. In no time Sheriff Bruce Kelly had the room barricaded. Outside, an ambulance, the fire brigade, police and inevitably the media, with cameras, began taking up positions. Until the police had made their way to the room, a couple of sheriff officers kept watch, ordered not to try any negotiations. And then Jake changed tack. 'I want Joyce,' he said. Major Joyce Harmer, who had sat in court with him the day before.

Somewhere in the complex Joyce heard her pager. 'Come quickly,' she was told. Emerging from the lift into the foyer outside the Legal Aid office, Joyce found a milling crowd that included Hilton.

'That bloke in there is going to jump. It's Jake, and he wants you.'

Bruce Kelly was fearful about letting the diminutive Joyce go anywhere near Jake. But he had to let her if she insisted, and she did. He warned her that on no account was she to go close enough for Jake to grab her. He might jump and take Joyce with him. He might make her a hostage. 'It's all right,' was all Joyce would say as she moved calmly into the Legal Aid office.

'I went right over to him,' Joyce recalls, thinking what might happen if he jumped before she got there. 'Listen here,' she said to him. 'Give me your hand, Jake.' Jake was uncertain, glancing across at the officers on the other side of the room and then down to the street below. Then he stretched out a hand to Joyce. 'Now the other one.'

They were facing one another, holding hands: the huge, frenzied young Jake, balancing on a window ledge four storeys up, and a calm little grey-haired woman in a Salvation Army uniform, barely five feet in height in her comfortable flat court shoes. At the edges of the drama, court officers and Correctional Services officers milled about in the corridor outside, the Legal Aid staff froze at their desks and Sheriff Kelly held his breath as he watched from across the room.

'Listen, what do you think you are doing?' asked Joyce in a practical no-nonsense tone.

'I'm going to jump. I'm going to jump because I've just sacked my barrister and I'm going to jump. What the f— is going on down there?'

'Listen, just hold my hand. Now, don't be stupid. What are you doing up there? Come down and talk to me.'

Jake relented a fraction. 'I want the barrister back.'

'You want the barrister back. Right, keep looking this way. Whoever is over there, get the barrister. Go get the barrister.'

The barrister was there in a flash, in time to witness his client snarling at the figures outside the window.

'Look at those c— taking photos down there.'

One of the sheriff officers reacted. 'Do you want them to go?'

'Yes I do,' said Jake.

'Right, you stand back and I'll sort them out. Get those cameras out of the way!' he yelled out the window.

'Come on down, Jake,' said Joyce. 'The barrister is here. Come on down and talk about it.'

And then a few more quiet pleas from Joyce, and it was over. Jake jumped down into a chair, where he sat like a chastened child. He threw his arms around Joyce's waist as she stood in front of him, saying, 'I didn't want to do this, Joyce, in front of you.'

'All right, Jake, you're okay, so we're leaving now. Your barrister is here.'

Forty minutes or more had elapsed before Joyce led Jake out of the Legal Aid office, to the relief of the waiting Sheriff Bruce Kelly. Jake's case at the Downing Centre was immediately adjourned and it was agreed that Joyce would accompany him to the Supreme Court, where another matter was now to be heard.

'Don't say anything,' Joyce was heard to say. 'Hold my arm and stay with me.' With the barristers following, Joyce and Jake walked out of the Downing Centre into Elizabeth Street. Bruce Kelly crossed to the waiting media pack and instructed all media not to take any photos. But one photographer broke ranks, running up to Joyce and Jake while they hailed a cab to take them the five blocks to the Supreme Court at the end of Hyde Park. Joyce thrust her handbag over Jake's face. A photo of the handbag-covered face appeared the next day in one of the daily newspapers. When the brief Supreme Court hearing was over, Joyce escorted Jake back to the Downing Centre, where she explained their late arrival to the magistrate, leaving Jake in the hands of the courts. And, soon enough, he was back in custody.

By the time Joyce talked Jake down from the window ledge she'd been at the Downing Centre as court chaplain for six years. In that time, Joyce and Hilton Harmer had become a small two-band institution in the Central Court and the Downing Centre, and were known even more widely than that, as they sometimes dropped in on the Supreme Court or Magistrates Courts like Parramatta, Burwood, Waverley or Sutherland. Former Waverley magistrate Terry Forbes felt he knew the Harmers well, but for a long time it was just a voice and name at the end of a telephone. They eventually made real contact when the Waverley court was trying to clear the enormous number of drug cases that came before it each day.

'We had hundreds of cases a day,' says Forbes. 'I would catch Joyce for a few moments as she walked in a door or we caught a lift together.' Joyce would ask if she could look after a person if Justice Forbes might have to find against them. Perhaps there could be alternative arrangements made, rather than sending them to prison while their case was being decided.

Joyce and Hilton had become what barrister Charles Waterstreet calls 'a marriage that made up a team of twenty' round the courts. They had started from scratch, with just a little knowledge of the judicial system from the bail cases in their rehab days, but with a wealth of experience supporting people in trouble from substance abuse and life at the margins. They wore uniforms, like many in the courts, but their uniforms signified something quite different. In fact, some who work around custodial and judicial circles will speak of how alien such spiritual or godly influence is in the courts.

Jennifer Giles came to the Downing Centre as a magistrate in 1996. As a defence lawyer working for the Women's Legal Centre, she now admits to having at the time 'a working life motivated and bolstered by a certain amount of self-righteousness'. Then she came to the Downing Centre and 'was devastated by the absolute wasteland of the godlessness of working in the court system, a lack of faith in anything'. Until she met Joyce.

'I can't imagine how the court system had survived for as long as it did without a chaplaincy,' says Jennifer. 'As Joyce slipped in and out of the courts, her spirituality floated in her presence. I felt it inspiring and calming and uplifting in moments of huge despair about the hearing or sentencing before me. Joyce just knew. She was one of those people who could read people's auras. She could certainly see mine. And she would write little prayers for me on the back of cards and send them up to me on the bench. I almost weep with gratitude even now remembering how much they helped me at the time, to clear my head and focus on personal responsibilities.'

The Downing Centre's Chief Magistrate Derek Price can think of no service provided to people facing a custodial sentence and their relatives apart from Joyce and Hilton and the court chaplaincy. Certainly nothing so effective. 'They became part of the furniture here,' he reflected in 2004, just before their retirement. 'And those in custody or facing the possibility of going into custody need a large amount of support. One of the most unpleasant tasks that we have as judicial officers is having to sentence people to imprisonment. I have often observed Joyce in my courtroom sitting with a person who is facing a custodial sentence, or their family, and she helps them through that process, which must be a terribly traumatic time for them and their families.'

But some saw the need for a couple of Salvation Army ministers at the Downing Centre — used for anything from helping magistrates determine bail to minding babies in the court — as a sign of the abandonment of the local courts by the State government. 'It is a disgrace,' says one journalist who has been reporting in the courts for twenty years, 'that the government should need to outsource fundamental critical services. Joyce and Hilton, for all their incredible talents, were in many ways a Band Aid approach to a huge complex of human need. And to leave such a vast operation to just two exceptional people meant that when they were away there was nothing.'

Others found the style of the chaplaincy intrusive, preferring the impersonal ways of government-paid public services. The chaplaincy worked by seeking out people who wanted help, and that is a delicate operation. Some found it too much in people's faces; yet for others it provided essential relief, and Joyce and Hilton were like angels of mercy for those with nowhere to turn. The chaplaincy, of its nature, reached out, where a government service would simply be available. Joyce never sat in her office, waiting for the world to come to her. That's not the Salvation Army. It goes where no one else will. This naturally required Joyce to stick her nose into courts and groups of people. And not everyone found that easy. Not everyone wanted a hug or even to be approached.

Stephen Gibbs, who had worked the courts for years as a reporter for the *Daily Telegraph* and then the *Sydney Morning Herald*, was never put off by a Harmer warning. Joyce would sometimes take him aside and counsel him about ruining his health, what he calls 'a quiet chat', telling him, 'You've looked shocking all week, Stephen, you want to look after yourself.'

'Nothing could fool Joyce,' says Gibbs, as she'd seen about all there was to see of life at its lowest, either in her rehab work or in the courts. 'I remember seeing this tiny middle-aged lady in her uniform sitting calmly in court listening to violent and offensive language, transcripts of people calling each other c—s, nothing ever seemed to faze her. She sat through twenty minutes of a video highlight package on child molester Dolly Dunne, twenty minutes of a middle-aged bloke screwing eight-year-old boys. I remember a chap I worked with who saw it was distraught for days afterwards. Obviously, there were times when she went home and had a quiet cry, but in court she could sit through just about anything.'

With the strictures of the New South Wales *Bail Act* tightened, the 1990s saw a tougher stance by the government on crime and punishment. The Carr government's push for longer sentences and truth in sentencing posed a difficulty for magistrates, who faced more complex issues around individual offenders. Before long, magistrates and judges used the chaplaincy, Joyce and Hilton especially, to help them get around the government's revved-up law-and-order campaign. The Harmers' ability to argue on ways an offender could be rehabilitated rather than locked up often allowed the justices to grant bail, their actions sanctioned through the conservative approval of two officers of the Salvation Army. In the view of many professionals at the courts, it was always the most powerless who took the flak, unfortunate ageing alcoholics or young junkies, but never the big drug dealers or the chiefs of criminal rackets. Joyce and Hilton were a way of helping justice break through the political haze.

As court chaplain, Joyce maintained a strictly professional approach; having had a lifetime of sticking to rules she believed in, this came easily to her. Major Vic Bailey says, 'Joyce has always been a person of black and white mind, there's no compromise.' With this, she had her own spontaneous emotional and instinctive responses to situations in court, where informality is tolerated but where emotion can be triggered at any moment. The tightness of court discipline is part of the way the justice system not only appears to retain its objectivity but also keeps a lid on the pressure cooker of tensions behind many cases.

'Don't catch anyone's eyes,' Joyce would say on entering a court, preparing her visitor. One time she sat in the dock with a young woman who had killed her boyfriend in a violent attack with a knife. He had slept with the girl many times, only to tell her immediately after a final liaison that he was off to live with another woman. Joyce appeared all calm, even as she whispered desperately to the woman, her lips hardly moving, 'Don't look down, keep your head up and don't weep. You are doing well.'

And then, on rare occasions, Joyce would do something quite beyond the rules. She had supported Patricia through her son Mark's trial and time on remand. Mark, a club owner, appeared in court on serious drug offences and was sent into custody. While he was on remand for eighteen months before his trial finally began, his parents and children had visited him as often as they could, but he was very stressed. 'I'm here,' Patricia remembers Joyce saying in court. 'Have a hanky.' By the time Mark appeared for his trial he had palpitations from the tension. Yet moments of human empathy filtered through the harshness of the system when Joyce was present. Mark's aunt and uncle had come to the hearing with their baby daughter. Joyce came up to them, her eyes lighting up. 'Oh, a baby,' she cooed.

'Mark has never seen her,' said Patricia.

With that, Joyce picked up the baby and took her over to the dock.

'You can't do that!' Patricia and her brother gasped.

'Watch me,' said Joyce. She passed the baby to Mark and he held his little cousin for a moment till the judge entered. At the end of his trial, Mark was sentenced to five years, with parole after three.

The trust the Harmers inspired around the courts became legendary. It is not easy to gain access to the cells in the court complexes, but Joyce always got in. In no time, the Harmers were the angels of the cells. These cubicles with their peepholes in heavy iron doors are located in the forgotten areas of court buildings, often deep in basements, and are what many who work in the courts call 'the animal cages'. As the routines of a court day go by, here lie the men and women brought into custody. They huddle on their plank benches, more often than not curled into unrecognisable heaps of clothes trying to blot out their situation. Hilton would give out small packets of Smarties to prisoners as they waited to be called to the courts, small packets of cheer dropped into desperate hands.

Winston Terracini QC remembers leading an excursion of senior students from his son's school on Sydney's lower North Shore to visit the Central Court's cells. One went on to be a lawyer. 'I thought it would be helpful if they saw a young bloke not much older than they were being locked up like an animal in the old cell complex,' says Terracini. It was early morning, before the courts began the business of the day. In the dank and antiquated cells attached to the Liverpool Street court, the group found Hilton and Joyce going along the rows, notebooks in hand, chatting to the inmates through the small grates of holes in the doors, cut off from the city just above them, taking messages for loved ones and notes about any needs that were pressing. Hilton would drop the 'h' from words and talk in a vernacular common in the cells. Joyce, with more of a firm mother's touch, was understanding but also in charge. A druggie would ask, 'Can ya ring me missus? Please tell her it's all a mistake', and Hilton would take the number down. The 'missus' would most likely be a pregnant sixteen-year-old junkie with no means of support. Joyce even carried love notes between Lucy Dudko and John Killick. Lucy had helped Killick escape from Silverwater Jail, hijacking a joyride helicopter and landing in the prison's exercise yard. 'We always had to be careful the messages we took weren't coded,' says Joyce. 'But they were just love notes between those two characters.'

One young inmate Joyce asked especially to help was hardened and dysfunctional and hated anything to do with religion. Joyce began visiting him in Long Bay. He'd abuse her, to her face. She took no offence, repeatedly telling him he had to trust her because she was all he had. Hilton was worried Joyce might be harmed, yet she insisted on continuing. 'He just needs love and support,' she would say. The court date for his hearing was set. 'Listen, mate,' she told him, 'when you get angry with those bods up there in wigs and gowns, just squeeze on my hand.' It took about six months before Joyce won him over. She sat with him in court and eventually saw him relocated to a Salvation Army farm centre for rehabilitation.

Being taken into custody is especially rough on those without family or friends to lend support from the outside. Belongings are left in flats or houses where no one returns. Landlords are left looking for rent that won't be paid. Who will pack up the contents safely before another tenant moves in? Who will store those same contents if they are packed up? Without bail, there is no going back for months or years for the accused. Joyce and Hilton came to many in custody needing the help of someone outside. They packed away household effects, handed back keys, arranged storage, collected items for those in custody, and paid off rents owing. The system assumes someone else will provide the extras. Courts, police, Correctional Services are only involved in the crime, the hearings and the punishment. The lack of support in the system even extends to prisoners with only a few bare personal items of clothing from a summer arrest. Such prisoners would often be released in the thick of winter at 6 a.m., freezing. One of the myriad acts of mercy Joyce or Hilton performed was to provide clean and warm clothing for such releases, including warm socks and footwear. Small gifts to some, the difference of a world to those deprived.

Joyce was so often linked with moments of need in trials that Charles Waterstreet came to think of her as 'a bad omen dressed as an angel'. Waterstreet doesn't lose many cases, but observed that 'if Joyce sneaked into the courtroom, near to the verdict, you felt that there might be bad news ahead'. Joyce went into the courts to do social work, says Waterstreet, and came out a lawyer.

And verdicts are all over in a flash. With the word 'guilty', the accused is convicted. Those not in custody, who have arrived at the courts each day with family and supporters, will be immediately placed in the cells. One minute free, talking with family and friends in the court corridors, and the next there is no way friends or family can get near them. There will be screams and heart-wrenching tears; all sorts of emotional breakdown can unfold. But Joyce was always a rock of calm, often to the amazement of the professionals who worked in the courts.

Stephanie, then waiting for her husband's case to be finalised, recalls how Joyce handled a woman who broke down after a verdict. 'I had no experience of court and my mind was numb. Then I could hear a woman shrieking and screaming. She'd been given a jail sentence. And there was Joyce putting her arm around the woman and saying, "Come on, come on." The convicted woman had two little children with her, one a baby in arms and the other about three. And she was about to be taken into custody, just like that. Joyce just picked up the baby and somehow stopped the woman's sobbing. She has such a motherly manner. But I can still hear the woman's screams.'

The abruptness of having a loved one taken away is shattering for families. One little boy wanted to kiss his dad, lost to him in the cells below. Joyce went over to him and told him to kiss her hand and she would take his kiss to his dad for him, which she did. 'The dad kissed my hand,' says Joyce, 'and then we talked about his circumstances.' She then went back to the little boy with a message for him from his dad.

Barrister Greg Walsh observed Joyce at work over eight years with his clients and marvelled at her instinctive sense of when someone was floundering before the court processes and how to step forward just when needed. Some of his clients were accused of crimes that gave them little or no support from the public, and Joyce would talk to them. 'People can support another human being in a variety of ways,' says Walsh. 'By being physically present, with words of encouragement, by expressing positive comments that things will work out and by wishing them the best. I'd be in trials where she turned up every day for three weeks, sitting with the accused or their family, speaking to loved ones and with everybody seeing her do that, including the complainants and the police. In other cases, I watched her show tremendous support for the victims. She withholds moral judgment and offers unconditional support.'

A religious brother from a prominent college, accused of sexual crimes, had the tabloid press frenzied for colourful reportage. A journalist from the *Sydney Morning Herald* was ripping into Greg Walsh, demanding a statement. It was all very one-sided from the media's point of view, and then

Joyce walked out with her arm supporting the accused brother. To Walsh, this took guts and faith, and he recalls the stories of the Gospels where Jesus was criticised for sitting and eating with sinners.

'The philosophy of Joyce and Hilton is to be Christlike, to do their work in the community without fear or favour or ill will,' says Walsh. 'They would support someone without being concerned that they might be criticised. I believe the fact that they are Salvationists was very significant in the role they played in the courts. They would be down at the cells on weekends. They are unique human beings. I do a lot of work with people who are psychiatrically ill, like Rene Rivkin. People like this go to prison. They get no help or treatment in prison. The only people prepared to help them are the Salvationists.'

Many come to court not knowing what to expect, and not caring either. One young woman turned up in Magistrate Jackie Milledge's court wearing hipster pants, a midriff top and a stud in her belly. It was a style of dress that could have been interpreted as showing a lack of respect for the jurisdiction of the courts. Joyce stepped forward to help the girl get clothes that would cover her up, the best she could find on hand being a large hibiscus-coloured Hawaiian shirt, bright with palm trees, out of Hilton's locker of spare clothes. Eventually, with Joyce by the girl's side, Magistrate Milledge asked the police to think carefully about whether they really wanted such a person to go to jail for an assault while drunk, an act that was silly rather than malicious. After consideration of the situation and the support the girl had from the chaplain, and chatting with Joyce, the police agreed to drop the charges. 'Joyce basically became the facilitator for the case. I recall that she might even have given the police a bit of a hug when it was all over,' says Jackie.

It was nothing for Joyce or Hilton to race off and find outfits for clients who had no idea what to wear in court. Clients in custody would come in from the jails in prison gear, saying they couldn't get their civvy clothes in time, or they weren't given them when requested, and Hilton would find a suit, even go home and get one of his own. Justice Ann Ainsley Wallace says it was taken for granted that if a client had no suitable clothes for court, one of the court officers would immediately ring Joyce. 'Sometimes clothes for court would be sent to the wrong courthouse and there would be concern that turning up in the dock in a green prison tracksuit would prejudice a jury. Joyce would be called and she'd appear with a natty suit, shirt and tie. She did a load of practical things as well as hold people's hands.'

One heavily built woman with no interest in her appearance was given a complete makeover by Joyce before her day in court — clothes, hair, makeup — so much so that she appeared quite attractive by the time she entered the court, almost a different woman. On occasion, this sort of support might cause complaints from lawyers appearing for the prosecution. Barrister Greg Walsh recalls that a few prosecuting solicitors over the years occasionally remarked on Joyce's presence in the court beside an accused as unfair, or something they would prefer not to happen. For Joyce, it was God's work she did and the person needed her.

Retired magistrate Terry Forbes says history is littered with the burnout of social workers. Joyce never let people see her emotional weariness at the situations she faced. Dave Lennon marvelled at Joyce's strength in not ever intruding into the sentencing, although it must, time and again, have been a very emotional moment for her to get through. 'I think their faith plays a big part in it,' says Lennon. 'Hilton and Joyce are very faithful people. The good life they have obviously led; their keen desire to help their fellow man; and just their burning ambition to do good. I never saw her down, but I'm sure she must have been down often.' What people saw was sometimes a careful cover-up by the Joyce and Hilton tag team. Some days the exhaustion would get the better of them. Then Hilton would pack Joyce off to bed the minute she came in the door and make her dinner, one of his 'creations', which he would take in to her on a tray. When Hilton crashed, Joyce would take over in the cells and meet or ring the people he was supporting.

There were joyful moments too, even with their prisoner work. Fred was out on $20,000 bail and in the Harmers' care awaiting trial for 'electronic fraud'. He wanted to marry Bliss, who'd flown out from London to join him. Hilton became the marriage celebrant and went with Joyce to buy them rings. They had very little means for the nuptials. Joyce took Bliss to hire a wedding gown and Hilton found a nice little church for the service, where the wedding would take place immediately following the Sunday service. The Salvation Army officer finished the service and told the congregation a wedding would follow. They all stayed on. 'Those beautiful Salvation Army people in Earlwood were all excited,' remembers Joyce. 'The organ played and we had hired a stretch limousine to take them to the Intercontinental Hotel, where we had reserved a table. When it came time to cut the wedding cake, Hilton asked the string quartet to come over to us and play. He's such a thoughtful man, my husband, a darling. Fred was convicted and did his stint. On release, he rejoined Bliss in London. We still receive letters and Christmas cards from them.'

Many of the court officers themselves can recall going to Joyce or Hilton when in need. It might be a judge with a son caught up in drugs, where Hilton would offer some of his experience in rehab to the young man while Joyce would give emotional support to his mother. Others just found themselves calling them in times of sorrow and distress. Yvonne Cornish, a court officer, recalls that Hilton took photos of her father and mother on their diamond wedding anniversary. She'd only mentioned it in passing the week before when she had seen Joyce. Hilton's photos are the only photos the family has of that special day. Shortly afterwards, Yvonne's father was admitted, dying, to Calvary Hospital. 'At around 9.30 that night Joyce walked into the hospital,' says Yvonne. 'She said, "I won't be leaving if we're here all night." ' Yvonne's father died at around eleven. Joyce watched the last moments of the elderly couple together, observing, 'That dear wife closed his eyes. To me that was a very moving thing. His eyes were not closed properly and the wife gently brushed his eyelids down and I thought how it was a beautiful finality to a married life.'

'Joyce makes a difference because she doesn't let you ask, "Why me?" ' says Alice, whose handicapped daughter was one of the victims of a serial rapist and molester who had got away with his crimes for years while running a gymnastics school. 'She gives you the facts, which I love. She doesn't embroider things. To her, the system's the system; she just keeps the person going.'

Mandy, mother of four boys, watched as her son Josh went in and out of rehab for his drug-taking. After years of marijuana, at twenty-one he started on heroin and then began doing break-and-enters. When he was taken into custody, Mandy and her husband slept for the first time in months. Later, Josh went to the William Booth clinic and spent time at the Salvation Army's Morissett farm. These days he's the father of a young child and drug-free. Mandy now says she can see that good came out of those extremely troubled years, and not just for her son. 'We used to go to chapel at Morissett and at William Booth and we loved it.' She became one of the Harmers' team of friends. 'Hilton and Joyce rang up one morning and asked if I had a few spare hours. They had to clean up a unit where someone had been shot. I just hopped in some old gear and went over.' Many like Mandy have done the same over the years.

But not all clients, as Joyce and Hilton call them, were success stories. On one occasion, Hilton drove over 100 kilometres to collect an inmate's family and another 150 kilometres to take them to the Downing Centre, where the inmate was being incarcerated. Hilton waited there for four hours while the family visited and then drove them home, getting them all dinner at McDonald's on the way. Once home, the family piled out of the car with not a word of thanks. A woman Joyce had helped provided company in turn to a person who was alone in court. The hearing lasted three days, Joyce providing all expenses for morning teas and lunches. At the end of the hearing there was no thanks. The Harmers will say that it happened all the time, but it didn't stop them. No doubt some of these people felt the Joyce and Hilton team were all just part of the court service. And to Joyce and Hilton, in many ways, that was very true.

chapter 19

NOT ALL LOAVES AND FISHES

While the articles appearing daily in the mass media depict a hardened criminal class, replete with gangster wives and children, in fact the courts are thick with little-heard stories of ordinary Australians suddenly faced with the stigma of crime. Amid it all, Joyce and Hilton became people's strength when they had nothing else.

'Hi, love,' Joyce would say, sidling up to a person waiting outside a court. 'How are you this morning?'

'Not real good,' might come the reply.

'Going to court, are you?'

'Yes.'

'Are you there for yourself or for someone else?'

'It's my son, the one over there in the blue shirt. He thinks he might be in custody today.'

Joyce would work with wherever the conversation took her. 'You just sort of go with the flow,' she says. 'If they're desperate, you comfort them. If they're joking, you join in the fun a bit. If there's anything you can offer them, whether it be tea or coffee downstairs or taking them across the road and putting them on a train and paying for their ticket, you do whatever is needed. Some will say they're okay, they have good lawyers; and I'd say that's fine, anything we can do, the Salvation Army? Some might joke: "Can you gimme a hundred bucks?", and I'd say, "Not today." If you can laugh a bit it helps.' Where needed she'd hand over her business card. 'The majority of people gave me their phone numbers willingly and I would ring them up and chat with them. They would offload and talk and talk. Some I would pray with just as they were going to sleep. It depended on the circumstances.'

For many, the idea of court or crime has been far from their minds, when all at once it happens. Families whose experience with the police might have been no more than a fine for speeding can suddenly find one of their children or a partner is arrested and charged with a serious offence. It's devastating.

Some can barely bring themselves to tell their extended families that a husband or child has been charged. Sharon's brother had been under arrest and charged for two months before his wife could summon up the courage to tell his sister and family in England. 'I don't think she knew how to,' says Sharon. 'He wasn't even on bail. He has a small business that is now in debt and will possibly be declared bankrupt. They have two young children who are still trying to get through it all.'

Helen and Ken sat in court, sick with apprehension, at the trial for the murder of their son Chris, a seventeen-year-old who had gone out one night with his mates and an uncle and never returned home. He'd been shot in Oxford Street, in the Sydney suburb of Darlinghurst, after leaving a club, by one of a gang who had intimidated Chris's group and later tried to vandalise their car. He had died quickly.

It had taken a year to bring the accused to trial. Helen was six months pregnant with what she calls her 'miracle child' when the trial began. There had been intimidation all along, beginning with their son's funeral, when some of the gang supporting the accused had arrived among the mourners and made a scene.

In court, the accused's cronies smirked and made gestures to unsettle Helen and Ken, and the accused showed his contempt, even gesturing with his hand like a gun to the head when he thought the judge wasn't looking. The defence barrister tried every tactic he could to abort the trial. Ken and Helen were extremely shaken and upset.

Then they were told about Joyce. 'She would hold my hand,' recalls Helen. '"Just ignore that," she'd say. "Don't give them the satisfaction that you are crying, that you are upset, just hold on to your dignity." When the barrister walked his client in front of us she held me rigid, telling me to stay calm. She gave me heaps of hankies and hugs. She was our strength. Because we had nobody there. Everybody seems to disappear when something like this happens.' Joyce was there the day the accused's cronies had taken all the seats in the public gallery. Going up to the officers of the court, she soon had some seats cleared for the family of the victim. When the goading got obvious she would grab the couple and hold them firm.

'She is very strong physically as well,' says Ken. 'She can hold you still, and she did, almost dragged us both out of confronting situations outside the court. But she is so calming, so emotionally strong for you.' After the trial, with the accused found guilty and sentenced to twenty-seven years, Joyce kept in contact through the appeals, the ongoing hurt and the healing. 'For six years,' says Helen, 'every Mother's Day she will come and bring chocolates. She never forgets me.'

★　★　★

In mid-1999, Joyce was overjoyed at the news that Lyndall was expecting her first child. And then came the phone call — Lyndall had been confined to bed in the last weeks of the pregnancy. She was in danger of losing the baby. Joyce dropped her work in the courts and caught a plane for the United States, her final destination Colorado. Despite being a nervous flyer, she journeyed alone, paying for the fare with a credit card and knowing that Hilton would work long hours cleaning at night to pay it off. Joyce walked into Lyndall and her son-in-law Kevin's home and took over the reins, cleaning, cooking, shopping, making sure that Lyndall had no reason to get out of bed. Through the experience, mother and daughter bonded strongly. Lyndall believes her closeness to her mother began at that time. She had grown up seeing herself as Daddy's girl and was not always as considerate of her mother as she might have been. But, now she was very sick and heavy with a child threatening to be born prematurely, her mother was not only her backstop but also a confidante and friend. They laughed together during the day so much that the doctor warned Lyndall she might bring on contractions. And when Lyndall did go into hospital with complications and dreadful haemorrhaging at 2 a.m. one morning, Joyce helped Kevin get her into the car and then went back to change the bed linen and clean up. Until the birth of Kevin Junior, on 16 September, Joyce stayed with Lyndall at the hospital: 'my live-in roommate', as Lyndall describes her. 'She got to know everyone and asked all the right questions. She helped me count down the forty-eight hours before the C-section. I remember, as they wheeled me into the operating room, she was loaded with all our belongings heading for the room next door to wait for us, no doubt praying every minute of the time.'

Out of the hospital, Joyce helped Lyndall settle into the routines of mothering, bathing little KJ at first when Lyndall felt too apprehensive about holding him in the water, showing her daughter what she should do. Hilton came to join them, and he and Joyce would take care of KJ some nights so Lyndall could sleep. The greatest joy for Lyndall was having her father do KJ's dedication. 'At any point,' says Lyndall, 'I could have lost my baby, even both of us might have died. I had complete *placenta previa*. That time I had with Mum was very special.'

Realising they would only ever see their daughter and US grandson on special occasions, mostly when Lyndall and her family might get to Sydney, or more rarely when the Harmers might manage the airfare to visit the United States, Joyce and Hilton found the trip back a sad one. But Lyndall and KJ were flourishing and Joyce's prayers had been answered.

It's hard to quantify such giving without question and even without having to be asked. And always with no fear of taking the initiative. Joyce is known to not ask how, but just to do instinctively. One morning, aboard a Sydney bus, Joyce and Hilton were coming to work in the court when a baby vomited, leaving a vile smell. At the Marrickville shops, the bus driver pulled over, got out and began talking on his mobile. When Hilton asked why they had stopped, the driver said they were not moving with that smell. He would get another bus. Joyce wasn't impressed. She took off, going in and out of several shops, finally emerging with a bucket, mop and a can of air freshener. She handed the bucket and mop to Hilton for the clean-up, while she talked to the amused passengers and sprayed the air freshener around. The bus driver was delighted and asked for their business cards. A few weeks later, Hilton and Joyce received a letter of appreciation from Sydney Buses and a free pass each for one return journey to the city.

Joyce returned from Colorado to a backlog of people in court needing her. The cases filled the lists each morning of the week and, in her usual way, she went through them with Carol Steele, the sheriff in charge of juries, who supervised twenty-five court officers. 'Joyce kept up-to-date with all matters listed in the District Court,' says Carol. 'Court officers would advise me on the volatile or sensitive matters in the courts, where family members were hostile or there was a potential problem, or where there were persons on trial that were upset.' Joyce's instinct was often to attend sexual assault cases and those involving women, but not always. She had long since balked at nothing.

Many recall how Joyce, on her rounds of the courts, would approach them in the most natural way. Sue had come through five weeks of a trial in which her husband Peter was charged with a white-collar crime of which they both believed he would be found innocent. She had endured day after day, spending a lot of time in a small room because she was also giving evidence. It was late in the afternoon, after the courts had closed towards the end of the trial, when she saw Joyce walking towards her.

'I thought, oh dear, is she going to be a bit pushy, telling me God loves me and all that sort of thing? And she came up to me and said, "Oh I really love your shoes!" And I just said, "Thank you." She said, "Do you need to contact me?" I replied, "Not at the moment, but I might need you tomorrow."

She gave me her card and said, "I'll look for you tomorrow." Literally, that was it. Off we went. After that she'd come and sit with us while the jury was out. An awful time. It was terrible.' The verdict was 'guilty' and Sue was floored. 'They just take you away,' she says five years later as if it were happening all over again. Outside the courtroom Joyce appeared from nowhere. Immediately noting the distress, she went to see Peter in the holding cells, taking messages from Sue and returning with messages from Peter. 'I was devastated,' says Peter, 'but I was more worried about Sue.'

For Charles Waterstreet, Joyce was the guiding hand for so many in the New South Wales justice system. 'Joyce was the buffer zone between the brutality of the State and the reality of the sentencing. Time and again, but for Joyce, the suicide rate would have quadrupled. She nursed the poor fish through to the open sea. Words cannot portray how savage the sentencing of people is, just with the words "guilty" or "not guilty", and people are not in control of their emotions at these times.'

Waterstreet watched as Joyce corralled the highly emotional family of a Lebanese man who had come in guilty on two counts but innocent of the first. So they had heard 'not guilty' and must have sighed with relief for a second, only to have their feelings go wild with despair at the next two 'guilty' verdicts. They grabbed at the accused, trying to stop him from being taken. His eighty-two-year-old father, shocked and horrified, was what Waterstreet describes as 'quelched like a Wettex going across a bar'. But then Joyce came round to them, got them together, and let them mourn with her, and somehow they all quietened slowly. At such times, Joyce would intercede with the Correctional Services officers to let the family have a little more time to say goodbye.

Barrister Greg Stanton marvels at the impact Joyce and Hilton could have on a court full of tension. 'The Harmers brought tranquillity to the most stormy and tumultuous circumstances. What propels them is their faith, and it's an inescapable conclusion — even for those that are not practising Christians nor even understand Christianity — that no earthly power, no worldly concept and no material possession could inspire people the way they are inspired.'

Ann Brown, the officer in charge of the Darlinghurst courts, recalls the case of a young boy accused of murder. 'There was a child who had killed someone. A child of twelve. The Harmers were here. That little kid was sitting there, playing, not a clue what the business around him meant at all. That was scary, and even scarier for the barrister. It's a closed court with juveniles, but Joyce and Hilton came along with the families. When we had verdicts, I'd ring Joyce. Because the minute you say to the cops that there might be problems they'd be on the job but it could go either way. Having Joyce and Hilton there meant you were saved a big blow-up.'

Courts see a lot of upset but prefer dead calm. Magistrate Jackie Milledge is not a mother and admits to finding all children wild. In court, Milledge always found Joyce's effect on babies miraculous. 'There'd be a child screaming in court, and Joyce would be there, and the next minute she'd be rocking the baby and the screams would stop.' Two little boys in school uniforms spent a whole day with Joyce on one occasion. The father, needing to appear in court on charges the boys' mother knew nothing about, brought them with him. Perhaps he thought their presence in court might soften his image, or perhaps he just couldn't manage to take them to school and turn up for court at the same time.

'Two ladies came to me one day,' recalls Joyce. 'A baby had been born to an addict and the baby was addicted. But, of course, the mother was not capable of looking after it. I was able to find them advice as to how they could use Legal Aid to get the baby passed to someone in the family who could care for it. Sometimes, though, it wasn't possible to help. I sat in court with a mother who had been struck with postnatal depression and thrown her baby over a banister. The baby didn't live, but I was able to support the mother, who was in a very stressed state. I've had postnatal depression and I know exactly how it felt.'

She and Hilton sometimes accompanied the sheriffs as they did evictions, a task that can be a mean justice but one required by the law. Joyce recalls visiting an elderly lady who refused to pay a backlog of rent. She had locked herself in her bedsit. 'I knocked on the door,' says Joyce, 'and said, "It's the Salvation Army, would you like to open the door for me?" And she said, "No, I don't like the Salvation Army either!" So I thought, oh well, there you go, I've done my dash already.' Eventually the tenant had to be carried from the flat. Joyce found her a bed for a night with friends and the next morning, in pouring rain, moved her to alternative accommodation. But in time she was back in her old bedsit, had changed the locks and paid the rent she owed.

Court officer Richard Wilson can only sing the Harmers' praises when he reflects on the contribution they made in the courts. But he also acknowledges, with his own personal experience of years in the courts, that some cases defy any sort of crusade. A couple Joyce tried to help, supporting them through their court appearances and advising them from time to time outside, were involved in the mess of a marriage breakdown that had led to violence on the part of the wife's lover. The case, however, was one that said much about the inured caprice of some. The wife had spent time with her lover at her parents' home, then the boyfriend had become violent, which exposed her trysts and led her to take out an Apprehended Violence Order (AVO) against him. Joyce had sat with her at the hearing, holding her hand and offering her comfort. Meanwhile, the wife resumed her relationship with her husband. In time, however, she returned to the lover, who subsequently torched the husband's home where her children were living. By the end of it, even Joyce admitted to not being able to influence some situations for the better. Not everyone is capable of change. And this was something Joyce had to accept as she moved around the courts. 'They had to pull back on expectations a lot of times,' said one journalist who watched them in action around the courts for years. 'There is a limit to what anyone can do in so many cases.'

A bad business partnership brought Sandra into contact with Joyce during a long period of court action that left Sandra with debts, and out of which she crawled by sheer hard work in a new business. 'I was in the witness box and my husband saw this tiny lady with a beaming smile coming up to him,' says Sandra. 'She was so upright, he said he thought she had on a starched bra. He told her that I was in the witness box and he was worried about me. She pushed her way into the court and came out shortly after. "Oh yes, she's crying," Joyce said, "but don't worry about that. She'll be okay." When I came out, she handed me her card and said if I ever needed her, day or night, just to ring. And I did need her, desperately, one night. Our younger son was trying to kill himself. Nothing to do with my business problems. And I rang her.' Joyce got the son into the William Booth clinic for ten months. 'She saved his life,' says Sandra.

In some tragedies, the best to hope for was some sort of reconciliation, like the case where the driver of an overloaded truck had not been able to brake before ploughing into a number of other vehicles, which then caught fire. A ten-month-old boy was burned so badly that he died shortly afterwards in hospital. His mother had escaped with one child, only to hear the screams of her baby strapped in the back of the car. 'It was the sort of brief,' says Greg Stanton, 'that when you read the police statements from witnesses it brought you to tears.'

In the court Joyce stood by both sides, but particularly the driver of the truck and his wife, who underwent enormous stress. The media attacked the driver mercilessly and his wife sobbed while giving evidence, saying to the parents of the dead baby, 'Every night we light a candle for your son and we are so sorry for the pain we have caused you.' Joyce took the wife's arm as they left the court to face the glare of the media. After the trial, at which the driver of the truck was found guilty, Joyce sat with his wife and the parents of the baby who had been burned to death and they made peace with each other.

'The courts are a cruel place,' says Stanton. 'There are no winners. People are deprived of breadwinners and family members. And it's a brutalising institution, jail, which expects rehabilitation but in most cases strengthens the criminal element. But I guess that also strengthened the resolve of Joyce and Hilton.'

In February 1999, a woman had abducted her fifteen-month-old son from his adoptive parents, stabbed him and thrown his body into a dam. It was a brutal murder by a very disturbed person. Her strict Italian parents and brothers had forced her to give the child up for adoption when they discovered she was pregnant, saying that it was an embarrassment to the family. After he was adopted out, the baby had never been referred to again. Taking the tragic background into account, Justice Graham Barr surprised most people by giving the mother a two-year suspended sentence. Joyce Harmer supported the woman throughout her trial, from the day Hilton rang her from Central Court to tell her about the case. Joyce sat in the dock with the accused and then asked the Correctional Services officers if she could go with the woman into the tunnel to the cells. The woman had gripped Joyce and hugged her hard, so desperate was she for the feeling of support. This was a person despised. After her trial, the woman left the Supreme Court holding on to Joyce in the face of a mob of media.

The brutal effects of a court and jail experience can take years for many relatives to get over. Joyce would keep in touch for a while and then gently let go as people found the strength to face life again. Vera, whose husband served some four years in jail while she tried to maintain the family home and a livelihood in one of Sydney's garden suburbs, will always regard Joyce as someone who became her friend. 'From the first day when she said to me, "He's not the only one", I felt I could cope a little better. It's something you never think you'll have to deal with. Joyce and I sometimes have lunch in the city; back then [right after his sentencing] it was probably every two or three months. Many times I would think of ringing Joyce but eventually you have got to get over it yourself. And as I did, she wouldn't ring me so often. Once Hilton tried to coax me to confront the courts, to scare off the demons, by telling me about the Christmas crib and saying I should come and have a look. And Joyce said, "Oh no, Vera can't cope with going in there", but I thought to myself that I had to do it one day so we went to have a look and I was fine.'

The night Sue's husband Peter was sentenced, Joyce and Hilton were waiting for them outside their house when Sue arrived home with her two adult children. 'They came in with us and we ended up around the piano, singing. My daughter is musical. It was quite late but they waited for us and it made us feel almost happy for a little while. They came all that way and probably hadn't even been home.'

Hester, mother of two young boys, continued to resist the idea that their lives would be tainted by the fact that her husband was doing time. She found it too difficult to ask for help and rejected any suggestion that she might develop the prisoner's wife mentality. So Joyce worked through others around Hester to keep in touch. 'They are just innocent victims,' says Hester's sister. 'It's much harder on the prisoner's family, and they're not even the instigator of the crime.' Hester's husband had pleaded guilty in the end, and she was spared any court appearance whatsoever. But keeping family life intact meant years of pain and adjustment, with long trips to visit Dad in prison. After being attacked inside, Hester's husband was moved to the protection of Kirkconnell prison farm. His children became used to giving up whole days of weekends to visit Dad.

'Three hours there and three hours back; that's how the boys spend their weekends,' their aunt reflects. 'Sitting in a car, visiting their father. At eight and ten you don't want to be doing that so they get very angry and quite resentful. And it's very mixed feelings when it's your dad.' Hester's husband, to spare her as much trauma as possible, will not speak about his life in jail, so while visits to see him are emotionally charged for Hester and their sons, the father always puts on a brave face, seeming entirely philosophical about his dilemma. Keeping conversation flowing is hard, the boys growing old beyond their years in these awkward and forced meetings. 'It will leave a lot of scars,' says their aunt.

Part of Joyce and Hilton's work was to make known to people the many support groups they could tap into as their experience of the courts and custodial sentences took hold of their lives. Joyce would refer inmates to the work of the Karios program, available to each prison or correctional centre through the chaplaincy service. Volunteers working for Karios are vetted by Correctional Services and begin by attending eight weekends of education and training. Volunteers are then assigned inmates they follow up — even after discharge. They especially help those who have no contact visits. There was also the halfway-house program run by the Salvation Army, which assists with rehabilitation of discharged prisoners. It's a strict program, often used by those convicted of offences relating to alcohol or drugs. The program has helped many, including some who have missed out on literacy skills and have therefore been unable to start any purposeful employment. It gets many into jobs, allowing former inmates to begin productive and effective working lives.

Joyce often found herself being called out to domestic violence situations to help a mother and her children. On one occasion, Cathy, the wife of a court officer, rang the Harmers after a cry for help from a friend. The woman had taken the rough of her husband's brutality over years. Then, after one alarming incident, she grabbed a few belongings and put them into backpacks and ran with her children to a new address. But they had nothing in the house in the way of furniture, bedding or cooking implements, not even any heating, and it was bitterly cold. Joyce told Cathy to go to the mother and tell her that the Harmers would arrange for them to stay in a motel for a few days while furniture, bedding and other goods could be collected for the house. The family were freezing and huddled together when Cathy went back to them, with one baby asleep covered by nothing more than a towel. They relocated to a motel and Hilton and Joyce then made plans to move the family's possessions while the father was not at home. Cathy and her husband went along to help.

'I had heard of the Salvation Army so many times,' says Cathy, 'but never before did I see it in action. Joyce and Hilton had so many contacts, people on the spot to help. It happened like clockwork. My friend and I packed and Hilton turned up with a truck and some guys from Foster House. There was even a friend of Hilton's in a car, watching the street in case the husband came home. Then, while the men loaded the truck and moved everything, we went to take out an AVO against the husband. Joyce's daughter-in-law minded my friend's children for the whole day. At the new house, the men unloaded furniture, rewired things, reassembled beds, the lot — and all in a few hours. The husband's currently in prison, and the family will never be completely safe when he is released. But they are okay now, thanks to Joyce and Hilton.'

Being able to put up money for extras like a few nights in a motel for a mother and her children made a wonderful difference in work with the needy. It was money the Harmers valued and it came from a handful of benefactors who supported their work and made sure they would always have enough to make the phone calls, buy the meals, and provide the clothing and sundry items for a basic new start in life.

'We managed,' says Joyce, 'with the help of some very wonderful people who supported us in a marvellous way over the years. We had loaves and fishes. We turned water into wine! It all happened. They were friends of ours, personal friends, who would not leave us without anything we needed. And there were certain things the Salvation Army would reimburse us for when we provided the receipts.'

It was a two-thousand-year-old message from the Christian Gospel played out yet again in a modern setting. But it was a phenomenon that left some asking why it had to be left to the sterling character and conviction of a couple of wonderful people when governments and taxpayers should, and could if there were a desire to do it, support all citizens in trouble. Why were prisoners released without a basic kit? Why was it left to people like Joyce and Hilton to provide small amounts of money to pay for fares on release, to bring tea and coffee to the cells in court complexes while prisoners waited out the days for their cases to be heard, to offer their mobile phones for a call to a loved one in a desperate moment?

Late at night, Hilton would often tune in to John Kerr's midnight-to-dawn radio program. He'd listen to the cries for help of voices down the end of the line who from time to time rang in. And then he'd ring in and a lot of times make a difference. So much so that John Kerr got in touch off-air with both Hilton and Joyce and worked out how he and the program could make use of their willingness to help whenever they could. 'At two, three, four or even five o'clock in the morning I have detected people who have been in serious trouble and we've contacted Joyce and Hilton. They have invariably got themselves out of bed, depending on the seriousness of the problem, and gone to help. If people are outside Sydney they've been able to refer them to the Salvation Army wherever it was.'

Barrister Greg Stanton sees Joyce and Hilton's winning combination at the courts in the light of having grown up a Catholic and of his understanding of the New Testament message. 'Their motivation is Christ, and they will tell you that, sunup to sundown. Their faith never wavers and they always believe they are doing what Christ would do in any situation they find themselves in. They don't cast stones; their love is not discriminatory; they don't take sides; their compassion is equal and binding. They are beautiful, patient people.'

After seven years, Joyce was regarded as a first-class court counselling professional. In 2002, however, she found herself taking on the first of two cases that would test both her faith and her non-judgmental compassion.

chapter 20

CLOSED COURT

'Who is this Salvation Army woman in every picture?' queried court reporter Cindy Wockner's editor after days of trying to find new angles on a story to which the *Daily Telegraph* was devoting pages each week.

'That's Joyce Harmer. She's doing nothing different from what she's been doing for years at the Downing Centre.'

'Can we do a story about her?' asked the editor.

'At that point,' says Cindy, 'everybody started doing stories on Joyce and the way she was looking after the girls in the rape trials.'

Joyce Harmer had been at the Downing Centre for seven years. She was a court veteran, often spotted holding tightly on to the arm of a defendant as they left the courts. In photos she was ubiquitous, small, grey-haired. Often editors cropped her out of the picture. Television footage was momentary, the commentary focused on the accused or the story of the crime. Then came the notorious Sydney rape trials of 2002, and editors started to notice.

These trials caused the sort of sensation welcomed only by the media. Four trials conducted over several weeks in a closed court brought together three female victims and a number of accused of Lebanese background. The pack rapes had been brutal and unprecedented: some of the perpetrators never apprehended, girls literally plucked off trains and out of shopping centres, with members of the gangs called to the scenes of the would-be crimes by mobile phone hook-ups. Although both sides attempted to suppress or play down the race element in the cases, evidence given at the trials made it clear that during the rapes the attackers had used a heap of abusive language laced with racial slurs to demean their victims. The girls weren't just called 'sluts', but also 'Aussie pigs'. At least one attacker declared, 'I'm going to f—k you Leb style,' and asked, 'How does Leb c—k taste? I bet it tastes better than Aussie c—k.'

With just snippets of what the rapes involved published in the media, they became more than brutal crimes in the minds of the public. Australia, some said, just didn't want to know about a familiar phenomenon in many Western countries, where Muslim youths had increased in number. The French even had a name for it. They called it 'tournante', meaning 'take your turn' — a young white woman, the girlfriend of a Muslim man or picked up by one, is taken to an isolated spot, where she is given over to a pack of mates who rape her one after the other. Some blamed Muslim intolerance of the way women dress in the West; others saw it as inexcusable, racially motivated violence. Stories of the growing incidence of such pack rapes spread across Sydney from 2000 to 2002. A few commentators claimed that serious racial problems had hijacked Sydney's Western Suburbs, where a cluster of Middle Eastern immigrants were settled and where the minarets of mosques were becoming as familiar as the spires of Christian churches. In August 2003, a rape trial of three Muslim men resulted in lenient sentences and special comment from Judge Megan Latham that there was no evidence of a racial link. This only further inflamed the debate. Could the peaceful multicultural society that had welcomed the 2000 Olympic Games be sustained? Or had the doomsayers, like the racially motivated political aspirant Pauline Hanson, been right? Had the clash of cultures arrived for Sydney residents in the form of Lebanese gang rapes?

Joyce Harmer had little of these political implications on her mind when, in June 2002, when she was approached by Crown prosecutor Margaret Cunneen, who asked if she would be present at the trials of four men about to begin in a closed court at the Downing Centre. 'I knew my boundaries,' says Joyce. 'And generally, unless you are a carer of the victim or have some special reason, you are not allowed into a closed court.' Joyce replied that she wasn't planning to.

'Oh, that's wrong, you're the very person who should be in there,' came the Crown prosecutor's reply. 'I want you to be in mine. To support the girls.'

Margaret cleared the way, through presiding Judge Finnane, for Joyce Harmer to be in the closed courtroom. There was no objection from the lawyers, who knew Joyce well from past cases. Then the prosecutor introduced Joyce to the girls. They met in the small room off the side of Court LG4 where the trials would be held — just two of the girls, their mothers, Joyce and Margaret Cunneen. 'This is Major Joyce Harmer,' the Crown prosecutor told them. 'She will be with you during the trials, inside the court.'

The crimes of the four accused in these gang rapes were brutal. Two girls, seventeen and eighteen, had been lured from a Chatswood shopping centre to Greenacre, where they were repeatedly raped and forced to perform oral sex on eight men. Then there was the eighteen-year-old, lured from a train and subjected to violation and rape over six hours, at first in a Bankstown car park toilet by four men, then at the Bankstown Trotting Club by three others, then at Chullora, where she had an industrial hose turned on her in the cold of winter, was held at gunpoint and raped again by another five men before being released. The group who had taken her from the train had played along like friends for a while, and then the heavy groping started. One of the men took the girl's mobile phone when a friend rang her suddenly. He told the caller she would be home within twenty minutes. Then he had switched the phone off and put it down his pants. At a nearby toilet block, the taunting started: 'You won't get your phone back until you f— me.' She'd replied, 'F— the phone, I'm going home.' The first rape took place shortly after that, inside the toilet block. More rapes and assaults then followed from the other men. When the girl fell to her knees during the assaults, one of the men forced her to perform oral sex. Then the men left; the girl staggered out of the toilet block and found a woman approaching her, asking for money. Thinking the woman would help her, the girl gave the woman money for a taxi. The woman led her to some young men standing near a black car. The girl thought she was safe and they would take her to the police. In the car, though, she found herself under attack again. And so it went on for six hours, cat and mouse, the attacks becoming more violent, the violations of the girl more extreme. At around 10.30 p.m., she was left outside Lidcombe station to find her own way home. Her mobile phone had been returned, but the gang leader had demanded her phone number and rang her several times in the next hour — threatening her if she went to the police.

Joyce recalls that she approached the girls as she had other clients over years. Like a human horse-whisperer, Joyce has instincts in her methods and an ability to communicate with troubled people that defy theories. Crown prosecutor Margaret Cunneen explained what Joyce did in the courts and how long she had been doing it, and said she thought having Joyce with them could help them through the trials. It was Margaret who advised the girls and their mothers that Joyce could make a difference to the stress about to hit them. 'They thought the world of Margaret,' says Joyce, 'so anything she suggested was great. So they were happy.'

Joyce admits to having no apprehension about being with the distressed girls after her years in drug and alcohol rehab and with traumatised people. 'It wasn't anything new to me,' she says. The girls were dreading what was coming, although at that point they wouldn't have had any idea how hard it would really be, even though Margaret Cunneen had briefed them.

At the initial meeting with Joyce, there were also a few first impressions to overcome. Dressed in the Salvation Army uniform, she could appear more than just a person who would support the girls. As for many who had watched Joyce approaching them in court, the uniform could trigger both positive and negative connotations. One of the girls remembered being in Salvation Army Sunday school. The other, known only to the public as 'Miss C', was of Koori background. She had no previous connection with organised religion. The uniform came across as strange; what was she to expect? But it was only a small hurdle and it wasn't long before Joyce had assured 'Miss C' that she was merely a person there to support the young women. They could call on her day and night for anything they needed. She would be with them and their families in court. They only had to say the word and she would find what they required, whether it was a glass of water or a box of tissues, or a hug, or someone to sit with while they sobbed so wretchedly the sound went through walls. She would be a presence so they would know that they were not alone. Joyce's very instinctive movement around the courts exuded a seasoned experience that told the girls she knew where to find whatever was needed. 'At night I would pray to God,' Joyce recalls, 'to ask that I would be sensitive at all times to their feelings, that I could be truly their friend and know when I might be offending them, know what I should not say and what I should.'

The stories the girls told were graphic, but evidence had to be tested and the minutiae of the acts and events on the days of the rapes gone over by prosecution and defence counsel. The girls would have to be examined in the dock for accuracy and credibility and each case treated as a separate happening, so that no evidence from one rape could affect the judgment on another. One girl was in the witness stand for the whole of a week. The rapes had occurred on three separate dates in 2000: 10 August (two complainants), 12 August (one complainant) and 30 August (one complainant). There were accused common to all.

In a paper entitled 'Prosecuting Sexual Assault — The Complexities and Difficulties', dated 11 November 2004, Margaret Cunneen pointed out how uniquely in sexual assault cases the shame and humiliation of the crime engulf the complainant as much as and sometimes even more than the perpetrators. *The unlikelihood of pleas of guilty means that persons alleging sexual assault are almost always required to give evidence in court and muster resources necessary to give an account of the events, maintain it when challenged and continue to be composed throughout searching cross-examination about their lives (some of which may do them no credit) with which the accused is well-acquainted because of the association between them,* wrote Cunneen. To which she added, *Sexual assault trials inevitably involve a broad-ranging and sustained attack on the major witness's credit.*

The trials went on for three months. Joyce remembers that she had to put much of her other work on hold or catch up in breaks from the closed court. 'I was always loaded with hankies,' she says. 'When they needed water I would get it; coffee or tea, the same. I also gave them their space. When they were distressed during court breaks, and they were in the anteroom, I would stand back. If I felt that I was uncertain of what I should do in a moment then I wouldn't move near them. You need to allow personal space to people who just want their family around them. So then I would leave the little anteroom and stand outside with the detectives and the police officers and the sheriffs, but I was nearby should they need me.'

Court LG4 is specifically designed for the trials of multiple accused and as a closed court. The public gallery at the back is separated from the main courtroom by a thick panel of shaded glass. There are just two rows of chairs. During the rape trials, the public gallery could hold only the families of the victims and accused, so the media used a tiny room off the entry foyer of the court, where they could listen but not see the trial inside. The atmosphere in the public gallery, Joyce recalls, was ugly, even poisonous at times, with tensions running high as families, bitterly divided, occupied the small space together. None of which was helped by the behaviour of the accused, who laughed and jeered at the girls from behind their glass-panelled cubicle, diagonally across the courtroom from the public gallery. This would intensify as the girls came to the witness stand, when the accused would twist their microphones and tear up their paper cups to grab the court's attention. Time and again Judge Finnane cautioned them and brought them to order.

During the lunch breaks, the girls would go to a special safe room on another level and Joyce would go to her office or to a rest room and have a weep over the whole trauma. These girls just wanted the ordeal to be over. Throughout the giving of evidence she watched the pain on their faces. No one could give the details of the evidence but them, and it left Joyce feeling helpless as never before. 'For me it was horrific, simply horrific sitting through it all. I had seen a lot but these were gang rapes and it was more than I had experienced. Being with the girls was part of that, how much they suffered. These trials and the Kathleen Folbigg trial affected me like no others. I always kept dead calm in the courts or I would be of no use to anyone. Later, I would fall on Hilton when I went home.'

The tension was palpable across the court. The trauma for the victims was absolute. But the families of the four gang members were also undergoing all the stresses known to other families Joyce had supported over years. Disbelief, loyalty, anger all played their part. And shame at what these young men were being accused of. Added to that, a sense of cultural divide, that feeling of being outcast as alien by a population they had tried to join. Margaret Cunneen watched as Joyce, at times, would slip across to the families of the accused, much as she had always done in other trials. 'I noticed that sometimes she was there with the families, the innocent members of the families of the accused,' recalls Margaret. 'And she spoke with them, she held their hands, put her arms about them. And they welcomed that. They were obviously not from her faith and were wearing the symbols of other faiths, but they still recognised her as a person of spiritual authority. Someone who was kind and compassionate to the core, someone with them in a completely non-judgmental way, who was different from any other functionary of the courts. Joyce was there, as always, to give the love of God through her actions to everyone — and not to take sides.'

Joyce's spiritual essence had also quickly touched the victim who had no religious background as the tension mounted and she needed strength. 'At one time,' says Margaret Cunneen, 'I saw "Miss C" with Joyce, and they were together seeking God's help or the help of some spiritual being, help for her to have the courage to go on. Joyce does that without offending, she never proselytises.'

Joyce was there at all times when the girls were in court. Court journalist Cindy Wockner believes it is a testament to Joyce's reputation that Judge Finnane had allowed her to sit in a closed court. Courts, like royalty, do not bend the rules easily. Yet Wockner remembers the judge commented from the bench that Joyce was a respected member of the court and he thought it was a good idea for her to be present.

The court was secured tightly during the trials. Correctional Services officers and police from the task force in charge of the investigation were in attendance. Many waited outside in the small foyer adjacent to the media room or the room where the girls could go for a break if they collapsed during their evidence. It was an intense experience. Joyce noticed individuals being affected by the unrelenting experience of the trials, one detective taking leave afterwards, another moving from Sydney to live in a quieter location, one disturbed by the thought of the world his own daughters were living in.

Judge Finnane presided throughout, a measured figure looking down from the bench, the witness stand a little below him, the jury along the wall beside that to his far right and the accused on the opposite wall to his left behind their protective glass panel. In front of him, the prosecution lawyers on the jury side and the defence lawyers on the side of the accused stood and sat making their arguments, directing their questions, haggling over points of law. If the judge looked across the heads of the barristers and their attendant solicitors to the back of the court, he would catch sight of the troubled families behind the glass, and directly in front of that, in the far left corner of the courtroom, a small woman in navy and white whom he knew as Major Joyce Harmer. From the witness stand, as the defence questioned the girls and tried to put them off balance, the girls would be facing left, directly in line with the accused, who sat smirking and gesturing, albeit behind shadowed glass.

'Those girls were very brave,' recalls Joyce. 'They had to sit in the witness box, which put them eyeball to eyeball with the defendants, unless they chose to look slightly away. There they sat, judge, court staff to record everything, the court officer who does the running about, the bar tables in front, the sheriff at the door next to the dock. When any of the girls got distressed I stood, and the mother came out and around very quickly. I was told the accused smirked at them a lot, making fun of them, but I didn't see that, as I had my eyes on the person I was there to care for. Those girls were very brave, just a few steps away from faces that they knew from a terrible experience, hearing the events in graphic detail all over again. I believe they hurt and re-hurt every day of those trials. They could well have given up halfway.'

Cindy Wockner first noticed Joyce's involvement in the trials when one of the girls became particularly distressed during the proceedings. With court closed, the media had no pictures of what was occurring, apart from what the words they heard might conjure up.

Joyce had told the girls to ask for a break whenever they felt they needed one. And they did — particularly 'Miss C', the girl with the Koori background, who was determined never to give the slightest hint she was close to breaking down. 'It was horrible listening to it,' recalls Cindy Wockner. 'The most gruesome part of it was the distress the girls themselves were under giving their evidence. They were so upset. And worst, for me, was not actually what happened in the court but what I heard from one of the girls outside. This girl would never get upset in front of her attackers. She would simply say, "Can I please have a break?" And then she would come out of court with Joyce and go into a tiny room next to where I was sitting, and she would just absolutely howl, almost like an animal in pain, a dog that has just been knocked by a car. She was so distressed. Hearing it through the wall was the most disturbing thing I've ever experienced, because I was hearing the pain she was feeling, pain she did not want the court and her assailants to know about. And there wasn't much Joyce could say to her, because she was in the middle of giving her evidence. I know that, because I've talked with the girl about it. But Joyce would be there with the nicely laundered hankies, giving her a bear hug, letting her sob it out. And always with her mobile phone in case she needed to call someone. That was her role. She was a tower of strength.'

'There are no winners' is a common saying about violent crimes that come to court. Margaret Cunneen, playing her part as prosecution counsel, could also observe the accused as pent-up, young and angry, at times a little like caged animals — not, as she adds, in a pejorative sense, but because of having to endure sitting in the confined space of the dock, four of them with their own rivalries and divisions, their own squabbles about blame and cause. Behind the glass of the public gallery, their friends and relatives came to give their support, and people who weren't so friendly signalled and gestured to them. Like the women complainants, they were rookies in court, not understanding the routines and pedantries and having to come back week after week to face the tedious proceedings. 'They tended at times to let out some vituperative sort of bile,' says Margaret, 'some of it directly offensive to the complainants, those who said the accused had sexually assaulted them.'

This added to the burden of court for the young women. In the witness box, they also had to endure full exposure to the usual onslaught from the defence counsel. 'I was crying and screaming,' one girl was saying.

'No, you weren't, you were moaning with pleasure, you were enjoying it,' the defence lawyer said back to her. And as he said these words, her attackers just a few feet away looked on as if to agree.

On one occasion, the girl who refused to cry in the court decided she had had enough. 'I'm not going back in,' she told Joyce. 'I'm just not going back to put up with any more of that.' She had undergone six hours of unspeakable abuse and rape two years before and it was as if she were going through it all again with no one believing her, while the men accused, whom she knew had done it, looked on, smirking, enjoying her trauma. Joyce comforted her, let her anger cool, gave her some time to think and shared a prayer. Composed after a break, she went back in for further cross-examination.

Joyce herself almost needed to flush the day's hearing from her head the minute she got home. The crudity, the bile, the physical violence, the violation of such young women. Going home on the train early one evening she found herself watching a young girl and a male companion holding hands and flirting together. She remembers thinking, 'This is the train they took the girls from, the same line.' As she got out she tapped the girl on the shoulder and said, 'You might think you're okay but do be careful.'

Sexual assault cases are made more complex now, partly because of the use of electronic and physical surveillance, listening devices, phone records and the like. The trials of the gang rapists in 2002 went on long after the complainants had given their evidence, with the accused still in the dock. Denying that they had been involved was useless when mobile phone records could pinpoint their location at a precise time. The gang had made frequent use of their mobile phones both during the rapes and later, one suspect leaving a police station and ringing a mate who had also been involved. A phone interception of the call was then used to implicate both the suspect and the mate called. But these more thoroughly policed investigations also make sexual assault trials more complex and drawn out. With each area of evidence under legal scrutiny, there is increasing argument over the use of such evidence, whether it is fair to admit it, whether it has been obtained legally or illegally and so on. Appeals against a verdict can be successful over minute amounts of fact rather than the whole. The letter of the law then extends the tentacles of the courts, regardless of whether justice is done or even seen to be done.

The four men were found guilty. On the day of the sentencing, Judge Finnane took his time. At 12.30 p.m. the court was adjourned while the judge determined the length of the sentences. After 3 p.m., when the court was due to resume, the public gallery was full and the girls waited behind its pane of glass, watching the bench and taunted by jibes from supporters of the rapists. It was not until 4.15 p.m. that the judge took his seat and began his summing up. Just before 5 p.m., a sentence of fifty-five years was imposed on the ringleader of the gang, who screamed an obscenity at the judge, his mother collapsing in front of him and his girlfriend running from the court.

For the victims it was relief and joy. They had withstood the weeks of the trials and won. Outside the courts they beamed, with Joyce beside them. The verdict resonated in the columns of scribes and critics and great slabs of the city's *Daily Telegraph* and *Sydney Morning Herald*. As if a bottle had been uncorked, air breathed into the story, debate sharpened by a sudden freedom in the media for frank discussion of what had happened. And the photos came out, large and bold, of Joyce Harmer smiling and walking with the three joyful figures of the young women, faces still blurred to hide their identities. That Salvation Army woman from the courts was now a media item.

'It was a nice bit of recognition,' says Stephen Gibbs. 'I'd take the mickey out of her a bit after that, saying she had become a bit of a star, her head on the television or in the papers. For those of us who had watched her for years, it was a little bemusing, as if she was some recent discovery when she'd been there nearly a decade doing the same thing every day. Here was this angel in the court who seemed to appear out of nowhere. In fact she's quite an earthy creature, not some saintly type. She's definitely no shrinking violet.'

Ask Joyce how it felt being the focus of media attention and she'll say it was nothing different from any other day in the courts. She had given her time to the girls as a priority when they needed her throughout the rape trials. That didn't mean she neglected others. She was well aware of the many people who knew the girls and came to support them: family, detectives, Margaret Cunneen. 'A good crowd, good friends,' is how she describes the group around the young women. Joyce never let the glare of the spotlight distract for a minute. 'I couldn't be occupied with socialising, all the chit-chatting as if it was the only case. I had thirty-two courts to run around and keep track of.' So when there was a crowd of supporters gathering at the morning and lunch breaks, Joyce would zip off to check the other courts. Just as she had always done.

On the day of the sentencing for the gang rapes in August 2002, as the media scrum followed the girls away from the court, one could imagine Joyce in the background saying a quiet prayer of thanks to the One who for her made it all possible, then ringing Hilton to say she was finished at the Downing Centre for the day and arranging where to meet him. As she waited for Hilton she would have been checking her mobile phone message bank to see what calls were there waiting for an answer.

chapter 21

MRS FOLBIGG

Some time late in 2002, the Harmers received a request from a legal team, led by defence barrister Peter Zahra, preparing for a trial to be held in April 2003. Their client was to be tried for the murder of her four young children, deaths that had occurred over a period of ten years. Her name was Kathleen Folbigg and she had no blood relatives. Her only family, both adopted and in-laws, as well as most of her friends, now shunned her because of the charges of murder hanging over her. She had no one who could be her support during the trial. Estranged from Craig Folbigg, the father of the children she was accused of killing, Kathleen lived in Singleton, in the Hunter Valley. She would also need accommodation while in Sydney for what promised to be a long trial.

The Folbigg case was to be no ordinary trial. If Hilton and Joyce agreed to support Mrs Folbigg, they would be responsible for her outside the court whenever she was in their company. She was not in custody, but if, for example, Hilton and Joyce took her for a day out to help her cope with the stress, they would be responsible for seeing that she did not abscond.

Hilton and Joyce arranged to meet for lunch with the thirty-five year-old Mrs Folbigg. They needed to get a feel for the woman. If there was a genuine rapport, they would agree to take the case.

The three ate sandwiches and drank tea in a café in the heart of Sydney. *I immediately liked her*, wrote Kathleen Folbigg in 'About Joyce', a three-page recollection sent to Hilton from Mulawa Women's Prison a year after her trial. She added that it wasn't hard, as many will confirm. The lunch was a success, Joyce and Hilton immediately finding Kathleen Folbigg sane, sensible and quite normal. Kathleen's recollection of the meeting is that it was 'congenial and polite'.

A woman of average frame with short curly auburn hair, Kathleen Folbigg could react to her circumstances either impassively or with lively animation. The conversation about small things flowed naturally over lunch. They all had the spontaneous frankness of people with country backgrounds. The Harmers had been Corps officers in Maitland in the mid-1970s, and they had also worked as Corps officers in Newcastle. For all three, the Hunter Valley and surrounds were familiar territory. They swapped impressions of Singleton, noting changes since the Harmers had lived in the district.

'She was absolutely 100 per cent normal,' says Hilton. 'So we said okay, and I agreed to book her a place with the Salvation Army.' In one phone call, the Salvation Army's Foster Street manager agreed to the use of his personal unit, a flat set aside for emergency nights when the manager has to stay over. Kath Folbigg could stay there for the duration of the trial. Then, as the date of the trial neared, Hilton phoned Kathleen in Singleton to ask if she would be staying in the flat alone.

'Occasionally I might have some of my women friends with me, but nothing more,' was Mrs Folbigg's reply.

'Only women?' asked Hilton.

'Well, basically.'

This was enough to give Hilton, with his sense of proper behaviour, second thoughts. 'At Foster Street there were a number of secure areas to get through and there were some ninety men in the place. I didn't want the institution to have to make concessions just for us. So I found a family who could put her up for 200 dollars a week. Joyce and I offered to go halves with Kath on the rent and we paid it all up front.' Just before the trial began on 1 April 2003, Joyce and Hilton met Kath, as they now called her, near the Goulburn Street car park in the centre of Sydney. She unloaded her luggage from a friend's car into theirs and they drove to her accommodation. On the first day of the trial, presiding judge Graham Barr placed a suppression order on the release of any information relating to the whereabouts of Kathleen Folbigg's Sydney accommodation. This would be no ordinary trial.

On 19 April 2001, Detective Bernie Ryan of the New South Wales Police had driven to Mrs Folbigg's house in Singleton, where she was living with new partner Tony Lambkin, and arrested her for the murder of her four young children. This was the culmination of extraordinary sleuthing work on the part of the detective, who had been called in to investigate the death of Kathleen's fourth child Laura, a little girl aged nineteen months. Just twenty-three hours before her untimely death at home alone with her mother, during the late morning of 1 March 1999, Laura had been videoed laughing and playing, a picture of health and vitality. Her sister Sarah and two brothers Caleb and Patrick had all also died, suddenly, while in the care of their mother — each Folbigg child a little older than the one before. Two of the children had died while alone with Kathleen during the day, while their father Craig Folbigg was at work, the other two after Kathleen had got up to attend to them as Craig slept. Craig Folbigg never woke at night and had left Kathleen to do the night-time feeding and settling of the babies. The Folbiggs' second child, Patrick, had also been discovered close to death at night, hardly breathing, when he was four months old. Kathleen had given him a feed and then said she had woken to find him almost dead. He was left epileptic and blind, only to die at nine months of asphyxia.

The deaths of the first three children had been put down to a combination of Sudden Infant Death Syndrome (SIDS) and various minor health problems. No one had ever suspected their mother until Laura's death. Laura was older and had communicated to her father, in her childish way, and her fear of her mother's mood swings had been palpable in the days leading up to the child's death. The day Laura died, Craig Folbigg had been apprehensive enough to sit with her before going off to work after he witnessed Kathleen's rage at the child in her highchair when she refused her breakfast. In fact, Laura had frequently been emotional about being left with her mother in the days immediately prior to her death. When questioned later, Kathleen's foster sister Lea Brown said she had also witnessed Kathleen's anger with Laura when she wouldn't sleep or eat as her mother wanted her to. It was a wild anger, spontaneous and violent towards the small child.

Then there were the telltale signs at the house on the day of Laura's death, which Detective Ryan could not make sense of.

Why were the child's sandals and drink bottle in the lounge room at one end of the house if, as Kathleen said, she had carried Laura sleeping from the car straight to the child's bed? Over the months that followed, as Ryan investigated, he discovered that Craig Folbigg had covered up important circumstantial evidence surrounding the death of his third child Sarah. It was evidence that could implicate Kathleen in Sarah's death. Later there had been the first of Kathleen Folbigg's diaries, which the police obtained from Craig Folbigg. Strangely, Kathleen had left them in her estranged husband's possession almost as if she'd forgotten ever writing them. Those diaries, and others subsequently acquired by the police, became crucial evidence of Mrs Folbigg's involvement in her children's deaths.

Like many accused, Kath Folbigg proved a complex character. Her appearance each day of the trial was a mixture of held-back emotion and shrug-of-the-shoulder surrender to the rollercoaster ride she was on. Always well made up and dressed in businesslike jackets or shirts, the wispy pieces of hair she combed onto her forehead and cheeks gave her a coquettish touch that belied her abject misery. To Joyce and Hilton, as they supported her, she was apprehensive, although capable of being vivacious and friendly, of seeming to be what they still describe as quite normal under the circumstances. Only when the trial was over was the full story of her abusive past as a child and the contents of her diaries revealed to the public. Her lawyer Peter Zahra observed that throughout the trial, while his client was able to 'put on a façade or exterior in order to exist', there was obviously 'turmoil beneath'. The fact that an exhaustive study of Kathleen Folbigg and her psychological state of mind, undertaken for the trial, could not find that she was in any way psychotic or mentally disordered is a relief to the Harmers. That's how they found her, and still find her as they visit her in prison — sane, sensible and intelligent. Their instinctive judgment was not mistaken. As Joyce told Mark Bannerman for ABC TV's *The 7.30 Report* after the trial, Kathleen was always 'a very normal mother . . . a mother that if you saw her in a shopping centre you would not even distinguish her as different from any other mother walking through the shops'.

On that basis, Joyce proceeded as she always did. She and Hilton accepted Kathleen as yet another person who found herself surrounded by a tragedy that she had to get through. They made no judgment of her guilt or innocence. Their job was to give her support; the court would do the rest.

'We never thought of what anyone had done,' is how the Harmers put it. 'That's the only way you can do your work. If you thought about what people might have done, you wouldn't do it. A man drowns his three children in a bath, and you are in a cell with him, speaking to him, giving him courage to face his trial. He isn't happy and you don't go back. But you say you will be in court and if he ever wants to see you he only has to look up and he'll know you'll be there to support him.'

The Folbigg trial had been delayed, with the defence attempting to have the four children's deaths tried separately. This was refused. Kathleen Folbigg would have to appear at Sydney's Supreme Court in Oxford Street, Darlinghurst, accused of four murders before one jury.

Crown prosecutor Mark Tedeschi pulled no punches in his opening address: 'The accused had a very low threshold for stress, and she was also deeply resentful at the intrusions that her children made on her own time and, in particular, on her sleep, her ability to go to the gym and her ability to socialise, including going out dancing.' To this he added the accusations that Kathleen was constantly tired, resentful against her husband for not helping her with the children, and frustrated with her weight gain because she could not get to the gym. The Crown asserted that Kathleen Folbigg had intended to kill 'during a flash of anger, resentment and hatred against her children, or, alternatively, that she deliberately sought to render them unconscious in an attempt to put them to sleep, either so that she could get to sleep herself or so that she could have some time to herself'.

Joyce Harmer approached her client with the usual caution. At first, as the trial began, Kathleen was withdrawn and didn't want to talk much. 'I had to find my way and discover whether it was better for me to stay with her entirely or for me to leave her a little space each day. We sat in the anteroom when we were not in court,' says Joyce. 'Then I discovered she didn't need space. She just needed me to be there. So we would have lunch together and talk.' The women chatted about anything but the trial. The weather, clothes, losing weight, the kindness of the lawyers, some trivial thing that might have been amusing for a moment that day. Anything but why Kath was there.

On weekends, Joyce and Hilton also tried to get Mrs Folbigg out as much as possible, both to distract her from brooding and to give her hosts where she was living some time to themselves. So it was arranged that on Sunday Hilton and Joyce would arrive to take Kath for a day out. She sat in the back of their car alongside a woman who'd been around the courts a long time, an alcoholic and wild card who had served several prison sentences. 'She [the woman] had been placed in the Rozelle Psychiatric Centre under the *Inebriates Act*,' says Joyce, 'and she couldn't leave unless we took her out. We told her that when Kath got into the car she was not to say anything about Kath's alleged crimes. Now, she is notorious for her outbursts and the way she can intrude on people. She's been in and out of jail and through the courts for years. And prisoners hate people who hurt children. But during our days out with Kath, she would sit there and not say a word.' It was certainly an incongruous party on the road on Sunday in the Harmers' car: two ministering angels, a woman being tried for the murder of her four young children and an institutionalised inebriate, all four dropping into the Salvation Army for services from Congress Hall to Hurstville and Dulwich Hill, after which they might take a drive to places like Nowra or Berry for a view of the pretty coastline that spans out below the Southern Highlands escarpment.

On many mornings of the trial, over seven weeks, the Harmers would collect Kath for the day and later drive her home. Other mornings, when she was required to be in court early, she'd catch a train with her solicitor. On one occasion, Hilton met some of Kath's friends at Hornsby station and drove them to their Sydney accommodation, which he and Joyce had arranged. 'We set out to be as helpful as we could, whenever,' says Joyce. All the while, Kathleen Folbigg was consulting daily with her lawyers, Peter Zahra and Peter Krisenthal, in their chambers, after which they would make their way to the Supreme Court, where Joyce would meet her for the day's proceedings.

'My role happened then, as she arrived,' says Joyce. 'We would enter the court, and I made a point of sitting right where she could glance at me and know there was someone there for her. She was in the middle of the courtroom and the media block were watching her every move. I also needed to know how she was coping. If I could have sat with her I would have. But that wasn't the situation. When the morning session was over, we would all stand and Judge Barr would leave the bench. Kath would leave the dock and I would come straight round to be beside her. The public attention was so intense. You could feel it as we left. But we would move directly to the small anteroom where we had our lunch. Out through the front door, past the media and onlookers, relatives of Craig Folbigg grouped together in support. At the end of the day, Hilton would be ready for us outside the court. We would collect our belongings and head for the car.'

The coming and going to court each day cemented relationships. The protection of the car became a time to bond and be normal in a whirlwind of public attention. Both Folbigg and lawyer Peter Krisenthal remember how getting to know Joyce and Hilton brought them into close contact with people who were remarkable, people they couldn't match with any others, always available to assist wherever. No high-profile event was a distraction for the Harmers in their daily work. There were streets of needy everywhere and they were still on call. Peter Krisenthal tells of how, as they left the court one day during the trial and were crawling in peak-hour traffic along Oxford Street, they passed a couple brawling. 'Joyce told Hilton to stop the car,' recalls Peter. 'She just got out and Hilton left her there and drove around the block. In ten minutes, Joyce had resolved the whole situation.'

It had been quite an emotional day, says Kath Folbigg in 'About Joyce' of the Oxford Street incident. *She dived out of the car, or at least in my stupor from the day that's how it seemed. Joyce had heard the screams of a woman in trouble. What sort, no one knew. So out of the car she gets, brandishing her smile and courage. We went around the block. Once returned where we left Joyce, she opens the door and our gladiator dressed in blue has returned triumphant. She has helped and that's all she needs to do.*

In the early days of the trial, Joyce and Kath Folbigg had tried to be normal at lunchtime by going out for lunch at busy Taylor Square across from the courts. It was hopeless. Stopped at a set of lights, they were media prey. 'We couldn't move,' says Joyce. 'It became terrible very quickly. I talked to the lawyers and they decided we should stay in the court. At first I took to going out for a takeaway lunch; then I brought sandwiches and a Thermos. Others also brought lunches for Kath. We went out only for the bathroom, and even that wasn't without the clicking of cameras, like seagulls trying to get a chip off the sand.'

Joyce hadn't yet realised it, but with the Folbigg case her life's work had reached an emotional and public climax. The cameras captured her outside the old sandstone court firmly holding the arm of a woman who was slowly becoming known as one of Australia's most notorious offenders. At the court, early on, Joyce had talked with Craig Folbigg and his relatives. She had assured them it wasn't a 'them and us' situation. They understood that, admitting Kath needed Joyce. Joyce would stand by any accused she felt she could support, and would do that to the end. And all this in spite of the heartbreaking tears she would shed for the lives of 'those dear little angels', the four Folbigg children, 'taken in the way they were', as she put it. If only Kath could have known the joy she and Hilton had had in their own four children, in watching them grow. But here was a woman on trial for what her own lawyer Peter Zahra describes as 'extremely serious crimes that most of the community, obviously, find extremely abhorrent'. Crimes of a woman who had become so enraged at her small child of eighteen months whimpering after her and calling 'Mum, Mum' that she'd knocked her down by spinning around and saying, 'Piss off.' Kathleen had admitted this to Craig Folbigg when he returned from a day out. Laura had been in shock and Kathleen herself had been thrown by her loss of temper.

The story of Kath at these moments reminded Joyce of her own blackest time, fighting postnatal depression after her daughter Lyndall had been born, when she'd pleaded, 'Hilton, don't leave me alone', all those years ago in Mt Isa. She knew what it was like to have thoughts that scared her, dangerous feelings she could not explain, behaviour she felt capable of that was not natural. It had been a medical condition, not a moral one. She had been saved by Hilton, who had reached out to her and understood she needed help and time to recover. And even so, recovery had taken months.

Kathleen Folbigg was a woman ostracised in both her public and private domains even before the verdict of the court had been reached and the full details of her alleged crimes could be known. But Joyce thought too of the images in the Christian Gospels, images of a woman accused of adultery about to be stoned to death by her peers. The faith Joyce believed in said, *Let they who are without sin cast the first stone.* As media interest and public condemnation intensified outside the court, Joyce held Kath's hand tightly and ran the gauntlet.

Joyce, writes Kathleen, *guided me, protected me and never once hesitated.* Kathleen still cherishes the support Joyce was to her. *The foremost impression came when the media behaved as they usually do. When the scent of blood is in the water. And who is walking proudly, head held high and parting the sea as she walks through? Quite the sight — five feet nothing and the appearance of a lovely little lady who wouldn't hurt a fly. I followed suit quite readily. That is Joyce, teaching in a sublime non-aggressive manner. You don't even realise you've learned something. Her kindness of heart and soul is never-ending, and no one seems beyond her touch. She reminded me of a pilgrim with strong messages but a soft style.*

Kathleen had caught the Joyce Harmer infection, what Peter Zahra calls the Pavlovian response to goodness, what he recognises as reflected in the grin he gets on his face whenever he sees Joyce. The strain of being so strong certainly had its effect on Joyce, but only in private did she collapse. The days of the trial were an exhaustion Joyce never showed in public. 'I had to be strong for them,' she will say. 'And the Lord gives me that strength.' In the car, alone with Hilton after dropping Kath off on the way home or after they had entered their own house, she might sob her heart out. Hilton would put his arms round her, holding her still, and then suggest she climb into bed and he would bring her dinner. As Joyce had been for him so often, Hilton became her strength.

The verdict of the jury on 21 May 2003 was 'guilty'. The Folbigg diaries, a damaging interview with Detective Bernie Ryan on video that was shown to the court, the lack of substantial medical evidence to prove that the deaths were natural, with each child taking some four minutes to die, the motive, the circumstances and opportunity for the mother to be the perpetrator all added up against Mrs Folbigg. Throughout the trial, she had sat and watched and listened. What she was thinking was anybody's guess. The assembled jury, officials, media and public gallery only heard her speak when a video of her interview with Detective Bernie Ryan, made in July 1999, was shown to the court. Joyce had rushed to her side after the showing of the video. Kathleen had collapsed, her feet going from under her as she had attempted to leave the dock only to be ordered back by the judge.

'I would have dearly liked to have been there with her in the dock,' says Joyce. 'Just to put my arm around the back of her and to hold her hand.' Folbigg needed medical attention after the video incident. As soon as Joyce could get to her, at the little door through which she was finally allowed to leave the dock, Joyce had taken her round to St Vincent's Hospital and she was excused from the court for the day.

Later that month, when the verdict of guilty was read out, Kath Folbigg broke down again, in a flood of tears, and Joyce once more rushed to her side. She had now to assure her client that she would still support her, even as a convicted murderer. A few moments later, in the chilly cells with hugs and hankies, Joyce told Kathleen she would never desert her, just as the van came to take Mrs Folbigg into the years of confinement that were now her fate. They had had over two months in each other's company, highly pressured time but as relaxed as Joyce and Hilton could make it. Moments of banality, of comfort, of small things, of life at its most practical. For the first time in her life, Kathleen Folbigg had felt the embracing power of unconditional love. A kinship that teaches without preaching, that guides and fashions and moulds character. A love that some who came before the courts would witness suddenly in their own parents. But it was a love that Kath Folbigg had never known until her trial and until the company of Joyce Harmer.

At the sentencing, on Friday, 24 October 2003, sitting impassively with her hair longer, untended and bushy, Kathleen Folbigg received a sentence of forty years in jail and a non-parole time of thirty years. A lifetime in custody, which would be served in isolation for her own protection. In his sentencing statement, Justice Barr concluded that Kathleen Folbigg could never admit to her guilt or the part she played in the deaths of her children. Should she do so, she would probably kill herself. Her own early life as a child had been most tragic. Her father, Thomas 'Jack' Britton, a small-time criminal who had killed her wayward mother before she was two, had so badly misused her sexually as an infant that as a two-year-old, when taken briefly into the care of her mother's sister and husband, she had shocked them badly with her behaviour, even at times involuntarily masturbating by trying to insert objects into her vagina. She would scream when stopped.

In this summing up of Kath Folbigg's early life, the judge had released to the public for the first time information from Department of Community Services records relating to an assessment made by a Dr Spencer of Kathleen Folbigg as a three-year-old. The information shocked listeners. Then, drawing extensively on the report of Dr Guiffrida, one of the three psychiatrists who had interviewed Kath Folbigg on sentencing, Justice Barr quoted at length in an effort to explain Mrs Folbigg's detachment from her children at the times of their deaths. In the words of Dr Guiffrida, *Kathleen Folbigg in her first three years of life [. . .] suffered a profound and probably irreversible impairment of her capacity to develop any meaningful emotional bonding or attachment, [this impairment contributing] in part at least to her total inability to relate, care for and protect her own children.* In spite of many years of normality as she grew up in the care of loving foster parents after the age of three, the seed had been planted in her psyche by a corrupted early experience at the hands of her natural parents. Around children in her care, she was, as a result, a walking time-bomb, whose behaviour no one could predict. Her calm could momentarily snap and her frustration turn to dangerous anger. Kathleen Folbigg was not to be around children nor bear them ever again.

Joyce heard the sentencing statement from Judge Barr, the judge who, at the conclusion of the trial, had taken a few moments to commend Joyce Harmer on the way she had supported Mrs Folbigg over the trial's duration. As the judge read out his ninety-minute summation, Joyce had not moved in the seat where she sat in support of her client. Kathleen did not turn round to glance at Joyce. Cowed and broken in spirit by her four months of prison life, she appeared matter-of-fact, unresponsive, ready for the worst. The judge's lengthy recapping of evidence and argument, laced with extracts from Kathleen's diaries and accounts of her childhood, drew the picture of a tragic background. The child, left without parents at eighteen months in violent circumstances, and then in care, had grown to cope over the years by moving on quickly from her hurts and upsets without looking back. With each of her children's deaths she had similarly moved on, so much so that she could barely remember their faces. But Joyce could not let it go that easily. Walking in Hyde Park after the sentencing, unable to go back to the Downing Centre, Joyce wept copiously before ringing Hilton.

No one could hear the full story of Kathleen Folbigg and her children and not be moved. ABC TV's *Australian Story* brought the tragic images to the screen in 2004, with home-movie footage taken over years of a happy Kathleen and her babies, of little Laura laughing and playing with her parents over many months of her infancy and then a much more subdued Kathleen a few months before Laura died, finally refusing to appear at all with Laura in the video made the day before the child's death. Six months after the sentencing, Detective Inspector Bernie Ryan received a Commissioner's Commendation for his work in bringing Folbigg to trial. Asked how he felt about it all, he played down suggestions he had been a hero. 'It's a story of misery, really.' But, for all the negatives of the trial, Ryan could isolate one pearl. That was Joyce Harmer. 'The Folbigg case was and is a tragedy for all involved, including Kathleen Folbigg,' he commented late in 2004. 'Kathleen needed and deserved support throughout the trial and that was forthcoming in the form of Joyce and her husband.' To Ryan, what Joyce did for Kathleen Folbigg was 'nothing short of amazing'. It was a pleasure to be in the company of a person like Joyce, he said. 'If you could measure a person's wealth on the good they have done in their lives, I am sure that Joyce would be a very wealthy person.'

Joyce comes to see me as often as she can, wrote Kathleen Folbigg from her cell in Mulawa Women's Prison, six months after her sentencing. *And always greets me with a smile and listens and allows you [to] be heard. She has also spread her arms around me and created a warm, safe space that invites you to expel all that may be hurting or just to enjoy a hug. An age-old remedy if ever there was one. I know I shall always cherish meeting Joyce Harmer. An eternal effect on my life. Joyce is a gladiator of the word. She eagerly undertakes all that is demanded or asked of her. Spreading kindness and peace into hearts that are open and ready to receive. I was one of those recipients. Bless Joyce, for she would be one that is truly deserving of all praises. And when I see her again, a smile I shall have.*

On 17 February 2005, Kath Folbigg's appeal was lost, but her sentence was reduced to thirty years and the non-parole period to twenty-five years. It was still a very harsh sentence. On a visit to Kath in Mulawa Women's Prison, Joyce had promised Kathleen she would attend the judgment on the appeal, which she did. In a letter sent from the prison that same day, Kathleen Folbigg wrote: *Joyce has revived my faith in the kindness of humanity. Her selfless, simple acts can mean the world to someone like me, a hug that is pure and meant as it should be, comfort and support. Smiles that convey enjoyment of your company. Her generosity. The bond she shares with Hilton amazes me and the comfort they have in their lives I envy. But with the guidance and help that I've received, I have changed and now know the strength I carry is something that I've always had.*

chapter 22

CHRISTMAS WITH THE HARMERS

Happy Christmas, my darling, wrote Hilton to Joyce in a note on 25 December 2003. *I wanted to give you this gift in the privacy of our own bedroom, because it is a gift with too much spiritual significance to just place under the Christmas tree with other gifts.*

The note Hilton left for Joyce put into words his ongoing esteem for his darling wife, for the life she embodied and what it meant to him. *On a daily basis (seven days a week if required) you constantly place yourself at the disposal of 'complete strangers', as well as your family and friends. When you show such compassion you are showing it to Jesus*, he wrote. *When you give a handkerchief or wipe away a tear from the face of a troubled person, or take notes from loved ones to prisoners and then a message back to the family, you are doing all these things for Jesus.* Hilton's present to Joyce was his devoted recognition of her work and faith in God, *a hundred and one ways that you express the compassionate Christ each day.* As she woke on Christmas Day, here was Hilton's precious Christmas package, acclaiming her special attributes and life choices, gifts within herself that he hoped she would always treasure. *Of course, we know that you obtain your capacity to do these things in the mornings when you are surrounded by your library of books and have your devotional time . . . I consider myself ever so blessed to have you as my special partner for all of these years.*

Asked on Network Nine's *Today* show, in June 2004, to explain how they managed to greet each day with energy and spirit, to continue their work in the face of exhaustion and emotionally draining circumstances, the Harmers replied that some days were not so easy. But they did it. And their unfailing impetus could be put down to beginning each day with their private prayers and Bible readings. While the Harmers might seem, in passing, simply a devoted married couple, still in love after forty-five years, what makes them different is that their first love has always been God, a God they worship and seek to emulate in every waking moment. A God who said to them, in the words of Matthew 25, *I was hungry and you gave me meat, I was thirsty and you gave me drink, I was a stranger and you took me in, I was naked and you clothed me, I was sick and you visited me, I was in prison and you came unto me.* From this and other Biblical teachings in both Old and New Testaments came the faith that made what they did a passion. It gave them a zest for life, intoxicating to the observer.

After the Folbigg trial, Joyce became a public figure. 'The Salvation Army woman who was with that Folbigg woman in that trial,' people would say to explain who she was. 'Oh, yes,' would come the reply, 'heard about that.' They would have a vague recollection that there had been something in the news about Joyce, even if they didn't recall her name exactly. The Folbigg case became a standout in the public memory relating to Joyce.

Then, as time passed, Joyce became the interest. Hungry for new angles, people wanted more. Stories done on Kath Folbigg early on had included Joyce in a supportive role. Now they swung onto Joyce as the subject. The *Australian Women's Weekly* for July 2003 titled its feature piece by Michael Sheather 'The Sinner and the Saint'. From that, readers could be excused for thinking Joyce had bestowed her goodness on the wrongdoer in a 'lady bountiful' fashion. Nothing could have been further from the truth. In person, Joyce kept on doing what she always did, out of the limelight. She walked the levels of the Downing Centre as usual, sitting in on trials and talking to people here and there, picking up the signs of where she could be useful. She left her unique and intimate perceptions of Kath Folbigg to herself. Her reaction to Matthew Benns' comprehensive account of the story in his bestselling book *When the Bough Breaks* in late 2003 was cursory ('Nothing new there'). But the public, with little knowledge of the trial and needing an explanation for such a mother's actions, had wanted the story. Benns' book gave them that.

As their retirement drew close in mid–2004, those reflecting on the Harmers' exit from the justice system began to realise that Joyce and Hilton had taken the Sydney courts to a new level of expectation. There was widespread public interest in their departure. In a letter to Commissioner Les Strong on 6 July 2004, just a few weeks before their official retirement date, Hilton Harmer wrote: *Since 24 June, Joyce and I have conducted nine radio interviews, five television interviews and three newspaper interviews.* The media slots were still coming in as he wrote: *On all the media occasions*, Hilton continued in his letter, *we have sought not to glorify ourselves but to give glory to God for the way he has led us, and to the Salvation Army as a Movement for its care and compassion and the opportunities that have been ours simply because (and for no other reason) we have been part of the Salvation Army.*

The Harmers, with their outstanding talents and personalities, had come to court chaplaincy work by chance. Had Hilton not upset the powers-that-be in the Salvation Army all those years before, who knows where they might have ended their careers? Many who knew them before their falling-out at Congress Hall assumed they were capable of very high office in the Army. It didn't happen and their life journey instead took them to the courts. They revelled in the work there, but such was their output that it was unlikely ever to be replicated. At times it had even got the better of the Harmers themselves.

Joyce Harmer told the *Today* show that their work in the courts had been 'double gold' to them, an amazing opportunity in their lives. But what she had not added was that it came with days of wrung-out exhaustion and sometimes collapse. Hilton's sickness was never far away, and while he might often ring in to the midnight to 5 a.m. show on 2UE radio, making offers of help to callers, he could just as easily need time out with a day of ill health. It never showed at the courts; Joyce could cover for him as he could for her. But Joyce herself could be so tired at times that she could not stop herself from saying so to those who knew her closely. A note she scribbled for Hilton on one occasion is revealing. It shows how there were times she felt circumstances were at breaking point but managed to carry on. Under a heading on the notepaper, *You came into my life*, she wrote:

> *My darling Hilton, I love you more than I can say. The pressure of work is getting to us, honey. I just needed to 'go out' to give my brain a break today. Please 'slow up' before it is too late, darling — I need you, we need you, and I want to be with you for a long time yet. Your health will give in if you are not careful. All you do, we value and are proud. All my love, sweetheart, you are precious and very valuable to me. Your loving wife, Joyce xxxx*

The Harmers' gift of giving reached a visual climax each year in the courts at the end of November. It was then that Joyce and Hilton brought Christmas to the justice system. What began as pepped-up decorations soon became weeks of organised gift-giving and spreading the message of Christmas to all. Within a year of starting their chaplaincy positions in 1995 they had commissioned a small Nativity scene, which was developed over the years until in 2003, courtesy of Jerry, a Lebanese friend, a life-sized version replaced the more modest crib the Army used at the courts. Each year, this stable of wood and its figures of Mary, Joseph and baby Jesus, with animals, wise men and shepherds, was placed in the Downing Centre's massive foyer to the right of the spiral staircase on the ground floor. Joyce then organised an arrangement of taped, round-the-clock Christmas carols to herald in the Christmas spirit. With the courts closing down by mid-December, they started on the first working day of December every year and made their mark. The courts had seen nothing like it. This was no modest, tucked-away display for an occasional passer-by to glance at. This was Christmas, on tap and in your face, in the cheeriest way possible. The sign went up, bright and large, *Jesus is the reason for the season*. It was the only evangelising as such that Joyce and Hilton actually did at the courts. In all their other work, they never so much as asked whether a person believed in God. They simply did their job of helping in whatever way they could. Only at Christmas did they proactively spread the message.

'When we started at the courts,' says Hilton, 'I thought, how can we make some kind of statement for the Christian faith in this place? I thought of carolling and of giving a little gift. After it got going, all sorts of people would come in and help put up the Nativity set. With a portable CD player and amplifiers we played carols for a whole month. From 7.30 a.m. It was no good starting at nine in the foyer, as by then half the staff had gone up to their offices. And you only get one chance to make a first impression.'

They put up greetings from the chaplaincy in the foyer, and around their office on level five. 'Children would wander in and out,' says Joyce, ever aware of the real joy of Christmas in their young eyes. Then there was the Harmer gift-giving day. Almanacs rolled up by the thousand and given out with the help of the Harmer grandchildren on the last Friday the courts would be fully open. 'All sorts of people helped roll them up,' says Joyce. 'For many years they were done in the sheriff department's control room at night when it was quiet. But then security was tightened over the years and we couldn't distract the officers on duty. After that we had all sorts of people helping.' For years, each Christmas Joyce and Hilton bought small gifts for all the workers in the courts, from the justices to the Correctional Services officers. These were wrapped over hours, with help from friends like Beverley and Graham Edwards, who owned a small factory where the Harmers could spread out the job and store the hundreds of little packages. One year it might be a desk stand with a piece of scripture or poetry, another year a special candle, or a picture of the three kings with the message *Wise men still seek Him*, and there would be practical items like socks. Small reminders of the season created to give and spread goodwill.

Armed with their stack of goodies, they would start off on the last Friday the courts were open, their grandchildren singing carols by the Nativity scene at 8.45 a.m. Hilton would play his piano accordion and they'd all sing with the gusto that comes from regular church attendance. There might be a sheriff in the group, and others playing different instruments. One year it was a saxaphone; another, a member of the Sydney Philharmonic Orchestra joined them. At a minute before nine, Joyce and Hilton would head for the lifts with their loaded trolley, accompanied by a sheriff to unlock doors on the way. They took the lift to level six and began distributing gifts, working their way down the floors. Joyce would lead them into an office or room with 'Come up, folks, here's something for you!' If the atmosphere was welcoming, and it mostly was, she'd add, 'How about we sing a couple of carols?' All to the smiles and amazement of the staff, who readily joined in — and then the Harmers gave out the small gifts and wished everyone a merry Christmas. 'God bless you all,' they'd finish. 'Have a happy and holy Christmas!' Some laughed, some even cried. One lady said to Joyce soon after it began, 'You know, there's never been anything here at Christmas, not in the past eight years I've worked in the courts. You have brought Christmas to us.'

'We would keep on going down the levels until we reached the cells,' says Joyce. 'But here we couldn't give the prisoners any actual gifts, so we would hand out Smarties and sing. And then we headed up to the Supreme Court. To Darlinghurst.' On one occasion they used a utility, with a friend driving and Joyce in the front, while Hilton lay down in the back so the police wouldn't catch sight of him with no seat belt. Then they took to using a 'Megamate', an elaborate trolley, to push the pile of presents up Oxford Street for their Christmas greetings at the Darlinghurst courts. Court sheriff Ann Brown can never forget how it was, the cheer they brought and the atmosphere they created as they carolled and distributed gifts. 'And then we had to get back to Central Court by 11.30 a.m.,' says Hilton. 'It nearly killed us.'

For Joyce and Hilton, the best thing of all about the Christmas season was its universality. They would be down in the cells at Central, with their half-light and old iron grates on heavy tomb-like doors, where so often each day they would move along the rows, looking in on figures curled up like sick animals in a zoo, lying on their pallet strips in the corner of bare cages. Striking up the notes, Joyce and Hilton would begin 'Away in a Manger' and some of the fellows behind the bars would start to join in. 'It was absolutely gorgeous,' says Joyce. But they had little time to linger. It would already be morning-tea time for the magistrates in the courts above them. Up Joyce and Hilton would go, and within minutes would be passing round the cheer, with dancing and singing, in the justices' chambers. From prisoners to magistrates, the message was the same.

One year a magistrate asked them to sing carols in her court at 11.45 a.m. 'There was a protected prisoner giving evidence, a Code Nine,' says Hilton. 'He was sitting in the docks with mega-security. "Well, gentlemen," said the magistrate, "We're going to hear from the Salvation Army. They are going to sing a couple of carols before we start proceedings." So we sang, "*Silent night, holy night . . .*" and the looks we got from the defence lawyers and Correctional Services officers! We did a second carol. And then the magistrate said, "Could we have another one, Major?" '

Joyce recalls how at first there was a degree of reserve about what they were doing in the courts at Christmas. 'In the beginning someone said to us, "Oh, you can't go in there, making a noise." But we said, "Oh, yes, we'll be all right, we're going to sing carols." Anyway, they got to love it after a while.'

'But we did have to sort of push our way around a bit at first,' adds Hilton.

'People would be talking business on the phone in an office,' says Joyce. 'And the next minute you could hear "Hark the Herald Angels". Others would nearly die as I put a gift onto their table. But to us they were like friends. In the street they would kiss me on the cheek and ask, "How are you, Joyce?" It was that kind of atmosphere. And it's good to be reminded that it doesn't hurt to stop for a second. We had a wonderful time.'

'It was just so Salvation Army,' muses Hilton. 'And often we'd see the little gifts that we'd given them still on their desks, like Paddy in Correctional Services at Darlinghurst, still there after nine years.'

Christmas 'inside' came next. Meeting up with prison chaplains Connie and Stan Hindle, Joyce and Hilton would go from wing to wing in the jails, or outside the recreation yards. On one occasion Joyce got inside the yard. 'We were at Parklea and we had the protection of staff,' she says. 'I gave them gifts. One guy asked me to pray for him. I just took his hand and prayed.'

Then there would be the exits of the subways in the city. 'I'd leave at five in the morning,' says Hilton, 'and be at the exit by six. I'd play and collect from six till half past nine. Or ten.'

'While you're playing carols, people will usually throw in a coin,' says Joyce.

By Christmas 2004, Joyce and Hilton had been retired for five months. They had at first swung along on the high they got from their Congress Hall 'salute' afternoon and from having Lyndall with them from the United States for a few weeks with her little boy KJ. 'We'll be doing a lot of the same things in our retirement,' Joyce had told the *Today* show in June, 'but it won't be in the courts.' Messages had come in to them from around the world, from people they had helped or their relatives. Messages of thanks, good luck and affirmation.

From Linda in Houston, Texas, whose daughter had been arrested for smuggling cocaine into Australia in 2003. Her daughter had served a three-year sentence and Joyce had supported her. Wrote Linda: *I cannot put into words what Joyce did and meant to my husband and myself during that time. I can only say that I feel so terribly grateful that God brought her into my life and I will never forget her.*

From Wende, who was accused with Linda's daughter: *I was arrested at Sydney airport. I had spent the night in a police station and the following morning was taken to Parramatta Court cells. Needless to say I was in a terrible state, very upset and nervous about my future. Joyce was ministering to the prisoners. I looked up to see someone in a Salvation Army uniform. It threw me back a bit. My grandparents were Salvationists. I felt such comfort in that uniform. Joyce talked and comforted me, took my parents' names and phone numbers. I thought that would be it, yet I continued to receive mail from Joyce throughout my incarceration. She came to visit me as well. When I was able to get day leave, the Harmers agreed to be my sponsors. They would pick me up once a month and take me out for the day. I am truly blessed having the Harmers as a presence in my life.*

From Robert Somosi, a barrister retired from the law who found himself in court over tax evasion charges: 'What Joyce did for me by turning up at my own case showed me that what she did for others actually worked. She helped me that day, and it fitted in exactly with my belief about what she was doing with distressed people in court over the years I had known her there. And it was given totally freely. On one occasion I was late for a day in court. I happened to mention to Joyce, by way of explanation, that I had been with my mother who'd been taken to hospital after a heart attack in Katoomba. She asked me about the hospital and I thought nothing of it. Within hours of telling her that, she was at my mother's bedside in a Blue Mountains hospital. Amazing. But wonderful. That approach is very humbling.'

From a young graduate whose father was sentenced to eighteen months' jail for fraud and whose family had never experienced a day in court before: *Joyce found us sitting in the court, bewildered. She said a prayer with us and stayed with us the whole day. None of us were expecting my father to go to jail and we had no idea what to do after he was led away. Hilton gave us the advice we needed to keep in touch with him and what was happening with him in custody. They were like angels. Angels appear when needed and then leave. We don't see them often, but whenever we are at a really low point Joyce will call unexpectedly and make things better. I get goose bumps just thinking about that.*

They left the courts at 9 p.m. on the last night of their appointment, Friday, 30 July 2004. They had finished cleaning their office ready for their successor. Their son Peter had called them on their mobile phones and said that they deserved to be clapped off like sporting heroes leaving the field, and that they should listen, as he had recorded his own slow clap for them.

Joyce and Hilton were moved to tears. They knelt at the chairs in their office and gave thanks to God for His grace and care and the opportunities they had been given and then rededicated themselves for their retirement years. They then walked into the darkness with a cold wind blowing, down

Elizabeth Street to the parking station where they had left their car. Two text messages, also from Peter, beeped onto their mobiles: *Easy to be proud of, thanks for a lifetime of service to Australia; gone soon from public life but never forgotten — Peter.* Then, *It's all over, well done, worked hard, played strong, with the motto 'just do it' — Peter, 30 July 2004.*

In their retirement, Joyce and Hilton have slowed the pace somewhat, but are still very much on the road wherever they see a need. Yet they have more time for each other now. Time to spend together. Time for Hilton to tend his garden and for Joyce to get into housework that has been waiting for attention for a long time. Joyce wants to spend time looking at the gifts they have received over forty-two years, beautiful items that dot their furniture and mantelpiece and hang on walls in their home. She wants to reflect on the giver in each case. As Joyce puts it, 'My life's journey taught me to trust God to move mountains, but also that I had to do my part and keep climbing.' Now there's time to consider where the two of them have been and what they've done. For reflection on the people they've helped, worked with and befriended.

Joyce and Hilton now relish the extra time to be grandparents in the true sense of the word. Like the day they organised to take the grandchildren, nine of them in Australia, ten-pin bowling while the parents were on a Sydney Harbour Bridge climb. Joyce and Hilton hired a minibus for the day and planned it like a school excursion.

'Neither Hilton nor I have any desire to go on that long retirement holiday,' says Joyce, 'because our whole life has been a "going" experience for forty-two years. And it is just beautiful to be able to stay at home.' She adds also that she will visit Kath Folbigg as long as she has the health to do so. For the moment, they are supporting many with prison sentences, along with relatives waiting on the outside, mothers with children who have no dads, who might need a lawn mown, a day out for the kids, whatever.

Strangely, on the eve of their retirement there was a pre-emptive move by one Army Major to take away Hilton's 'pass' for the prisons as a representative of the Salvation Army. Sitting down at his computer once again, the slow typist he is, Hilton fired off a pointed letter to a more senior commanding officer. It was his last territorial battle with Army bureaucracy. There he was, in the month of their retirement, still fending off elements of the organisation he and Joyce had given their lives to. Joyce kept her counsel, but wondered what could possibly have triggered the move against them. Wrote Hilton to his senior officer: *The question still remains in my mind, what legitimate reason could there possibly be for you to attempt to prevent me from ministering to these dear people whom I know so well, and who are away from home and loved ones, and why after [forty-two] years of service would you want to 'disown me' now?*

Hilton retained his pass.

Phone Joyce or Hilton in their retirement and you might well discover that all their numbers are on message bank. You can guarantee they are visiting someone behind bars. Each time they visit they are searched thoroughly; everything with them, including handkerchiefs, is put away in a locker, fingers going over Joyce's blouse and waist to check she's not carrying banned items. 'But that's the thing about security,' says Joyce. 'The person whom you trust is the one who might carry the contraband in.' They continue to care for numbers of incarcerated people in various centres as they have for years. Many of Australia's most notorious have been among their clients.

Phong Nho, convicted of the murder of John Newman MP in Cabramatta. 'In the cells, he would always put his hands together and bow and not say anything except when I asked if there was something I could get for him,' says Hilton. 'Then he would say, "A cup of water." That's all he used to say.'

Snapper Cornwell, notorious gambler and drug king, described by the press as a career criminal. In 2004, he received a sentence of twenty-four years after a previous eight-year stretch in jail and other arrests for major drug trafficking. 'When I first met Snapper,' recalls Hilton, 'he was a different man from what he is today. During his first incarceration, he was exercising in Long Bay when he got belted unmercifully. He nearly died. His skull was broken, and his jaw. I visited him later and he was in a bad way. After he was released, he asked us round for dinner. His dear old mum cooked lasagne.'

In 2001, Hilton received the Anzac of the Year Award for service to the community. In 2003, Joyce was nominated for the prestigious Justice Medal, given as part of the Justice Awards by the Law and Justice Foundation. She was subsequently nominated for the 2004 Australian of the Year Awards. In December 2004, Joyce and Hilton both received a letter from Lisa Curry Kenny OAM congratulating them on being nominated as Australian of the Year. These community acknowledgments make each of the Harmers very proud of the other. But no acknowledgment matches the daily joy they receive from seeing something they can do to help a person in need. Hilton recently took on the job of Sydney Congress Hall Chaplain to the Inner City, a ministry one could say he has been doing unofficially for years in the Jock

Geddes tradition. And they still sponsor people in jail for day leave. After forty-two years and more, that's the adrenalin in their system, that and their mutual love of God.

Barrister Charles Waterstreet says that Joyce gets a thrill out of her media acclaim, and he believes she should. 'She loves being on the cover of those magazines, and why not? For her, it's the sheer pleasure of giving, that's what it is. So she gets back infinitely more. And as we all know, in the end you do from giving.' To which he adds, with a touch of mischief, 'You might even say it's a little selfish: she's getting all that back because she gives more than anyone. But she deserves far more publicity than she gets. She should have her own chat show.'

The Harmers are an established team now. Their reputation has gone far beyond their immediate Salvation Army circle. They now have requests from numerous organisations to be guest speakers at functions. Their most recent came from a church in the United States, a connection developed through a family they had helped years before. They have also been invited to speak in New Zealand at various locations. And Joyce is developing a project of her own to assist Salvation Army officers who are having difficulties. A sort of Joyce 'at home' service, where officers can come for a meal and a chat and share a little of the Harmer experience of getting through the tough times. The opportunities are multiple. Joyce will never be bored.

Writing to a group of Salvation Army cadets in September 2003, just before they were to spend time with Joyce and Hilton at the courts, Hilton Harmer drew their attention to a few verses from Ezekiel 37. No words he might have chosen could better sum up the life he and Joyce have lived in their ministry:

*The hand of the Lord was upon me, and carried me out in
the Spirit of the Lord, and set me down in the midst of the
valley which was full of bones, and caused me to pass by them
round about, and behold, there were very many in the open
valley, and, lo, they were very dry. And He said unto me,
Prophesy upon these bones, and say unto them: O ye dry
bones, hear the word of the Lord. Thus saith the Lord God
unto these bones: Behold I will cause breath to enter into you,
and ye shall live. And I will lay sinews upon you, and will
bring up flesh upon you, and cover you with skin, and put
breath in you, and ye shall live; and ye shall know that I am
the Lord. So I prophesied as I was commanded, and as I
prophesied there was a noise, and behold a shaking, and the
bones came together, bone to his bone. And when I beheld, lo,
the sinews and the flesh came up upon them, and the skin
covered them above; but there was no breath in them . . . So
I prophesied as he commanded me, and the breath came into
them, and they lived and stood upon their feet, an exceeding
great army.*

Joyce and Hilton Harmer will continue to journey until their
last day together. Like they did on Christmas Day 2004. On
Christmas Eve, a woman had turned up at their door loaded
with chocolates, from The Chocolate Pot in Brookvale.
Taking these upmarket chocolates to the back streets of
Woolloomooloo the next day, Christmas Day, Joyce and
Hilton distributed them to people there who live on the
street. They shook hands and handed out chocolates for most
of the morning. 'The handshake was probably more
important than the chocolates,' says Joyce. Then they took off
to visit a dear friend, Major Stan Hindle, just retired from

chaplaincy work but recovering, barely, from the effects of a serious car accident. As Stan clung to life on 25 December 2004, Joyce and Hilton took the highway to Gosford to visit him and his wife at the hospital. 'There was nowhere to eat our Christmas lunch,' Joyce said, 'until we found a place with an outdoor table at the Gosford Showgrounds, after a long search. And we stopped there, under the gum trees, with our turkey and soft drinks and Christmas pudding from the car. It was lovely. Just Hilton and me.'

They have a plot set aside for their burial, with a water view. Neither Joyce nor Hilton is planning to use it in a hurry. They have no fear of death, though. Like all those with a firm belief in an afterlife, in the totality of their existence in both the material and spiritual order, they are relaxed about death. It's part of their passage, whenever it arrives. The ultimate destination, with their Creator. From time to time, Joyce and Hilton have been known to visit their tiny plot, the only piece of real estate they have ever owned and which they affectionately call 'the property'. They once sat and enjoyed a cup of tea in a café near the spot where their bodies will eventually lie together for always. 'No point in waiting till we are dead to be there,' says Joyce. 'Why not enjoy it together while we can still talk to each other and give each other a kiss and a hug?'

One day, as they were inspecting 'the property', a beautiful snow-white dove flew down and walked on the ground near them. Then it flew to a tree branch above. 'We felt that this was the Spirit of the Lord telling us it will be all right,' says Joyce. As it always has.

Acknowledgments

From Major Joyce Harmer

I acknowledge the funding of the New South Wales Attorney General's Department, which made it possible to establish the court chaplaincy service that brought me into contact with thousands of people, and our two wonderful friends Mr Phil Purdie and Mr David Robertson, whose continuous love, loyalty and financial support made it possible for me to say 'yes' to the many and varied requests made for assistance throughout the nine years that I served as chaplain in the courts.

I would also like to acknowledge the co-operation of judges, magistrates, sheriff officers, Correctional Services officers, police officers, probation and parole officers, solicitors, barristers and general court staff whose endless assistance made my ministry so much easier, and an absolute pleasure. I miss them all!

I have tried to be honest and open about my life's journey in this book, and in so doing have touched a raw nerve on many occasions. However, if you are to know me through this book, and why I have been passionate about caring for people who were passing through difficult circumstances, and why I have been so dependent upon faith in Jesus Christ, I needed to tell it as it was, and is.

I felt that areas of my childhood were clouded in unhappiness, and following the birth of our precious daughter

Lyndall Joy in 1968, I suffered the severe debilitating effects of postnatal depression. It was in later years, whilst in the court chaplaincy ministry, that I faced the challenge of menopause, with all its emotional turbulence. These circumstances have given me a deep understanding of and empathy with people whose journey in life has taken them the way of such experiences and more.

Over the years I have discovered that this business of serving people is never a one-way street. The more I have loved people, the more I have been loved. The more I have served, the more I have been served. I am extremely grateful to those who empathised with me along the way.

I have discovered that we are never alone when we have a faith in Jesus Christ, who has promised never to leave us or forsake us, and I have found that Jesus cares and understands.

I have shared my life story with you in the hope that you will be blessed, and that the faith of some will be strengthened, so that they seek to be led in the 'day-to-day things of life' by the Holy Spirit of God.

I have discovered that it is not what happens to us in life, but what we do with our experiences that matters. There is hope, and there is a light at the end of the darkest tunnel, and for me that light has been a faith in Jesus Christ and a commitment to serving my fellow man.

My mother would often sing these words whilst attending to her home chores:

> *Got any rivers you think are uncrossable*
> *Got any mountains you can't tunnel through*
> *God specialises in things thought impossible*
> *He can do what no other power can do.*

In John 8:12, Jesus said, *'I am the light of the world. Whoever follows me will never walk in darkness but will have the light of life.'* As you read this book you will discover that Christian commitment is not an insurance policy against heartache and sad experiences, but I give testimony to the fact that in the darkest of my circumstances Jesus was the 'light of life' to me . . . may it be so for you.

It has been an honour and a privilege to be given this opportunity to share the story of my life with you. May Jesus Christ, the light of the world, illuminate your pathway.

From Anne Henderson

The story of Major Joyce Harmer (née Lipke) and her husband Major Hilton Harmer could not have been pieced together without their frank and candid co-operation. I am indebted to their honesty and openmindedness. Likewise, to the Harmer children, Peter, Bruce, Lyndall and Athol, a special thanks for sharing their memories of Mum and Dad and the experience of growing up with parents so dedicated to the work of the Salvation Army. To the extended Lipke and Harmer families, I am especially grateful for many anecdotes from Joyce's and Hilton's early lives. For details of family historical record, a particular thanks to Val King and Keith Lipke.

My thanks are due also to the serving and retired officers, soldiers and adherents of the Salvation Army, and other friends and colleagues of Joyce and Hilton Harmer, who gave me their time, along with insights in interviews, as I researched the work and structure of the Salvation Army and the place of the Harmers within it. In evaluating the outstanding contribution Joyce and Hilton Harmer made in the courts, I would like to thank the lawyers and magistrates, court and Correctional Services officers and many friends of Joyce and Hilton Harmer who knew them in the courts. Last, but not least, a particular thanks to the members of families of both victims and accused who spoke to me.

Many interview transcripts went into this book. I am indebted to the work of Lalita Mathias, Alice Grundy and Tanya Goldberg, who typed out the transcripts, at times against tight deadlines. And to Gerard, my longtime partner at home and at work, thanks again for support, patience and adaptability when the deadlines arrived.

At HarperCollins, it was Helen Littleton's inspiration that Joyce Harmer's life be written, which allowed me to meet and know a very special Australian lady, and her remarkable husband Hilton. Thank you, Helen. And to Amruta Slee, who grappled with my early drafts, my gratitude for perseverance.

Those who would like to contact Joyce Harmer can find her at: PO Box 72, Earlwood NSW 2206.